Suffering Scholars

INTELLECTUAL HISTORY OF THE MODERN AGE

Series Editors
Angus Burgin
Peter E. Gordon
Joel Isaac
Karuna Mantena
Samuel Moyn
Jennifer Ratner-Rosenhagen
Camille Robcis
Sophia Rosenfeld

Suffering Scholars

Pathologies of the Intellectual in Enlightenment France

Anne C. Vila

PENN

UNIVERSITY OF PENNSYLVANIA PRESS

PHILADELPHIA

Copyright © 2018 University of Pennsylvania Press

All rights reserved. Except for brief quotations used for purposes of review or scholarly citation, none of this book may be reproduced in any form by any means without written permission from the publisher.

Published by
University of Pennsylvania Press
Philadelphia, Pennsylvania 19104-4112
www.upenn.edu/pennpress

Printed in the United States of America
on acid-free paper

10 9 8 7 6 5 4 3 2 1

Library of Congress Cataloging-in-Publication Data
ISBN 978-0-8122-4992-7

Contents

List of Abbreviations   vii

Introduction   1

1. Medicine and the Cult of the Thinker, 1750–89   20

2. The Ardor for Study: Inwardness and the Zealous Cerebralist   46

3. Passions and the *Philosophe*   68

4. Corporality and the Life of the Mind in Voltaire and Diderot   92

5. Melancholy, Genius, and Intellectual Identity: The Cases of Rousseau and Stael   123

6. Refashioning Intellectual Pathologies in the Wake of the Revolution   150

Epilogue. Not So Singular, After All?   176

Notes   183

Bibliography of Primary Sources   239

Index   253

Acknowledgments   265

Abbreviations

DAF   *Dictionnaire de l'Académie française*, 1694 and 1762 (accessed via the ARTFL Project, https://artfl-project.uchicago.edu/content/dictionnaires-dautrefois)

DPV   Diderot, *Œuvres complètes*, ed. Herbert Dieckmann, Jacques Proust, Jean Varloot, et al. (Paris: Hermann, 1975–) (34 vols. anticipated)

ENCYC   *Encyclopédie, ou dictionnaire raisonné des sciences, des arts et des métiers, etc.*, ed. Denis Diderot and Jean le Rond d'Alembert (accessed via the ARTFL Project, http://encyclopedie.uchicago.edu)

OCV   Voltaire, *Oeuvres complètes de Voltaire / The Complete Works of Voltaire*, 143 vols. (Geneva: Institut et Musée Voltaire / Toronto: University of Toronto Press / Oxford: Voltaire Foundation, 1968–)

SGL   Tissot, *De la santé des gens de lettres*, 3rd rev. ed. (Lausanne: Grasset, 1775)

SVEC   *Studies on Voltaire and the Eighteenth Century*

Introduction

A Strange Idea: The Singularity of the "Poetically" Organized

Few characters embody the myth of the suffering scholar more dramatically than the mysterious protagonist of Honoré de Balzac's novel *Louis Lambert* (1832), "that poor poet who was so nervously constituted, often as vaporous as a woman, dominated by a chronic melancholy, entirely sick from his genius as a girl is sick from the love for which she yearns without knowing it."[1] Lambert is certainly a striking figure, endowed with a brilliance that is both dazzling and strangely pathogenic, and his creator is arguably the modern writer who did the most to popularize the idea that intellectual endeavor could be dangerous to your health. Balzac was, in fact, the author who first got me thinking about one of the central notions underlying this book: the idea that sustained mental effort comes at the cost of the body. Where, I wondered, did he get the idea of "thought killing the thinker," which determines the fate of various characters in the *Études philosophiques* cycle, including the brilliant but doomed Louis Lambert?[2] And what factors were at play in this conception of thought as capable of sapping the life force of the person who engaged in it too intensely?

Balzac did not invent the strange condition of being sick from one's genius. Concern about infirmities tied to study dates back to Aristotle's famous problem XXX, which linked intellectual superiority to melancholy. The topic was also discussed by early modern writers like Marsilio Ficino (*De triplici vita*; Three books on life [1489]), Robert Burton (*The Anatomy of Melancholy* [first ed., 1621]), and Daniello Bartoli (*Dell'huomo di lettere difeso et emendato*; English trans., *The Learned Man Defended and Reformed* [1660]).[3] However, it was during the century directly preceding Louis Lambert's creation that the persona of the ailing scholar really took hold in the

French vernacular, a phenomenon illustrated by the popularity of works like Samuel-Auguste Tissot's *De la santé des gens de lettres*, first published in French in 1768. Though hardly limited to French-speaking Europe, the link between mental endeavor and disorder was embraced with particular vigor in that context—as was the tendency to imbue cerebralists with an aura of otherness and detachment from the world. Oddly perhaps, an important strand of French Enlightenment thought portrayed intellectuals as peculiarly susceptible to altered states of health as well as psyche.

That situation looks less odd if we recall that the eighteenth century was also an age of great anxieties, many of which revolved around health. Compared with the centuries that preceded it, this one was relatively healthy: mortality rates declined in France and longevity rose, due to factors that included a reduction in famine, fewer wars on French soil, and the declining frequency of the waves of massive epidemics like the plague, which had been a regular fact of life.[4] However, people still lived in fear of falling victim to other diseases recognized as transmissible, like smallpox, dysentery, and syphilis. They also faced such potentially grave conditions as consumption; excretory obstructions (the term sometimes applied to cancer); apoplexy, gout, and gastric disorders (more prevalent at the high end of the social spectrum); fevers and other sorts of pathological heat; and the dangers of pregnancy, childbirth and breastfeeding.[5] Last but not least, they were exposed to various "manufactured" diseases, an expression that Dr. Théodore Tronchin used to describe the vapors, but which could also be applied to onanism (the century's most notorious invented pathology) and to the *maladies des gens de lettres*, the disease syndrome explored in this book.[6]

Viewed against the backdrop of the period's health anxieties, the Balzacian-style cerebralist comes more fully into focus: although obviously a reflection of Balzac's own vision of the life of the mind, this figure also had roots in eighteenth-century ways of thinking about thinkers. In the eyes of numerous Enlightenment-era commentators, the passions and pathologies of intellectuals and artists made them singular—not simply as individuals like the original genius (a new type of being, born during this period) but also as a group of people bound together by their working habits and their devotion to the life of the mind.[7] Much of the discourse written in this vein was medical, but just as much belonged to the realms of moral philosophy and imaginative literature, like moralist accounts of the passion known as the love of learning, autobiographical reflections on mental application, and fictional portrayals of meditators in the grips of cogitation.

Singularity, we should note, carried both positive and pejorative meanings at the time, an ambivalence illustrated by the entry for *singulier* in the 1694 *Dictionnaire de l'Académie française*: "Unique, particular, that which has no peer, rare, excellent. . . . It is sometimes used negatively, and signifies 'bizarre, capricious, affecting personal distinction.' "[8] That ambivalence was apparent in the celebrity culture that took shape around the mid-eighteenth century, when, as Antoine Lilti has shown, a particular set of factors converged to make certain people a focus of intense public curiosity.[9] Fame was, of course, bestowed upon many types besides intellectuals: some of the greatest stars were actors, opera singers, courtesans, and political figures. However, the mantle of singularity was particularly associated with those who distinguished themselves through their ideas, as Charles Secondat, baron de Montesquieu, emphasized in "Mes pensées": "As soon as a man thinks, and he has a personality, people say 'he's a singular man.' . . . It must be that singularity consists in a refined way of thinking that escapes other people; because a man who can only distinguish himself by wearing a particular sort of shoe would be deemed an idiot anywhere."[10]

Montesquieu's larger point was that people who actually thought for themselves were in the minority in the conformist milieu of polite society: "Most people resemble each other in the sense that they don't think: they are eternal echoes, who have never said anything [new] and always repeated."[11] That remark brings to mind various critiques he made in his novel *Les Lettres persanes* (1721), like the character Rica's wry comments on the French nation's slavish devotion to the latest sartorial fashions, and the tale he recounts of the two aspiring *beaux esprits* who take turns uttering empty witticisms they've practiced in advance. However, like many contemporaries, Montesquieu attributed the uniqueness of genuine thinkers to more than just their social comportment: he held superior minds to be exceptional in physical organization as well.

This period's blanket term for intellectuals, *gens de lettres*, encompassed many sorts of knowledge seekers, but it was commonly evoked to single them out as a group in terms of their habits and temperament. Thanks to the rise of the *maladies des gens de lettres*, the singularity of intellectuals and artists came to entail more than their unique ways of thinking or behaving: it also derived from the special constitution they supposedly possessed. This book is designed to tell the story of how the bodily as well as moral exceptionalness of the learned was represented and debated from the early eighteenth century to the era of Balzac. It also explores the complex web of interconnections created between the life sciences and literature around that idea.[12]

Background Currents: Sensibility, Psychology, and the Mind/Body Relation

Obviously, French culture has long given privileged status to intellectuals. Even today, the mythology of Frenchness endows thinkers with a "marvelous singularity" more glamorous than that which most other nations bestow upon them.[13] Just as obviously, the perceived connection between high intelligence and illness is not unique to the period studied in this book, which runs from the 1720s into the 1840s. However, something happened during this era to endow cerebration with unprecedented pathogenic powers, powers that both worried and fascinated authors throughout Europe. The shadow of disorder that loomed over intellectuals also had a moral component: *gens de lettres* were considered prone not simply to bodily sickness, but also to reclusiveness. Although such views might seem difficult to reconcile with the promotion of reason and social engagement for which the Enlightenment is best known, they were nonetheless pervasive; and they had the effect of complicating the persona of the knowledge seeker in intriguing ways. They also played a significant role in the so-called cult that surrounded great intellectuals: the mental intensity and somatic frailty of *gens de lettres* proved both the privileges and the perils of knowledge seeking and creative endeavor.[14]

Various aspects of eighteenth- and early nineteenth-century French culture contributed to the perception of the intelligentsia as diseased in a figurative or literal sense. One factor was the struggle for control over public opinion between the *philosophes* and the *anti-philosophes*: both sides delighted in throwing verbal bombs at the enemy camp, sometimes denouncing its beliefs as poisonous bile or the product of deranged minds. Pathological rhetoric was commonly used in debates over the state of the Republic of Letters. Whereas Rousseau tied book learning to physical and moral degeneration in the *Discours sur les sciences et les arts* (1750), Elie Harel branded "la nouvelle philosophie" as a disease in his counter-Enlightenment tract *La vraie philosophie* (1783).[15] Another factor was the belief that sustained mental work really was dangerous to one's well-being, for reasons that included its physiologically taxing effects, the stale and overheated air of the scholarly workplace, the delicate stomachs to which scholars seemed prone, and their excessive attachment to their studies. The notion that intellectual activity could imperil health was, in short, commonplace, so much so that it would be impossible to document every instance in which it occurred. A more fruitful approach is to ask what, in the philosophical, ideological, and social currents of the period, made sustained mental application a possible way to be or to become sick.[16]

Chief among those currents was sensibility, a concept widely perceived as the key to understanding both the workings of the living organism and the interactions of the physical, moral, and social aspects of human life.[17] Medical vitalism, the doctrine of holistic vitality that Théophile de Bordeu and other Montpellier physicians promoted from the 1750s on, provided an important framework for theorizing sensibility in French-speaking Europe.[18] Whereas German and Scottish theorists made sensibility nerve- and brain-centered, French and Francophone Swiss biomedical investigators located it diffusely throughout the body.[19] Their diffuse perspective suited the ways in which laypersons typically thought and talked about their bodies: even after the old humoralist psychology of fixed characters had been largely abandoned, a loose brand of humoralism persisted, both in the rhetoric of "flows" and "evacuations" that was used by patients to report pain and other symptoms to their doctors, and in the vitalist notion that local body parts had their own passions or modes of sensibility.[20]

Another important current was the idea of "the physical and the moral," a conceptual pair established well before Dr. Pierre-Jean-Georges Cabanis featured it in the title of his *Rapports du physique et du moral de l'homme* (1802). The notion of an essential linkage between the physical and the moral (the latter understood as a notion encompassing the mental as well as the passional) was crucial to the biomedical theory of holistic vitality, which influenced the emerging fields of anthropology and psychiatry. The resulting "science" of man treated mind and body as fundamentally interrelated, a point stressed by Elizabeth A. Williams: "The science of man did not generally reduce the psychic domain to the physical, and thus was neither 'monist' nor 'materialist.' Most physicians who worked within the tradition accepted some kind of distinction between the mind and body and between willed and unwilled action. But they taught nonetheless that these realms of existence and experience were closely interdependent."[21]

A similar emphasis on the interdependence of mind and body pervaded eighteenth-century French literature. Many libertine novelists staged the physically arousing effects of erotic art and storytelling, whereas more proper writers like Mme de Graffigny (*Lettres d'une Péruvienne* [1747]) employed morally induced diseases to shape the fate of their protagonists. In the *Confessions*, Jean-Jacques Rousseau sketched a plan for what he called a "morale sensitive, ou le matérialisme du sage," that is, a program for controlling all of the impressions made upon the sensitive system, physical as well as moral, in order to put or maintain the soul "in the state the most favorable to virtue."[22] More mischievously, Denis Diderot had his sleeping d'Alembert character undergo a philosophically inspired wet dream in the fictional dialogue *Le Rêve de d'Alembert* (written around 1769).[23] What connected all of those examples was the conviction that the mind or soul was not an entity separate from the body: it was holistically attached to it, operating through a complex play of actions and reactions that involved the world outside the mind as well as the inner, organic world.

As Vladimir Janković emphasizes, the conception of the human being as a reactive organism, acutely vulnerable to its surroundings, had a profound effect on both medicine and moral theory: it reoriented the quest for the causes of illness toward the environment around the individual; and it tapped into the larger idea that contemporary European society was itself pathogenic, an argument that particularly targeted city life.[24] In some ways, the supposed sickliness of *gens de lettres* was a subset of the more general syndrome of pathogenic nervousness, which Michel Foucault has aptly characterized as "falling ill from feeling too much."[25] Heightened feeling was integral to this era's sense of its own modernity, a condition that was both exciting and perturbing. Theorists in a range of fields undertook to explain sensibility's moral as well as physical mechanisms, producing a number of fine-tuned distinctions among different sorts of sensing and feeling.[26] Those efforts contributed to the fashioning or refashioning of some of the period's iconic personae: the *philosophe*, the man of feeling, the libertine, the vaporous lady, and—as I emphasize here—the superior mind.

Of course, transcendently rational, dispassionate representations of the thinker can be found in certain eighteenth-century European sources, like Immanuel Kant; both Cartesian substance dualism and Christian apologetic approaches to the soul persisted.[27] However, voluntary rationalism competed with very different representations of those who devoted themselves to knowledge seeking. Notions of what constituted an intellectual were many and varied, as were the methods used to investigate nature and human nature—not to mention the genres used to disseminate the ideas that came out of those investigations.²⁸ Also crucially, the models of mental operations that held sway for much of the period I am considering gave considerable weight to the mind's physical underpinnings—and to the interactions of the physical and the moral.

This is particularly apparent in the field of psychology, which was at the time a form of natural history, a science that included "manifold programs for adopting an empirical approach to mind and its relation to body."²⁹ Psychological naturalism had a strong purchase among prominent French-speaking mind theorists, who included the Lockean-inspired sensationalist philosopher Étienne Bonnot de Condillac, the Swiss naturalist Charles Bonnet, and (more notoriously) Julien Offray de la Mettrie. Moreover, those who studied mental phenomena often conducted their investigations in the context of medical physiology and anatomy, which also oriented attention toward the body. In a typical physiological adaption of the sensualist philosophical tradition, the famous biomedical investigator Albrecht von Haller described mental operations as a chain of events that began with the impression of a body upon the "organ of the sensory" and built up from there, through the elemental processes of association, memory, and so forth, all of which thrust further impressions on the mind.³⁰ While usually taking pains to steer clear of materialism, mind theorists commonly invoked a simple "impressment" model to explain both the reception of bodily sensations and the generation of ideas. The presumption of a causal connection between the mind and its underlying physical substrate allowed them to use the same vocabulary of impressions or affections to talk about both. The mind/body relation, on this account, involved a network or economy of communicating parts.

As Tobias Cheung notes, the main operative building block at the heart of this networking model was the fiber, which around 1750 became "the first unifying principle of function-structure complexes of organic bodies"; according to its proponents, "plants feed through fibres, animals move and sense through fibres, and humans think through fibres."³¹ The designated "thinking" fiber was often the nerve, widely considered at the time to be the main intermediary between soul and body, but mind theorists sometimes spoke vaguely of brain fibers without describing them as neural. Take, for example, Bonnet, who first coined the term "psychology" in his *Essai de psychologie* (published anonymously in 1754) to refer to the study of how ideas are formed in the human understanding—and who declared in the preface to his *Essai analytique sur les facultés de l'âme* (1760) that the best way to reason about the way ideas combine and interact was to assume that "ideas are attached to the play of certain fibers."³² Bonnet described the seat of the soul as a "prodigiously composed little machine, yet simple in its composition. . . . One can envision this admirable instrument of the operations of our mind/ soul [âme] through the image of a harpsichord, an organ, a clock, or some other more complex machine. . . . The mind/soul is the musician that performs various airs on this machine, or who judges those that are performed, and repeats them. Every fiber is a kind of key, or hammer destined to render a certain tone."³³

In addition to showing the variety of instrument analogies that mind theorists used to model mental operations, Bonnet's description illustrates their emphasis on complexity and dynamic interplay—an idea often conveyed via comparisons between idea formation and music.³⁴ The musical metaphor that envisioned the human being as a sonorous body became ubiquitous in several fields around 1750, under the influence of a number of factors: the musical controversies of the period; interest in vibratory phenomena in both medicine and acoustics; and the idea of fibers that oscillate, shake, and resonate—a notion embraced by theorists of aesthetics and epistemology as well as by biomedical investigators.³⁵ Another heuristic model envisioned the mind as dwelling in the body like a spider in its web. Although best known today for its appearance in Diderot's *Rêve de d'Alembert*, that analogy stemmed from a long philosophical tradition and was used by French authors earlier in the century.³⁶ It was also related to the weaving or tissue-producing analogies that anatomists had employed since the sixteenth century to describe how organic bodies develop, subsist, and reproduce.³⁷

Montesquieu used such an analogy in the "Essai sur les causes qui peuvent affecter les esprits et les caractères," which he wrote around 1734–36 while preparing his magnum opus *De l'esprit des lois* (1748): "The soul/ mind [âme] is in our body like a spider in its web, which cannot move without shaking one of the threads that are stretched out in the distance; and by the same token, you can't move one of those threads without triggering a response in another thread. The more these threads are stretched, the more the spider is alerted; and if there are some that are slack, the communication will be lessened between that thread and the spider or between that thread and another thread; and the providence of the spider will be almost suspended within its very web."³⁸ According to this scenario, the tautness or slackness of the spider's threads (its body parts) directly affects the movements of the soul/mind, and a motion in one part triggers motion in another. The state of our *esprit* thus depends not simply on the brain but on the entire body: "It is hard to believe how many things affect the state of our mind. It is not simply the disposition of our brain that modifies it: the entire machine, sometimes all the parts of the machine, contribute to it, and often those that one would not suspect."[39] Montesquieu also argued that there was a constitutional difference between the two types of people called *hommes d'esprit*, those in the social world versus "the intelligent man among philosophers": whereas worldly wits regarded *esprit* as the art of weaving together disparate ideas, scholarly sorts engaged in fine-tuned distinctions.[40] Real thinking, as he defined it, was a mode of sensing or feeling that involved subtle, spontaneous discernment; this capacity arose from education, but it also depended on the condition of the material parts or fibers of the individual mind. Extending that logic, he concluded that thinking was carried out most "finely" by those who possessed the most developed, best-exercised nerves and brain fibers.

This emphasis on the tight interrelation between the moral and the physical clearly informed the approach Montesquieu took to social bodies in *De l'esprit des lois*, a work that inspired some later theorists to devise constitutionally grounded scales for judging qualitative differences in sensory acuity and mental aptitude among different groups of people.[41] Some echoed his premise that those who advanced the furthest in intellectual development (that is, Europeans, especially men of letters) had the liveliest, most responsive brain/nerve fibers, an advantage they gained both through physical circumstances—a favorable external climate, the right temperament, and so on—and through moral causes like education. They also echoed his idea that there was an essential tension between the kind of *esprit* that was valued in the world and the sort required to excel in serious intellectual application or artistic endeavor.

Medicine and Culture in the French Enlightenment

Paradoxically, perhaps, at the very moment when the Enlightenment movement was disseminating hopeful new ideas about human progress and perfectibility, doctors began issuing grave warnings about the dire health effects of sustained intellectual effort—and continued to do so for a good part of the nineteenth century. Equally striking is that so many *gens de lettres* embraced this anxious-making perspective on their work. I am not the first person to take note of this: historians interested in the persona of the eighteenth-century intellectual have discussed its medical aspect, at least in passing; so, too, have specialists of the period's most famous sickly writers, Voltaire and Rousseau.[42] However, existing assessments of the disease syndrome known as *maladies des gens de lettres* tend not to look beyond Tissot, and literary-critical treatments of a particular writer's health concerns generally don't venture beyond that writer's corpus. My study takes a more synthetic approach by considering the broad range of discourses in which the pathologizing vision of thinkers took shape.

It is worth noting here the special prominence of medicine in the culture of French-speaking eighteenth-century Europe. Whereas earlier writers tended to satirize doctors—Molière, for example, in Le Malade imaginaire (1673)—eighteenth-century literary depictions were generally respectful.[43] This may have been due to the heroic aura that surrounded physicians who took up controversial causes like smallpox inoculation.[44] Another factor was the active presence of physicians in the institutions and networks that structured polite society and the Republic of Letters, including courtly life, salons, academies, and epistolary correspondence.[45] Medicine also flourished in print culture: portable self-help manuals were widely available, and the rapidly proliferating Paris and provincial press publicized the latest ideas on health and hygiene (a mission also carried out in the pages of the *Encyclopédie*).[46] Some doctors even wrote novels and fictional dialogues to promote specific therapies.[47]

Physicians were particularly present in the lives of the affluent, some of whom were preoccupied with health for reasons that had less to do with disease than with "unwellness"—a state that was popular precisely because it was indeterminate: "Feeling out of sorts was an excuse to avoid social contact, refrain from exercise, elicit pity, or obtain professional help."[48] For those who dwelled in the eighteenth century's cultural climate of delicacy, nervous sensitivity taken to the point of infirmity was not just prevalent but chic, a marker of rank and refinement. The nervous body was a "type of corporeality attuned to the new cultural values of the social elite."[49]

In this secular-tending, pre-Freudian era, plumbing the depths of one's interiority often meant pondering one's nervous palpitations, visceral murmurings, odd rashes, or worrisome secretions.[50] Popular health manuals fed those anxieties by dispensing detailed advice on all sorts of topics, including domestic medicine, profession-specific dietary regimens, mineral-water cures, and bold new therapeutic methods. Patients were not passive recipients of the practices and remedies promoted through the eighteenth-century medical marketplace. There was a strong demand for medical goods and services, which strengthened in the century's final decades through mediums like advertisements in provincial *affiches* (journals).[51] Moreover, the soliciting and delivery of health care involved a dynamic, complex network of practitioners and caregivers.[52]

There was, however, more at play than health anxiety in this culture's receptiveness to medical warnings about excessive intellectual effort. As E. C. Spary has underscored, people living in the eighteenth century were "fascinated with new knowledge," and those who catered to that fascination drew on print, commerce, and their connections within polite society to establish credibility.[53] That point is useful for thinking about Enlightenment-era health claims: new biomedical ideas and therapies were publicly constituted, promoted, and contested in a very particular entanglement of science and society that depended heavily on writing in its various forms. In the case of medicine, this included not only published treatises but also a good deal of letter writing. Prominent physicians were, in other words, known as writers as well as practitioners—a double identity well illustrated by Tissot, who had both an extensive professional correspondence and a long string of medical bestsellers.

The doctors who wrote about *maladies des gens de lettres* were often strikingly literary in tone: they strove to display their humanistic culture by citing poets as well as fellow physicians. Literature, as they depicted it, was more than the brilliant outcome of the hours that *gens de lettres* spent huddled over their desks ardently communing with their muses. It was also a valuable source of information and corroborating evidence on the diseases that they were trying to define and classify. At the same time, these physicians engaged with literature for reasons that went beyond the desire to find famous examples of illness induced by overstudy or scholarly temperament: they also regarded it as a source of knowledge about human nature and, in some cases, as an antidote to melancholy.

The discourse on *maladies des gens de lettres* thus reflected developments both within and beyond medicine. It was an outgrowth of the expansion of the "medicable" into areas like hygiene, which underwent a marked rise in France after 1700 and triggered the growth of occupational medicine.[54] It was also tied to the popularity of individual or collective biographies of illustrious thinkers, which doctors tapped as a source of illness narratives. Finally, it emerged in tandem with a new, more individually embodied notion of genius: physicians were just as intent as moral philosophers on pinning down the attributes that gave rise to great intellectual and/or creative capacity.[55]

Gender and the Pathological Fashioning of the Intellectual

Although doctors who wrote about the ills of overstudy tended to employ the gender-neutral term *gens de lettres* to describe their subjects, they also reflected the period's larger, generally masculinist assumptions regarding the pursuit and production of knowledge. Those assumptions were, of course, vigorously challenged by the many women who strove to practice enlightenment overtly (like defending women's right to literary or scientific fame) or in less conspicuous ways such as conversations, reading, and pedagogy.[56] French women moralists widely championed the singularity of scholarly endeavor and the unique passion that drove it.[57] Echoing predecessors like Madeleine de Scudéry, Émilie Du Châtelet declared in her *Discours sur le bonheur* (written around 1746–47) that "it is quite certain that the love of study is much less necessary to the happiness of men than it is to that of women," because women were generally forbidden from striving for achievement in other public realms like government, the military, and commerce.[58] Châtelet earned recognition and respect as a geometer, physicist, and philosopher; however, her life story illustrates the power of gender to complicate and magnify the competing demands of worldly versus scholarly *esprit* during this period.[59] Female intellectuals who did not hide their learning were sometimes exposed to biting ridicule, a fate to which Châtelet herself was subject, despite her Promethean image.[60] Women were often blamed for civilization's ills in the wake of the late seventeenth-century quarrel of the "Ancients against the Moderns," and the ancien régime imposed a particular social stigma upon women who published openly.[61] Moreover attributing the term *philosophe* to a woman was just as likely to be an insult as a compliment.

Gender was, in short, a vexed question in the Age of Enlightenment: the movement that championed critical reason, service to humanity, and moral-intellectual improvement had a deep ambivalence toward women who made thinking, writing, and creative production central to their existence. Indeed, that ambivalence deepened in the final decades of the eighteenth century, when women's intellect was "naturalized" in newly limiting, biologically deterministic ways.[62] Gender was also an ambiguous element in the medical discourse on illnesses tied to overstudy. Although this discourse did not exclude women—Tissot, for one, cited cases of women scholars who made themselves ill from excessive reading or mental application—it was primarily concerned with restoring male intellectuals to health and active participation in society. Thus, when the nineteenth-century doctor Joseph-Henri Réveillé-Parise referred to scholars as humanity's most "heroic souls" because they labored in the field of ideas (thus straining every fiber of their "poetic organizations"), he mostly meant men; but he also included a few exceptional women, like Germaine de Staël, in this pantheon.[63]

Overt responses by scholarly laypersons to the *maladies des gens de lettres* syndrome also diverged, sometimes, along gender lines: whereas some male intellectuals—Voltaire and Bonnet, for instance—enthusiastically endorsed the link doctors made between serious mental application and ill health, their female counterparts either remained silent about that connection or, like Isabelle de Charrière, resisted it.[64] Women moralists and novelists were more concerned with such questions as marriage, education, happiness, social prejudice, men's authority over women, and the "inverse relationship between *amour-propre* and true learning."[65] Like their British Bluestocking counterparts, French women intellectuals struggled with "women's expected roles in the political, social, and sexual-emotional economy of the social elites."[66] Moreover, they had to put up with both old and new clichés about learned ladies. One reason was the enduring popularity of Molière's *Les Femmes savantes* (1672): the Marquise de Lambert, a prominent moralist and *salonnière* of the 1720s, began her *Réflexions nouvelles sur les femmes* by bemoaning the "shame" that this play had attached to women's scholarly endeavors.[67] Yet Molière's satire still cast a long shadow, particularly after its plot was repurposed by playwrights like Jacques Teisserenc (*La Femme philosophe* [1759]), Charles Palissot de Montenoy (*Les Philosophes* [1760]), and Jean-Jacques Rutlidge (*Le Bureau d'esprit* [1776]) to poke fun at philosophically minded *salonnières* as well as the *philosophes*.[68] It may be that women aspiring to acceptance in the eighteenth-century world of letters and learning could not identify overtly with the pathological fashioning of the scholar: shaping a public identity as a woman thinker in this cultural climate was already complicated.

That said, issues of sex and gender were integral to the unfolding debate about the consequences of studious work on both the individual body and the body politic. For example, expected gender roles infused Rousseau's polemic against the contemporary fad for learning, which he described as "denaturing" for both sexes. Norms of femininity and masculinity also underpinned the tension that many commentators perceived between the demands of sociability and the scholarly drive toward retreat, toward communion with one's muses (and with oneself).[69] Toward the end of the century, essentialist notions of the sexes became crucial to medical efforts to draw clear distinctions between three diseases often attributed to intellectuals: hypochondria, melancholy, and hysteria. All of those factors were part of the complex conceptual landscape that surrounded intellectual pursuit from 1720 to 1840.

Structure of *Suffering Scholars*

This book offers a six-chapter exploration of the ways in which the intellectual evolved as a medical, social, and literary figure in French-speaking culture over more than a century—starting in the 1720s and running to about 1840, the date after which doctors generally lost interest in the supposed special nature and health needs of scholars. It highlights three main themes in this period's representations of learned endeavor: an insistence on the complex interplay between mind and body, the belief that the solitary nature of intellectual production conflicted with family and civic duties, and concern over the pathogenic powers of mental application.

Chapter 1, "Medicine and the Cult of the Thinker, 1750–89," provides an overview of how *les maladies des gens de lettres* emerged and developed up to the Revolution. It pays particular attention to two of the syndrome's fundamental ideas: the view of thinking as a form of physical as well as mental labor, and the notion of "literary intemperance" or excessive zeal for learning. It also analyzes the logic and literary strategies underlying Tissot's *De la santé des gens de lettres*, the book that did more than any to popularize the image of the ailing scholar among eighteenth- and nineteenth-century European readers. By setting Tissot's book in a broader framework, this chapter shows that the discursive construction of diseases proper to the learned was very much a collective, interdisciplinary undertaking.

Chapter 2, "The Ardor for Study: Inwardness and the Zealous Cerebralist," builds from Chapter 1 by considering how intellectual zeal was represented by moral philosophers and literary writers. It surveys the themes and tropes used to talk about "ardor" for study, including the voluptuous language sometimes applied to learned endeavor, the widespread topos of contemplative detachment from the social realm, and the evocation of Archimedes to illustrate the condition of total meditative absorption. This chapter also explores the longing for solitude expressed by some of the most famously gregarious writers of the day, like Voltaire and Diderot. It ends with a short analysis of Montesquieu's musings in *Les Lettres persanes* on the fate of *hommes d'esprit* in contemporary European society.

Chapter 3, "Passions and the *Philosophe*," examines the role of the passions in texts that drew or redrew the social portrait of the iconic intellectual figure of the day: the *philosophe*.[70] I start with a consideration of how the figure was portrayed in plays like Pierre Carlet de Chamblain de Marivaux's *Le Triomphe de l'amour* (1732) and Philippe Néricault Destouches's *Le Philosophe marié, ou Le Mari honteux de l'être* (1727). I then turn to the different "manias" that were imputed to learning or the pursuit of intellectual celebrity, before examining the problem of envy, which many saw as the defining moral pathology of the contemporary Republic of Letters. That theme took on particularly complex resonances in Diderot's dark (and posthumously published) social satire, *Le Neveu de Rameau*, which also offers intriguing reflections on the ambiguities of genius and the *philosophe* persona.

Chapter 4, "Corporality and the Life of the Mind in Voltaire and Diderot," looks at the ways that two leading *philosophes* used notions of corporality to construct intellectual personae. As his correspondence shows, Voltaire crafted part of his own identity around his "bad stomach," linking dyspepsia in complex ways to wit and clearness of mind. He also put the stomach to creative use in satirical writings like *Les Oreilles du comte de Chesterfield* (1775), a tale that comically interweaves lower bodily functions, melancholy, and the destiny of both individuals and states. Diderot, for his part, emphasized the bodily side of thinking for reasons connected to the particular brand of philosophical materialism he espoused. He had a lifelong fascination with the inner workings of the mind, particularly the mind of geniuses—evident in texts like the *Rêve de d'Alembert*, the *Salon de 1767*, and the lesser-known "Sur la Vie et les ouvrages de Boulanger" (1765), written to pay posthumous homage to Nicolas-Antoine Boulanger, whom Diderot considered one of the unsung philosophical masterminds of the century.

Chapter 5, "Melancholy, Genius, and Intellectual Identity: The Cases of Rousseau and Staël," places in tandem two literary writers who were central to this period's refashioning of melancholy, a condition increasingly tied to genius at the turn of the eighteenth century to the nineteenth. Rousseau was an immensely popular clinical subject, particularly among doctors intent on fixing the precise medical meaning of melancholy. Although the pathographies they produced are sometimes dismissed by Rousseau specialists as simplistic, they are worth analyzing.[71] First, they illuminate the framework within which physicians theorized melancholy and related disorders; second, they draw attention to specific episodes in Rousseau's writings in which he, too, ventured theories on such conditions. One such episode is the Charmettes idyll recounted in the *Confessions* (Geneva ed., 1782–89), which interweaves the vapors with morbidity, frenetic mental application, and amorous bliss. Chapter 5 also considers Staël, who exemplified the peculiar tensions surrounding the intellectually superior woman—and who was regarded in her day as an authority on the connections between genius and melancholy. Key works here are Staël's reflections on the character of Rousseau (her literary idol) and her novel *Corinne, ou l'Italie* (1807).

Chapter 6, "Refashioning Intellectual Pathologies in the Wake of the Revolution," follows the story of the *maladies des gens de lettres* syndrome from the 1790s to 1830s. It analyzes how early French psychiatrists used the scholarly patient group to underpin nosographic distinctions between hypochondria, melancholy, and hysteria. It also explores how the body type deemed peculiar to male intellectuals was involved in emerging theories of human perfectibility and sexual dimorphism (or the belief that men and women had radically different moral and physical constitutions). Finally, it examines the hygiene treatises that two imitators of Tissot wrote for the intelligentsia of their era: Étienne Brunaud's *De l'hygiène des gens de lettres* (1819) and Réveillé-Parise's *Physiologie et hygiène des hommes livrés aux travaux de l'esprit* (first edition, 1834).

From the 1840s on, physicians stopped focusing on the supposed exceptionalness of *gens de lettres* as a unique patient group—even though writers and artists continued to enjoy a privileged aura of singularity in the cultural realm.[72] The book's epilogue sketches the factors involved in both developments, along with the new ideas and tensions that were invested in the persona of the cerebralist.

Some Methodological Considerations

One of the missions of *Suffering Scholars* is (to quote the historian Christopher Forth) to "put intellectuals back in their bodies."[73] My effort to recorporealize the figure of the Enlightenment-era thinker goes against the grain of some historical narratives: for example, those that see sociability as the defining quality of eighteenth-century French intellectual life. It also departs somewhat from constructivist approaches to the body, which emphasize the body's function as a text, a sign system, a symbolic and constructed object. Such approaches unquestionably open up new ways of thinking about embodiment—and resistance to embodiment—as modes of selfhood; and they shed light on the creative powers of language, literature, and art to create substance that transcends the physical.[74] They can, however, be difficult to reconcile with more biologically grounded perspectives on the body understood as a living, feeling, laboring, sometimes suffering entity—which are, in part, what I seek to recover in this book.

Much has been written about sex organs in historiographical studies of the body, and sex was unquestionably a factor in the construction of the intellectual during the eighteenth and nineteenth centuries.[75] The "sexual fix" does not, however, suffice to explain the carnal identity of *gens de lettres* during the period examined in this study.[76] Sex was only one way—and not always the most prominent one—by which thinkers were depicted as flesh-and-blood creatures: they were also bodies that felt, ate, moved about in space (or failed to do so), got older, fell ill, and eventually died. To recuperate the ways in which *gens de lettres* thought about bodies, including their own, we need to contextualize their views in relation to the period's dominant philosophical and medico-philosophical frameworks. Again, although the philosophical theories of this period included certain forms of dualism, the prevailing view of human nature was holistic: it assumed a good deal of mutual dependence between the two terms featured in the oft-cited couple "the physical and the moral." We also need to keep in mind the historical specificity of models of body consciousness.[77] Bodies, as I argue, mattered in multiple ways—not simply because they provided rich possibilities for creative discursive or conceptual construction, but also because, as flesh-and-blood machines, they were seen as simultaneously supporting and disrupting the intellectual (and other) activities of real human beings.[78]

At the same time, I am keenly attuned to the properly discursive aspect of the scholarly body as represented in the works I study here. An implicit question underlying my project is why the bodies of intellectuals became an object of concern, inquiry, and regulation at this particular point in the history of French culture (as they did elsewhere in Europe). To borrow the language of Foucault, one might say that the suffering-prone corporeal side of intellectual identity came to "exist" as a widely visible phenomenon through the combination of a distinct set of practices, discursive as well as therapeutic.[79] The cultural phenomenon known as *maladies des gens de lettres* owed a great deal to particular modes of textual circulation: these included not just works of medical popularization that specifically targeted intellectuals, but also the practice of epistolary medical consultation.[80] Particular discursive practices were also central to the making of the *maladies des gens de lettres* as a disease syndrome: its medical proponents used copious intertextual referencing and storytelling to support their claims. Dictionary writers and library catalogers of the next century further shaped the genre through the classificatory systems by which they grouped the illnesses supposedly prevalent among intellectuals. It is worth pointing out here that the government-commissioned *Catalogue des sciences médicales,* published between 1859 and 1889 by the Bibliothèque Impériale de France and then the Bibliothèque Nationale de France, must have been a gold mine for Foucault when he was doing his research for *Naissance de la clinique* and *Histoire de la folie à l'âge classique*: certain sections of both of those books proceed systematically through particular headings in this catalog, whose classifications were largely designed by the psychiatrist E. Frédéric Dubois d'Amiens (whom I discuss in Chapter 5).[81] Patients, too, played a part in the construction of "intellectual" pathologies. This is made amply clear by the consultation letters sent to Tissot by recognized or aspiring *gens de lettres* who believed they were afflicted with one or another of those illnesses.[82]

These are not, of course, the only sources that one could consider for a study of the ways in which knowledge seeking was conceptualized or experienced by individuals during this period. One could, for example, explore instead religious works like François Lamy's *Traité de la connaissance de soi-même* (1694–98) or Louis-Antoine de Caraccioli's *La jouissance de soi-même* (1759) and end up with a different story, one emphasizing mystical interiority and dualistic mind/body models.[83] The texts I study offer a window onto another, more physical sort of interiority: namely, the awareness of the body's inner workings, which many eighteenth- and nineteenth-century French thinkers viewed as a necessary part of self-knowledge.

A corporeal approach to the image and identity of *gens de lettres* sheds light on several aspects of European (particularly French) intellectual culture in the years leading up to and following the Revolution. These include the intertwining of invalidism and intellectual fame in the celebrity culture of the day; the physical etiologies that were assigned to diseases that we now view as largely psychological, like hypochondria and melancholy; and the corporeal quality that was commonly given to the emotions, including the cognitive emotions associated with sustained mental application. Restoring the somatic aspect of the scholarly person allows us to grasp with greater precision the ways in which nervous sensibility was held to operate in those who possessed it in the most refined forms. It illuminates the place of cerebralists in debates over the figurative health of the nation and the Republic of Letters—and the place of health, in the literal sense, among the preoccupations of the major players in those debates. Finally, it opens a new window onto psychology, a field that, as Fernando Vidal stresses, served as a key site for "the emergence of new ways of thinking about the relation between persons and bodies"—ways of thinking that differed from those that have held sway since the emergence of the "cerebral self," a perspective in which personhood is located in the brain alone.[84]

In that sense, this book is tied to the brand of intellectual biography that focuses on how knowledge and knowledge seeking have been incarnated by a particular writer, scientist, or philosopher.[85] Although I delve only occasionally into biography proper, I do cross the author/work barrier once held to be impermeable by theorists writing in the wake of Marcel Proust's essay "Contre Sainte-Beuve" or Foucault's "What Is an Author?"[86] Biography was central to the body-based views of intellectual and creative endeavor I study here. It was also central to the literary criticism done by Charles Augustin Sainte-Beuve and his disciples, back when the term "physiology" enjoyed a semantic plasticity that allowed it to be conjoined with a number of surprising qualifiers, from "intellectual" to "literary."[87] Although now largely forgotten, physiological literary criticism played a significant role in crafting both the French literary canon and illustrious French writers as national icons—individuals held to embody, through their persons as well as their writings, something essential about the spirit of the place and time in which they lived. As I shall argue in these pages, medicine had more than a little to do with all of those developments.

Chapter 1

Medicine and the Cult of the Thinker, 1750–89

Inventing *Les maladies des gens de lettres*

In a sense, the persona of the sickly scholar that became popular during the eighteenth century was a secularized version of the long-established Christian paradigm of suffering—with the frame of reference shifted away from religious belief and toward the realm of secular learning. Whereas Pascal called illness "the true state of the Christian," some Enlightenment-era commentators regarded illness as the true state of the knowledge seeker.[1] The latter idea illustrates a central paradox of the eighteenth century: the so-called Age of Reason, when intellectuals enjoyed unprecedented powers and influence throughout Europe, was also the era that gave birth to the nosological category of illnesses proper to the intelligentsia.[2]

Two themes pervaded the works that physicians wrote to define the distinctive traits of this new class of pathologies. The first was the idea that scholars were more susceptible to disease than many people because of the physical strains caused by excessive use of the mind. The second was a mixture of fascination and perplexity in the face of the intellectual passion that drove certain people to sacrifice their health through the relentless pursuit of knowledge. Both lay the groundwork for the emergence of later jointly cultural and moral syndromes like monomania and obsession, and both contributed to the creation of the various "sick heroes" who became prominent in French culture from approximately 1750 until well into the following century.[3]

Whether or not this suffering was heroic depended on one's perspective. In the eyes of François Jean-Pierre Letual, author of an 1810 medical dissertation on melancholy, losing one's health to the quest for intellectual or artistic fame was a noble sacrifice: "How many men of genius have paid, through the loss of their health, for a celebrity that is honorable but painful!"[4] For some of his predecessors, however, the ills associated with scholarly and creative endeavor were more lamentable than honorable. Jean-Jacques Rousseau took the most radical position on the subject: after denouncing the corruptive effects of the arts and sciences in his *Discours sur les sciences et les arts* (1750), he pursued the attack in later texts. In the preface to his play *Narcisse* (1752), he declared that "library work makes men delicate, weakens their temperament, and the mind [*âme*] is hard pressed to retain its vigor when the body has lost its own. Study wears out the machine, exhausts the spirits, destroys strength, weakens courage, and that alone shows sufficiently that it is not made for us. This is how one becomes faint-hearted, incapable of resisting both pain and the passions."[5] And in his *Discours sur l'origine et les fondements de l'inégalité* (1755), he contended that reflection led people far away from the simple, uniform life for which Nature had originally made humankind: "If she [Nature] destined us to be healthy, I almost dare to say that the state of reflection is an unnatural state [*un état contre nature*], and that the man who meditates is a depraved animal."[6]

Although extreme in formulation, Rousseau's warnings echoed the century's more general sense of social and moral crisis.[7] Overstudy was commonly cited alongside worldly dissipations like gambling and libertinism as a cause of the frailty that had beset most European nations. By the waning decades of the Old Regime, when the terms "degeneration" and "regeneration" became ubiquitous in French political discourse, learned people were standardly grouped among those judged to be burdened with a weak, oversensitive constitution. Indeed, they enjoyed privileged status as a patient group because doctors had invented a disease category, *les maladies des gens de lettres*, just for them.

This sort of medical writing is sometimes viewed as an overt expression of Rousseauism, partly because the Lausanne physician Samuel-Auguste Tissot explicitly quoted Rousseau's "Préface à *Narcisse*" in the best-known contribution to the genre, *La santé des gens de lettres* (first ed., 1768).[8] However, when Tissot revised his treatise in 1775, he cautiously retreated from endorsing Rousseau's polemical attack against learning. Moreover, he and the other doctors who wrote about illnesses associated with mental application were just as inclined to cite authors from antiquity or the Renaissance as their famous contemporary "Jean-Jacques."

Concern over the infirmities caused by intensive study was tied to the growth of hygiene, which became an important part of the medical curriculum during the eighteenth century; manuals on the art of conserving health became popular, and occupational medicine was born.[9] It was also related to the trend of "charitable" medical books, in which doctors assumed the posture of a specialist writing specifically for a nonprofessional public: the Jansenist Parisian physician Philippe Hecquet, for instance, devoted a chapter to the diseases of the learned in his posthumously published *La Médecine, la chirurgie et la pharmacie des pauvres* (1740).[10] Finally, it was connected to commerce: a blend of health activism and entrepreneurialism underpinned the effort to identify and treat the health problems of learned people, among other groups.

Like the period's more general discourse on nervous ailments, books that addressed *les maladies des gens de lettres* were sometimes designed to attract patients to a specific mineral-water spa for treatment, or to promote a particular diet or curative program. Take, for example, the well-known *Essai sur les affections vaporeuses des deux sexes* (1760), in which Pierre Pomme attributed vapors in men to "mental application of all sorts" and lumped together, in a single patient group, "gens de lettres, studious, meditative, and contemplative recluses" along with debauched libertines, drunkards, and people who consumed too much coffee or chocolate.[11] Dr. Pomme proposed the same cure for all of them: ice baths.

From a commercial perspective, the production of works on the special health needs of scholars was not as extensive as that of books about the vapors. However, *gens de lettres* sometimes appeared there, too. Like Pomme, the vapors specialist Jean-Baptiste Pressavin included studious application, especially the sort that involved abstract sciences, among the "distant" causes of the vapors; other causes Pressavin cited were excessive eating or drinking and immoderate sexual intercourse.[12]

Historians generally trace the rise of medical concern over intellectual pathologies to Bernardino Ramazzini's *De Morbis Artificium diatriba* (1700), translated into English in 1705 as *Treatise of the Diseases of Tradesmen*, whose Latin and English versions concluded with a long chapter titled "The Diseases of Learned Men." Ramazzini presented such diseases as the product of professional circumstances rather than innate temperament. After apologizing to scholarly readers who might "take it ill to find themselves rank'd in the Class of Tradesmen," he warned that they were just as susceptible to occupation-specific infirmities as were the metal-diggers, blacksmiths, washerwomen, and other artisans he also discussed.[13] Ramazzini singled out the sedentariness and bad posture of studious people: they were "as Slothful and Idle in their Body, as they are active in their Mind and Brain" (247), and spent too much time hunched over books. This was to blame for the weak stomachs they typically suffered (an ancient notion, first popularized by Aulus Cornelius Celsus), along with their susceptibility to compressed pancreatic juices and "Nephrtick and Athritick Disorders" (250). By classifying scholars in terms of the bodily effects of their labor, Ramazzini made their diseases medicable in a way that they had not been before: he inspired physicians to extend their attention beyond the scholar's specific dietary needs (an approach already well established in the European medical and moralist tradition) into other areas of the scholarly life and work routine.

Although the invention of this nosological category was an offshoot of professional medicine, it also had a special resonance for the physicians who contributed to its creation. Their worries over the dangers of mental application were clearly more personal than those they expressed about the work-related disorders of other at-risk groups like hatters, spinners, or goldsmiths.[14] We should bear in mind that when doctors took up the pen to warn the public about the health risks of mental work, they were also writing about themselves and their brethren: even when they did not publish actively, physicians belonged to the Republic of Letters through their academic affiliations, their membership in medical and philosophical societies, their correspondence, and the fashionable circles they sometimes frequented. Moreover, they actively participated in the campaign to bathe great thinkers in an aura of heroism via testimonials and eulogies—a mode of discourse that also contributed to the development of the "suffering scholar" syndrome.[15]

The first wave of physicians to heed Ramazzini's call for closer attention to the working and living circumstances of the studious were the English "hyp" doctors of the 1720s and 1730s, like Bernard Mandeville, Nicholas Robinson, and George Cheyne.[16] Contending that nervous disorders were on the rise among Britain's social elite, these physicians singled out learned people and other refined sorts as prone to "spleen," an ailment that involved bad digestion as well as depression. The causes they cited for spleen included both uncontrollable factors, such as individual nervous temperament, geography, and climate (England's cool, damp weather was a factor), and controllable things like bad habits, which for the scholar included sedentariness, neglect of the body, and a "labouring Imagination" that focused the mind unhealthfully on a single subject.[17] Cheyne, the most famous and professionally successful of the "hyp" doctors, gave a distinctly intimate tone to his famous treatise *The English Malady* (1733): he included an account of his own bout with spleen and used a "humanitarian" narrative style to elicit sympathy for the other suffering patients whose case histories he related.[18]

From midcentury onward, doctors on the Continent published a steady stream of works in the vernacular that addressed the physical and moral effects of study. A few were reassuring, like *La Médecine de l'esprit* (first ed., 1753) by the Parisian Doctor-Regent Antoine Le Camus, who offered precise dietary and hygienic regimens on how to reach and maintain one's full intellectual potential.[19] Alarmism was the more prevalent tone in the contributions made to the genre by two famous Swiss doctors, Johann-Georg Zimmermann and Tissot. Zimmermann included a long chapter on the effects of excessive mental exertion in his treatise on experience in medicine, *Von der Erfahrung in der Arzneikunst* (1763; translated into French as *Traité de l'expérience en général et en particulier dans l'art de guérir* in 1774), where he spoke of the love of learning as a noble but dangerous passion. Those who applied their minds too intensely were, he warned, liable to suffer digestive disorders, incapacitating headaches, weakened nerves, loss of vision and hearing, and hypochondria (a disease defined as physical as well as moral, and related to melancholy).[20] Finally, in 1768, Tissot published *De la santé des gens de lettres*. Filled with frightening tales of people who had destroyed their health because of excessive mental application, this book was read by some of the most illustrious members of the European intellectual elite.

Physicians who wrote on the health effects of mental application were aware of emerging theories of genius and sublime ecstasy—both of which tended to place certain sorts of thinkers, especially artists and literary writers, on a higher level of sentient existence. This view became more pronounced as the century progressed. Pierre Fabre included in his 1785 *Essai sur les facultés de l'âme* a long digression on the revolutionary effect that Corneillian tragedy had exerted on the physio-aesthetic sensibility of the entire French nation.[21] In 1800, Philippe Pinel identified several artists, musicians, and "versifiers enraptured by their productions" among the patients at the Bicêtre insane asylum but reported finding not a single naturalist, physicist, chemist, or geometer (he did, however, count a fair number of mentally deranged lawyers).[22] Finer distinctions between different sorts of mental work were also supported by the new doctrine of human types promoted by Revolutionary-era biomedical theorists affiliated with the Idéologue school, like Pierre-Jean-Georges Cabanis and Xavier Bichat. These and other factors led turn-of-the-century physicians to regard certain cerebral states, like poetic reverie or absorption in philosophical abstractions, as particularly apt to induce illness.

Prior to that, however, the discourse on intellectual pathologies had a leveling quality: it applied not just to philosophical, scientific, and literary luminaries but also the "pauvres diables" who had to write for a living, and to failed aspirants to intellectual celebrity.[23] Not everyone agreed with this lack of qualitative distinctions. For example, Ramazzini's French translator, Fourcroy, left out the chapter on the diseases of the learned from his 1777 *Essai sur les maladies des artisans, traduit du latin de Ramazzini*. Fourcroy's intent, as Dinah Ribard explains, was to make it more clearly "a book on the illnesses of the people, in the sense of the lower ranks of the social world (from which he sought to exclude those whom he didn't believe belonged there)."[24] Generally, though, physicians retained Ramazzini's labor-based approach to intellectual pathologies. Tissot, for instance, clearly read *De Morbis Artificium diatriba* in Latin, and he cautioned that heads of state and barristers could fall ill to the same ailments as metaphysicians if they strained their brains. So, too, could women who got swept up in the craze for novel reading, or people who applied their minds too intently to thoughts of God. As he emphasized, "One shouldn't think that study, properly speaking, is the only cause that can produce the illnesses I am describing; any strong tension of the mind can produce the same effect."[25]

Thinking as Labor: The Dangers of Mental Exertion

As any academic who circulates in the wider world can attest, the notion that thinking entails real, sweat-breaking work is far from universally accepted. Indeed, the perception of thinking as the very opposite of work is deeply ingrained in our culture because of the enduring popularity of *otium*, or philosophical leisure, as an element in the self-construction of the intellectual.[26] The eighteenth century was certainly not lacking in writers who embraced *otium* as a value. The Hebrew professor Jean-Jacques Garnier, for example, described the scholarly mode of leisure as radically distinct from—and superior to—the dissipated leisure life of the aristocracy.[27]

Indolence was also championed in works like Pierre Carlet de Chamblain de Marivaux's *Spectateur français* and Rousseau's *Rêveries du promeneur solitaire*.[28] In general, however, this was a deeply utilitarian period, and those who strove to portray scholarship as useful stressed the sheer effort it required. Such rhetoric sometimes had a sociopolitical dimension: borrowing metaphors of pain and exhaustion from the language of physical labor, apologists of intellectual labor argued that the scholar and the farmhand were equally useful and necessary to the healthy functioning of the state.[29]

We find an early example of the view of thinking as labor in Montesquieu's "Discours prononcé à la rentrée de l'Académie de Bordeaux" (1717):

> If we weren't driven by a beautiful zeal for honor and the perfection of the sciences, there is no one amongst us who would not regard the title of academician as an onerous title, and these very sciences in which we engage as a means more likely to torment us than to instruct us. An undertaking that is often useless; systems that are undone almost as quickly as they are established; the despair of discovering that one's expectations have been dashed; the continuous fatigue of chasing after a fleeting truth; the emulation that reigns with no less power over the minds of *philosophes* than does base jealousy over vulgar minds; the long meditations in which the mind turns in on itself, and fixes upon an object; the sleepless nights, and the anxious days passed in sweat that follow them: you will recognize there, Sirs, the life of men of letters.[30]

For a devoted polymath like Montesquieu—who, in 1717, was just as busy examining renal glands, sheep tongues, and the cause of echoes as he was analyzing the underlying principles of society and government—the quest after truth was exhausting and often frustrating. As he depicted it, studious life involved long and intense meditations, sleepless nights, and days bathed in perspiration, all of which would be a torment for scholars if they were not driven by the passion of emulation and zeal to contribute to the honor and improvement of knowledge.

Eighteenth-century commentators did not jettison all differences between manual versus mental work. Quite the contrary: a fundamental distinction persisted between the mechanical and the liberal arts, as did distinctions based on the exercise of intelligence within the category of *gens de métier*.³¹ For instance, although the Encyclopedists strove to integrate artisans into the collective enterprise of gathering together the various branches of human knowledge, they also maintained a hierarchy that placed *gens de lettres* above craftsmen in their capacity to articulate the *savoir-faire* involved in the mechanical arts; and Louis de Jaucourt's entry "Profession" carefully distinguished a merely "honest" profession like cultivating the earth from a "glorious" one like cultivating knowledge.³² Moreover, moralists and physicians sometimes used the figure of the laborer as a healthful countermodel to the frail, urbane *homme de lettres*, emphasizing the former's simple life and putative simplicity of mind.³³ However, according to the "Ramazzinian" perspective on the health of the learned, intellectuals were just as susceptible as manual laborers to the bodily fatigue and dysfunction brought on by the pursuit of their line of work. What mattered, from this perspective, was not the social standing of the worker or even the particular nature of his or her labors. Rather, it was the intensity of that work, along with its disruptive effect on the organism.

One consequence of this concern over study as work was increased concern about its ambient conditions: for example, the lighting, temperature, and air quality of scholarly cabinets. Yet doctors also paid increasing attention to the act of study itself, painting it in terms of threats that came as much from within the individual as from without. That sense of threat was inscribed in the very term used to characterize serious thinking: *la contention d'esprit*, or mental exertion. The application of the term *contention* to mental activity was a fairly recent phenomenon: *contention* had originally denoted battle or dispute.³⁴ By midcentury, however, the default meaning of the term was mental—as is illustrated by Denis Diderot's short entry in the *Encyclopédie*:

> CONTENTION [EXERTION] (*Gramm. & Métaph.*): Long, strong, and painful application of the mind to some object of meditation. *Exertion* supposes difficulty, importance on the part of the subject matter, and persistence and fatigue on the part of the *philosophe*. There are things that one can understand only through *exertion*. . . . There is only a difference of degree between *exertion* and application. *Exertion* is distinguished from meditation by the ideas of persistence, duration, and fatigue, which *exertion* supposes, and meditation does not. *Exertion* is the result of reiterated efforts.³⁵

No flesh-and-blood adversary is present in the battle described here: the struggle is solitary, internal, and cerebral. This brief portrait of the *philosophe* engaged in intense mental application emphasizes both the necessity of *contention* for grasping difficult ideas and the fatigue brought on by the effort. And fatigue, as Diderot underscored in a different article, was the inevitable effect of any "considerable effort"—whether the part at work was the body or the mind.[36] It is worth noting that the term *surmener* applied only to horses and other beasts of burden at this time: not until the 1840s was its derivative *surmenage* invented (in a veterinary context, according to the *Trésor de la langue française*); and not until the 1880s was its meaning extended to humans, to denote mental fatigue.[37]

This image of *gens de lettres* as exhausted by incessant mental exertion was promoted in a variety of contexts, including academic *éloges* and conduct books. The Parisian polygraph Jean André Perreau made this remark in his *Instruction du peuple* (1786): "It is true that only the common people undertake physical work, but there are other sorts of work that may not seem so tiring but may be even more. What, then, is this sort of work? It is the work of the mind, the work of business."[38] A similar view of mental work was promoted in treatises directed at medical students: Marin-Jacques-Clair Robert told those readers that major mental exertion triggered body-shaking spasms in the entire organism, creating enormous tension in the thinker who engaged in serious meditation.[39] The medical popularizer Charles Augustin Vandermonde also tied mental work to overexertion of the nervous system in the long section of his *Dictionnaire portatif de santé* (first ed., 1759) that dealt with the illnesses of scholars: "*Gens de lettres* typically err through an excess opposite to that committed by manual workers: they have their minds continuously strained and occupied, which taxes the nerves and makes the functions languish, the stomach lazy, and digestion slow."[40]

Dr. Paul-Victor de Sèze presented a full cascade of study-induced bodily events in the chapter on sex in his *Recherches physiologiques et philosophiques sur la sensibilité* (1786):

> At the moment when a man fixes all of his attention on the object of his research, his brain swells: its fibers stretch and attract a greater portion of the body's general activity. . . . However, the action of the brain does not suffice on its own: it must be reinforced by a

strong tension in the phrenic center, in the intestines and all of the viscera of the lower abdomen. One can see, when a person has meditated a long while, that the diaphragm, stretched and hampered in its movements, impedes freedom of respiration and even suspends it, such that the person is forced to sigh from time to time. The constriction of the epigastrum and of the entire intestinal canal supposes an effort that can be made only at the expense of the exterior organ [the skin], which remains inactive.[41]

Full concentration, as Sèze described it, virtually shut down the sense organs: "a man plunged in mental work does not see, even though he has his eyes open; his senses are inactive; only the head and the epigastrum are in action." If the scholar had the intestinal fortitude necessary to counterbalance the swelling and tension of his brain, then he could emerge relatively unscathed from the experience. However, if his viscera were weak, his intense mental action would wreak havoc by slowing down the functions of the abdominal organs.[42] Sèze then compared the brain's disruptive effects on the scholarly body to those created by the uterus in the female body, which was held to take its revenge for "unnatural," worldly living by causing hysteria (his purpose there was to discourage female readers from even attempting study).

The intense, exhausting mental effort that physicians attributed to the cerebralist did, of course, coexist with sedentariness, a condition doctors commonly sought to cure by prescribing exercise, including manual labor.[43] However, French and Swiss doctors referred less often to the dangers of physical inactivity for intellectuals than did their British counterparts.[44] It may be that, in the eyes of their physicians, French-speaking *gens de lettres* partook of the frenetic qualities that Montesquieu had famously attributed to his countrymen in *Les Lettres persanes* (1721), where he mocked the nation's presumptions to have reached one of the summits of human achievement by maintaining a social pace that (as his character Rica described it) was so overactive as to approach the superhuman.[45] Judging from the astounding rate of literary production among the French Enlightenment's most celebrated authors, the Republic of Letters in which they dwelled did, indeed, seem to operate at an exhausting pace. The view of thinking as labor was clearly in keeping with their self-image as heroically active.

Medical Warnings on the Passion for Study

Medical warnings about the pathogenic effects of intellectual work typically evoked some combination of physical and moral causes. Authors who emphasized the first saw the problem as residing in the mechanics of thinking itself: sustained mental work upset the overall animal economy, causing too much nervous fluid to be retained in the brain. Such a state shut down the senses, dried out the viscera, and suspended essential bodily functions like digestion and evacuation. However alarming, this view allowed its proponents to maintain that the damage of study could be corrected through gentle diets and exercise programs that would restore health and regularity to the scholarly body. The other, more morally slanted perspective on overstudy blamed more intractable causes for the rise of *maladies des gens de lettres*: for example, the zeal that some intellectuals exhibited for solitary reading, writing, and meditation; and the popularization of the sciences and arts, which had expanded the ranks of avid readers and aspirants to learning.

From the 1750s onward, intellectuals as a group were held to embody a dangerous combination of nervous constitution, bad hygiene, and questionable work habits. Passion played a role in this perception, in that doctors attributed the ailments rampant among *gens de lettres* not just to the work involved in study but also to the immoderate pursuit of intellectual pleasure. As Vandermonde declared, when the man of letters chased after the "insidiously flattering" pleasure of discovering truths, he strained his nerves beyond their natural capacity and harmed their spirits, by either corrupting them or draining them away from their normal channels. The damage done was easy to see: he cited, as proof, the heaviness and weakness that scholars commonly felt when they had worked too much, as well as their reddened, inflamed faces.[46]

The dangers of scholarly ardor were also singled out by the Parisian doctor Anne-Charles Lorry in the second, expanded edition of his *Essai sur l'usage des alimens* (1757). Lorry framed his discussion of the special dietary needs of intellectuals with sobering reflections on their generally frail health. Although he praised study as the source of humanity's greatest achievements, he emphasized the high price that scholars paid for their intellectual zeal: it led many toward a premature death. He then painted this dark portrait of a meditator: "If you look at the face of a man who is completely applied to his object [of study], you will see him in a sort of ecstasy. He neither sees nor hears, and he barely breathes. If you take his pulse, you'll find it even, well-developed, but slow. His evacuations are suspended; he doesn't perspire or urinate. . . . The state produced in the body by work and application can be compared only to the effects of chagrin and fear, in which the mind, likewise occupied by an object, can be distracted by no other."[47] Although he used the term "ecstasy," what Lorry perceived when he regarded a man lost in thought was the opposite of exaltation: he saw disruption of the bodily functions, suffering induced in the lowly viscera, and a fearsome fixity in the mind.

The passion for study was thus a significant factor in the etiology of the diseases to which scholars were deemed vulnerable during the Enlightenment. As Zimmermann put it, "The desire to acquire enlightenment or to make use of the knowledge which one has acquired can easily be ranked among the passions, because it is so strong in some people that it absorbs almost all their other passions."[48] Even while expressing admiration for those driven by this sort of desire (*volupté*), Zimmermann cautioned that it was appreciated by precious few in society at large.[49] Dr. Jean Jacques Ménuret de Chambaud likewise warned in the *Encyclopédie* that an unbridled zeal for certain intellectual subjects made people particularly susceptible to mania: "Those who are . . . endowed with a lively, penetrating mind, Poets, Philosophers, Mathematicians, those who give themselves over passionately to algebraic analyses, are the most liable to fall ill to this disease."[50]

In short, these doctors offered deliberately unpleasant portraits of people in the grips of the passion that drove deep cerebration. Their rhetoric even brings to mind the defamiliarizing techniques popular in exotic novels like Montesquieu's *Les Lettres persanes* and Graffigny's *Les Lettres d'une Péruvienne* (1747), where everyday things like city streets or scissors are transformed into bewildering objects when seen through a foreigner's eyes. These physicians aimed to offer their scholarly readers both an unsettling mirror in which to see themselves and some vivid lessons on the dangerous results of intellectual intemperance. Their descriptions read almost like an inversion of the popular sensationalist fable—put forth in Condillac's *Traité des sensations* (1754), among other texts—of the statue who came to life through the successive activation of the sense organs. Whereas the statue enjoyed expansive sentience starting with the smell of the rose, overzealous scholars became stuporous.

How to Cure "Literary Exhaustion": Tips from Tissot

> I rightly regard this work, so well conceived and so well written, as the breviary of *gens de lettres*.
> —Charles Bonnet, letter to Tissot

No single medical doctor was more effective at scaring eighteenth-century *gens de lettres* about their health than Tissot.[51] Trained in Montpellier and closely affiliated with many major scientific figures of the Enlightenment, he was a highly sought practitioner who attracted patients from all over Europe to his home city of Lausanne, a phenomenon noted by Isabelle de Charrière in her 1785 novel *Lettres écrites de Lausanne*.[52] However, what has kept Tissot in the spotlight was his fame as a medical writer. In addition to lending his voice to the campaign in favor of inoculation (*L'Inoculation justifiée*, 1754), he wrote the best-selling works *De l'onanisme* (1760) and *Avis au peuple sur sa santé* (1761) before turning to the problem of *maladies des gens de lettres*.[53] His works illustrate both a Calvinist cautiousness toward the high culture of the day and the extra-metropolitan geographic reach of the French-speaking Enlightenment.

Through the combined effects of his medical practice, teaching activities, books, and extensive correspondence, Tissot was "at the center of a dense scientific and worldly network that covered all of Europe."[54] One senses the complexity of that network in the pages of *La santé des gens de lettres*, a text that originated as *Sermo academicus de valetudine litteratorum*, which Tissot delivered in 1766 upon assuming the Académie de Lausanne's new Chair in Medicine. After the Latin oration appeared in 1767 in the form of a "detestable," unauthorized Parisian translation, Tissot rushed to translate it himself and had that version published under his watchful eye in 1768. After publishing a slightly modified edition in 1769, he produced a third, substantially revised, and expanded edition of the book in 1775. This edition is not as well known as the book's original French version, largely because most re-editions and translations are based on the 1768 edition.[55] It is, however, the 1775 edition that Tissot regarded as definitive —and that most clearly reflects his views on the health risks created by the studious life, along with his nuanced position on the moral implications of intellectual pursuit.

While acknowledging those who had written before him on the topic, Tissot claimed to be the first physician to offer a systematic account of the health circumstances "that differentiate the state of Scholars from that of other orders of society" (*SGL*, xii).[56] He aimed to make the book a collaborative work between himself, his medical colleagues, and the *gens de lettres* who read it. Toward the end of the preface to the 1768 edition (reproduced in the 1775 edition), he invited "that respectable segment of men who devote themselves to the instruction of others" to help him perfect his treatise by sending him "the important observations they may have made on their own state" (xii).

In fact, Tissot cited only a few letters from laypersons. One was an unnamed lady's account of the ills she had contracted from reading too late in the evening (92); another was a "very polite" letter he'd received from a lawyer who wrote to defend tea drinking, a practice that Tissot viewed as pernicious and far too common in Europe (197–99). The new observations added in 1775 came mostly from other sources: his medical practice, from which he drew the poignant story of the "progressive withering away" [*dépérissement successif*] that had claimed the life of his friend M. de Brenles, inserted into article 12 (34–43)[57]; academic eulogies and medical books he had recently read, like Johann Jakob Brucker's "Leibnitii vita" (1768) and Joseph Lieutaud's 1767 *Historia anatomica medica* (32–33, 52–53); and the preface written in 1769 by James Kirkpatrick, Tissot's English translator. One of the observations taken from Kirkpatrick is especially striking: "If one considers a man plunged in meditation, one sees that all the muscles of his face are stretched; they even seem at times to be in convulsion; and in the lovely preface he added to the English translation of this work, Mr. Kirkpatrick cites a fact that must find a place here: 'I knew,' says he, 'a gentleman with a very active genius who, when he thought intensely, had all the fibers of his forehead and a part of his face as visibly agitated as the chords of a harpsichord that is being played in a very lively manner'" (14–15).[58] Interestingly, in transcribing this anecdote, Tissot altered the sex of the person depicted, turning Kirkpatrick's "gentlewoman" into a *gentilhomme*.[59] This addition reinforced a long series of citations emphasizing the physical fatigue induced by thinking, which Tissot drew from sources as diverse as Plato, Ramazzini, Montesquieu, Bonnet, and recent issues of the London biweekly newspaper the *Adventurer* (he was often very precise in quoting them).

Clearly, through his arresting portraits of scholars laid low by what he poetically called "literary exhaustion" (*SGL*, 22), intermingled with frequent appeals to the culture of his readers, Tissot sought to address learned people as much as his medical colleagues. As François Rosset notes, "Tissot was, fundamentally, a typical *homme de lettres* of his time: he had a very solid classical training, knew several European languages, was involved in salons and worldly circles, and was open to current literary and intellectual events, despite having somewhat rigid tastes."[60] Throughout *De la santé des gens de lettres*, Tissot interwove his own ideas about the causes of illness in scholars with those of his medical contemporaries and notions that had been circulating since antiquity; and he incorporated multiple examples of poets, painters, philosophers, mathematicians, statesmen, and physicians who either had suffered from excessive mental application or had devised ways to counterbalance its deleterious health effects.

Milton was thus enlisted to prove the intellectual's susceptibility to temperature extremes (*SGL*, 204), whereas Corneille and Molière served to demonstrate that it is possible to produce literary masterpieces without the benefit of coffee (Tissot's counterexample here was the Swedish astronomer Celsius, who "killed himself through the use of coffee"; 202). Tissot also cited Rousseau as a patient, in a chapter on kidney stones: "no one is unaware of the cruel pains of this sort to which the illustrious and learned antagonist of the Sciences is subject" (80). In an addition made in 1775, he singled out the houses of Bernouilli and Cassini as exceptions to the general rule that overstudy so weakened men's seminal fluid that great thinkers rarely sired sons worthy of them (83–84). He even worked himself into the text as a patient on two occasions, citing the eye strain and stomach ailments he had suffered as a result of working too much (60–61, 229–30). Tissot's list of possible study-induced disorders included everything from poor digestion to more dire conditions like the sensory impairment observed in the renowned Greek scholar Madame Dacier, who, "while reciting Hector's farewell to Andromache, was so deeply moved that she lost the use of her senses" (19).

Clearly, storytelling was central to Tissot's effort to make these various ailments recognizable and worrisome to his readers. While many of his tales featured well-known scholars of the past or present day, some involved anonymous victims of excessive mental application. One particularly dramatic example was the case he took from his friend Zimmermann of a young Swiss gentleman who wore himself out by studying metaphysics. Although increasingly weak, the young man intensified his efforts; after six months, his ailment became so severe that "his mind and senses gradually fell into a state of utter stupor" (*SGL*, 22). His doctors struggled for a year to pull him out of his oblivion, but nothing worked until someone stood very close to the patient and read a letter in a thundering voice, which woke him up painfully, thereby unblocking his ears. That therapy was continued for another year until all of the young man's senses were restored: "he recovered completely, and is today one of our best philosophers" (24).[61]

Tissot intermingled success stories like this with rebukes to those who indulged in "literary intemperance" (*SGL*, 28). However, he refrained from pronouncing a purely negative judgment on the role of study in relation to health, because he did not want his book to be read as a polemical attack on scholarship. Much as *De la santé des gens de lettres* aimed to shock its readers by diagnosing the many illnesses that could be induced by study, the book's central mission was to remedy those ills.

Tissot made this clear in a passage added to the very last article of the 1775 edition, where he alluded to the "famous trial" that Rousseau had launched at midcentury with his *First Discourse*:

> My book offers a picture of the ills produced by an excessive attachment to study, but readers should refrain from concluding that I regard studying as dangerous and seek to put people off of it. This great question is unresolved, and I am far from wanting to enter into that famous trial which never should have existed; even if it were true, which I don't believe, that learning doesn't contribute to the happiness of society considered in general, one cannot deny that the knowledge of Letters increases the happiness of the person who possesses it, when he has not acquired it at the expense of his duties or at the cost of his health. (*SGL*, 240)

One of the puzzling aspects of *De la santé des gens de lettres* is, in fact, the seemingly paradoxical stance it takes in regard to Rousseau's already paradoxical "famous trial."[62] On the one hand, to lend credence to the argument that spending too much time hunched over books made *gens de lettres* fearful and melancholic, Tissot cited the passage from the "Préface à *Narcisse*" in which Rousseau blamed the arts and sciences for weakening men's moral and physical nature (31). He also assumed an overtly Rousseauistic tone in a long footnote to a later article, where he identified "the love of the Sciences and the much expanded culture of Letters" as one of the causes for the contemporary explosion of nervous maladies (185–89). Tissot clearly admired Rousseau: the two men exchanged cordial letters during the 1760s, and Tissot was greatly impressed by Rousseau when they met in person in July 1762.[63]

Yet for all of that, Tissot ended the 1775 edition of *La santé* with an emphatic defense of learned endeavor: "While reproaching those who devote themselves too passionately to study, I have not been referring to those who cultivate knowledge [*les sciences*] in a prudent fashion; and if one exposes oneself to the most unfortunate illnesses by sacrificing everything to the love of learning, one exposes oneself to shame by remaining in ignorance.... Let the detractors of study not be mistaken: one must adopt one or the other of these principles, either that the cultivation of the mind is a true good, or that the stupidest of animals is happier than man" (241). This passage directly echoed a remark Zimmermann had made in his treatise on experience: "The great benefit of knowledge [*les sciences*] for the individual is to save us from *ennui*, which I regard as the greatest enemy of the mind and body alike. Knowledge makes our lives less animal, less limited to the dust on which we tread."[64] In other words, the two Swiss physicians took a nuanced perspective toward Rousseau. On the one hand, they echoed some of his moral hygiene precepts, like his warnings on the influence of the passions over the mind, and his promotion of the curative powers of mountain air;[65] on the other hand, they did not agree with his argument that knowledge seeking was, in itself, pathological.

Curiously enough, Tissot provided a way of resolving this apparent contradiction in an earlier work, *De l'onanisme* (1760). In a recent reevaluation of that famous book, Patrick Singy refutes the conventional interpretation of *De l'onanisme* as a religiously motivated antimasturbation screed: he underscores that the "sinful" aspect of masturbation was *not* the main issue that preoccupied Tissot and the laypeople who wrote to him for advice on the health problems they associated with their sexual activities (solitary or otherwise).[66] The central problem, in their eyes, was not sex per se but, rather, excess: that is, the immoderate loss of semen, held at the time to be one of the body's most precious fluids. Singy emphasizes the particularity of the perspective taken by Tissot's correspondents: they "did not isolate sex from other problems that we, as modern people, would tend to keep clearly separated.... Bertrand Duclaux, who wrote for a sick friend, grouped together 'venereal acts,' the study of abstract sciences, and food.... Coffee, alcohol, food, studying, dance, gambling, hunting, late nights, hiking—and sex."[67]

The conceptual framework underlying this way of thinking was the ancient doctrine of the nonnaturals, which were defined as air, food and drink, exercise and sleep, bodily retentions and evacuations, and the passions of the soul (the last term was generally used by physicians and philosophers to designate moral causes and their bodily effects).[68] The driving logic of the nonnaturals doctrine was more quantitative than qualitative. According to this logic, excess in one hygienic category could be remedied through moderation in another, because all the nonnaturals had the same mechanical effects on the animal economy: depletion or restoration of a necessary vital resource. Too much sexual activity—whether it involved masturbation or "the use of women"—could therefore be compensated by giving up coffee and following soothing therapies like drinking *petit-lait* and taking tepid baths.[69]

A close reading of *De la santé des gens de lettres* leads to a similar conclusion: the central problem, in Tissot's eyes, was not study in and of itself, but rather an excessive "attachment" or "passion" or "love" for letters or the sciences (*SGL*, 32, 80, 185, 235, 240, and passim). This is consistent with the remark he made in an unpublished manuscript: "A wise doctor, consulted on the rules to follow to conserve health in a man with a good temperament, reduced them all to this one: avoid excess. Clearly, the term excess needs to be understood here in relation to age, strength, and sex."[70] Although Tissot recommended relative moderation in all bodily functions, he also believed that one could compensate for excess in one area through asceticism in another: for example, sexual—or intellectual—excess could be counterbalanced and corrected by dietary asceticism. A quantitative vision of health as the avoidance of excess pervades *La santé* just as much as it does *De l'onanisme*. It may, in fact, be this quantifying reasoning that most distinguishes Tissot's hygienic perspective on intellectual labor from the moralistic view of Rousseau, who condemned the pursuit of learning for all but the greatest geniuses.[71]

As Tissot's modern biographer, Antoinette Emch-Dériaz, points out, the thematic structure of *De la santé des gens de lettres* follows the standard categories of medical hygiene: the book covers all the ways in which scholars used and misused the six nonnaturals.[72] The topics of food and drink take up a good fifty pages of the book (articles 57–73, out of a total of 92), not including the discussions devoted to intellectuals' notoriously weak stomachs. Among other things, Tissot took scholars to task for their bad table habits, like hasty eating and inadequate chewing (*SGL*, 173). He considered them overly susceptible to fads and excesses of the gastronomic variety, like tea drinking.[73] He also warned against overeating, both in this book and in his *mémoires de consultation*. For Tissot and like-minded doctors, appetite was "the somatic locus where powers of mind might be overwhelmed by bodily desires."[74]

Tissot also had plenty to say about air quality, sleep, and bodily retentions and evacuations. He chastised scholars for their tendency to work late at night in the stuffy air of their studies (*SGL*, 89–94) and to delay urination and defecation, a bad habit he attributed to "the ardor for work taken to a *ridiculous and blameful excess* that does not allow a person to take the time to eat or drink" (97; my emphasis).

Quantifying reasoning is evident at many points in *De la santé des gens de lettres*, particularly in passages devoted to the laws of the animal economy (*SGL*, articles 14–17) or to the principles of sound hygiene. Take, for instance, Tissot's emphasis on the sensitivity of scholars to changes in temperature: "*gens de lettres* are living barometers who feel most cruelly all the changes in the weather" (83). This, he explained, was a result of a reduction in "subtle transpiration" (*transpiration insensible*), which afflicted learned people because of their physical inactivity. Another example is his suggestion that they would enjoy healthier, longer lives if they balanced the hours they devoted to their studies with time spent on civic duties (like the exemplary Professor Polier, the "ornament" of the Lausanne academy for over fifty years; 63) as well as on recreational activities. On the subject of exercise, Tissot encouraged *gens de lettres* to make a habit of strolling in the open air and playing lively games like tennis and pall-mall. One of the main reasons Tissot viewed scholars as prone to illness was purely physical: neglect of the body's basic needs had as much to do with their sickliness as did ardent mental work.

Few people, Tissot emphasized, were born with the strong constitution necessary to perform unremitting intellectual labor without suffering the unfortunate consequences. As he argued in another addition to the 1775 edition, this time alluding to Voltaire, "the example of an illustrious man who was already writing very pretty verses at the age of six, and who, at the age of eighty, is writing with as much fire and even more gaiety than when he was thirty, may be a unique example" (127–28). Considering that Voltaire's chronic health problems had attracted significant attention since the 1720s—not least through his very public self-fashioning as the "old invalid from Ferney"—this example merely reinforces the more general law that structures the argumentation in *La santé des gens de lettres*: thinking sapped the health of those who undertook it without sufficient precaution. Tissot directed that warning at both ends of the age spectrum: people of advancing age who became overly enthused for a new field of learning (122), and young people whose instructors pushed them precociously into intensive study. Too many talented young minds, he declared, had been ruined by such hothouse pedagogical methods: "I have seen children full of wit attacked by this literary frenzy beyond their years, and I have predicted with pain the destiny that awaited them: they start by being prodigies and end up as idiots" (114).[75]

However, despite the many pages Tissot devoted to diet and recreation, the most fundamental category of the nonnaturals at issue in *De la santé des gens de lettres* is the sixth one, the passions of the soul. The passions held serious health dangers for scholars because they were so obstinately attached to their studies, "too subject to go to extremes" about other things (including exercise; 150), and susceptible to intense, irrational fears because they overworked their brains. Passions are, in fact, the theme of the most dramatic tales Tissot recounted, like the vignettes of Tasso, Spinello, Pascal, and other famous thinkers, writers, and artists who went totally or partially insane (44–51). The chain of causation in their pathologies started in the mind, proving the general principle that "the mind long occupied has impressed too strong an action upon the brain and is no longer able to suppress it." In physical terms, prolonged mental application was like a "ligature" applied to all of the nerves at once (43); when the mind upset the organism to such an extent, the results were catastrophic.

Tissot's moralizing rhetoric is most pronounced in the article that marks the midpoint of *La santé des gens de lettres*: article 52, where he shifted from the grim recounting of ailments induced by overstudy into an explanation of the practical measures by which scholars could restore and maintain their health. Noting that *gens de lettres* were typically difficult patients to treat, he compared them to "lovers who fly off the handle when one dares to say that the object of their passion has defects; moreover, they almost all have the sort of fixity in their ideas that is created by study" (132). He also lamented their delusional belief that they could somehow escape the ravages of excessive mental work:

> Warn, reason, plead, scold, it's often a waste of time; they delude themselves in a thousand different ways. One counts on the vigor of his temperament, the other on the force of habit; this one hopes to avoid the punishment because he hasn't yet been punished; that one

justifies his behavior by citing outside examples that prove nothing about his particular case. All of them counter the Doctor with an obstination that they regard as a laudable firmness, and to which they fall victim. Far from fearing the danger to come, they don't even want to pay attention to the ill at hand, or rather, the greatest of all ills is to be deprived of their work. (132–33)

This strategy of incrimination continued in the next article, where Tissot compared *gens de lettres* to selfish gluttons: "most of them don't even have the public in mind, and devour study only as the gourmand devours meat: to assuage his passion. Too often, this leads them to neglect many essential duties. Rush them, drag them out of their *cabinet*, force them to engage in rest and entertainments that will ward off ills and restore their strength" (134–35). Interestingly, however, Tissot then did an about-face and declared that, by spending time outside of their libraries, scholars "will come back to their work with a new ardor, and a few moments devoted every day to leisure will be well compensated by the enjoyment of a long health which will prolong the time of their studies" (135).

In short, the key to health and longevity was not to avoid study altogether but, rather, to engage in it moderately. That meant avoiding "literary intemperance," a term Tissot used to refer to any sort of overly assiduous reading or studious reflection: "I have myself seen patients who were punished by this literary intemperance, first through the loss of appetite, the absolute cessation of digestion resulting in a general weakness, weight loss, atrophy, and then by spasms, convulsions, and finally the loss of all their physical senses" (28). Intellectuals *could*, he reassured his readers, cultivate their chosen specialty if they interrupted their studies often enough to restore balance in their lives and in their bodies (135). At bottom, it all came down to sobriety, broadly construed: *gens de lettres* had to learn to control their extraordinary appetites for learning. And when they fell ill, they needed to follow their doctors' orders and take their convalescence seriously:

> By neglecting their convalescence, *Gens de Lettres* risk never recovering their health altogether and making themselves incapable of any great literary undertaking. It is a bad calculation to sacrifice one's well-being to the pleasure of engaging a few more days in the object of one's passion, but passions are not calculated, and the passion for

Medicine and the Cult of the Thinker   41

learning is, perhaps, the blindest of all. *It destroys all the others*, as Aretaeus said, *the love of one's country, filial love, fraternal love, even the love of one's own conservation; what doesn't it destroy?* (235; emphasis in the original)

A key step was to overcome scholars' tendency to isolate themselves in their study and avoid social commerce. As he reminded his readers, "Men were created to be men; their mutual commerce has advantages that one cannot abandon with impunity, and it has rightly been observed that solitude leads to languor [CICERO *de offic. l. 3. cap.* I.]. Nothing in the world contributes more to health than the gaiety which society animates and which retreat kills" (99–100). Socially engaged intellectuals might end up succumbing anyway to overstudy, like Tissot's much regretted late friend M. de Brenles; their sacrifice, however, was noble and selfless.

Tissot and His Readers

Less than ten years after its first French edition, Tissot's book had already been translated into English, German, Italian, Spanish, and Polish. It was pressed into service by the Christian apologist Abbé Jean Sauri in his *Cours de philosophie: Élémens de métaphysique, ou Préservatif contre le matérialisme et le déisme* (1773), whose entire chapter on the influence of mental application on health consisted of passages lifted from *De la santé*.[76] Tissot's precepts on the hygiene of intellectuals were also subtly "anglicized" by J.-D. Duplanil, who translated William Buchan's *Domestic Medicine* (first ed., 1771) into French in 1775: Duplanil made Buchan's original chapter "Of the Studious" twice as long in *La Médecine domestique* by inserting numerous excerpts taken verbatim from *La santé des gens de lettres*. Some of these additions were duly attributed to Tissot, but others were close paraphrases (like a passage dealing with the bookish "gluttony" of the studious).[77] Thanks to this intertextual strategy, Tissot's opinions on the dangers of intellectual work intertwined with those of Buchan, one of the most famous medical vulgarizers of the day.[78]

De la santé des gens de lettres would continue to be reprinted regularly until 1859, when Dr. Guillaume-Scipion Bertrand de Saint-Germain reedited it in tandem with the *Essai sur les maladies des gens du monde* (first ed., 1770). In his preface, Saint-Germain emphasized both the book's continued utility and its historical value for understanding what he called "the feverish class of *gens de lettres*" that appeared in the eighteenth century, a time when "gens de lettres formed a militia, and took on the privileges of the vanquishing soldier, the disdain for all constraint, and the ardent pursuit of the pleasures of the mind and of the senses; . . . The alteration of health became an almost constant result of the intemperate cultivation of the arts and sciences."[79]

In 1895, the American doctor James Henrie Lloyd sized up *De la santé des gens de lettres* in these terms: "This essay is elegant in style but not always convincing in matter, because it has the still prevailing trait of ascribing too much to the alleged cause. In the cases of Tissot's scholars and literati, every ache, every symptom is to be ascribed to their occupation. The stone in the bladder is with him a concretion of learning. A most instructive case of hysterical sleep in a young man, lasting for a year, is an evidence of nothing but overstudy. The most notable part of his book is the description of neurasthenia (called by other names) due to mental overwork."[80] Lloyd offered a trenchant critique of the obsessively systematic causal logic that Tissot applied to the diseases that he imputed to overstudy. His use of the more modern term "hysterical sleep" to refer to the case of the young Swiss gentleman (*SGL*, 22) also provides a glimpse at one direction in which the discourse on *maladies des gens de lettres* would go in the nineteenth century: toward psychiatry, and the rise of neurasthenia as a disease syndrome (held, initially, to be particularly prevalent among Americans).[81]

We should note, however, that readers in Tissot's day were often quite fully convinced by the matter of his treatise. It was enthusiastically received by his scholarly friends: in a letter to Tissot, Charles Bonnet related that he had felt "goose bumps from head to feet" while reading it, and he complained that he had not yet succeeded in "evangelizing" their mutual friend Albrecht von Haller (a notorious workhorse) on the subject of the hygienic principles Tissot had established for the scholarly regimen.[82] It also got an avid reception from some of Tissot's patients, who were eager to see their own symptoms reflected in the pages of his book. Take, for example, M. Gringet, who wrote this to Dr. Tissot in 1784: "Sir, when your treatise on *La santé des gens de lettres* fell into my hands, I recognized myself with the greatest fright in the different symptoms that you describe with such precision. I saw myself carried to the tragic end of most of the examples you cite. . . . For as long as I can remember, I have been pale, sad, sensitive and timid, loving retreat, reading, painting and music."[83] Séverine Pilloud points out that Gringet may not have qualified for the title of *homme de lettres*, strictly speaking, given that he was an artisan; however, his love of reading—particularly, of reading medical books—allowed him to identify with the suffering scholars depicted in Tissot's work and to construct a personal narrative on that basis.[84]

In short, the way in which lay readers responded to *De la santé des gens de lettres* sometimes illustrated the syndrome of "pathogenic" reading, a mode of imaginary illness rooted in overidentification with the symptoms described in the pages of a medical book. This problem, widely recognized by contemporary physicians, prompted an amusing comment by Diderot: "There are no books that I read more readily than medical books, no men whose conversation I find more interesting than physicians; but that is when I am feeling well."[85] However, the risk of pathogenic reading did not keep Dr. F.-G. Boisseau, the editor of the 1826 re-edition of *De la santé*, from declaring: "Of all books of medicine, this is the only one that is without danger for *gens de lettres*, and the only one that they can consult fruitfully. The author has omitted nothing essential; few writers have better understood the difficult art of composing a book."[86] Writing forty years later, Émile Beaugrand likewise underscored the book's usefulness in a medical dictionary entry entitled "Lettres (Gens de), Hygiène": "From a practical point of view, this is still today the best work that has been written on the topic."[87] As we shall see in Chapters 5 and 6, Tissot's ideas about intellectual pathologies would be widely cited and imitated by various nineteenth-century physicians.

Even Rousseau, despite his general disdain for medicine and doctors, was an avid reader of Tissot. In the correspondence that followed their brief meeting in 1762, Rousseau not only expressed admiration for *De l'onanisme* and *Avis au peuple sur sa santé*, but also sought out the Lausanne physician's opinion on health problems—sometimes on behalf of friends and sometimes on his own behalf.[88] Although Rousseau generally disliked the tendency evident among contemporary physicians to transform him into a clinical case, he made an exception for his friend Tissot. In January 1769, Rousseau sent Tissot a consultation letter describing the stomach swelling and other symptoms he had been suffering for two months, and he ended his missive with a tribute and invitation: "Add this illness, Monsieur, to your registers if you think it is worth it, and may it provide you with some instructive reflections, either for the conservation of this short and miserable human life, or to teach men not to value it for more than it is worth.

For me, I will take some consolation as I see the end of mine approach if that occasion can attract some testimony of your remembrance and friendship."[89] If *De la santé des gens de lettres* can be taken as evidence, Tissot clearly regarded Rousseau's case as a source of highly instructive reflections.

In the end, however, Tissot's most significant reader was probably his friend and colleague Zimmermann. Despite the fact that they met only once in person (in 1775), Tissot and Zimmermann maintained a private correspondence that started in 1754, soon after the publication of Tissot's *L'Inoculation justifiée*, and lasted for over forty years. Each drew on those letters to craft pathographies of the other, which they featured in their publications. In *Traité de l'expérience*, Zimmermann evoked the six-week bout with brain exhaustion brought on by dyspepsia, which Tissot had endured in early 1763.[90] Tissot, in turn, used the case of Zimmermann to illustrate the horrendous headaches and vision disorders that could be caused by mental exertion (*SGL*, 53–54, 104). This exchange of letters seems to have served as a sort of sounding board for each man's thinking on the health and pathologies of *gens de lettres*.

One of the most remarkable traits of *De la santé des gens de lettres* may, in fact, be the extent to which it was shaped by the friendship between two of Enlightenment Europe's most prominent physicians—a friendship carried out in epistolary form, through writing, reading, and shared tales of suffering. Ultimately, it is this correspondence that shows most clearly the sentiments and judgments of Tissot and Zimmermann on the events, people, and great debates of their century—including the polemics surrounding the dangers and advantages of intellectual work. And even though they admired and felt sympathy for Rousseau, these doctors ultimately adopted a more Voltairian perspective that glorified the toll such work took on health.[91]

Tissot even went so far as to propose the reading of *Candide* (1759) as a remedy for Zimmermann when, as a Swiss ex-patriot practicing in Hanover, he suffered bouts of profound *Heimweh*, or nostalgic homesickness, complicated by a case of bodily hypochondria—that is, an illness affecting the organs and viscera of the lower abdomen. As Zimmermann related on September 26, 1768, "I am inclined to believe that I am corporeally ill, and that I have hypochondria to the greatest degree. . . . What I enjoy most is to recount my pains."[92] The treatments proposed by Tissot were a typical assortment for the time: cold or slightly tepid baths, moderate bleedings, mercury, and changes in diet, all accompanied by moral remedies. For example, Tissot encouraged Zimmermann to travel by accepting patients in neighboring cities, to focus his mind on educating his son, and to read entertaining books: "Busy yourself with the sorts of things that provide diversion without being tiring, and that are necessary to you in the state of despondency in which you find yourself. Read pleasant, lighthearted things like Horace, Petroneus, Montaigne, *Candide*. If Trimalcion and the six Majesties who went to spend Carnival in Venice don't make you laugh, I regard your hypochondria as incurable."[93] *Candide* did, indeed, help to alleviate Zimmermann's overwhelming depression, as he reported five months later: "Three Christian doctors, Mess. Muller, Meyer and Wichmann, and a Jewish doctor were assembled today in the room next to the Hole where I sleep. I had my wife tell them that I was sleeping deeply, whereas in truth I wrote this letter and read *Candide* cover to cover."[94] Unfortunately, the cure did not last long: Zimmermann's homesick melancholy soon returned, and within a few months his letters were given over to a new source of sadness, the deteriorating health of his beloved first wife, who died the following year.

Judging from the *Vie de Zimmermann*, which Tissot wrote shortly after the death of his dear friend, it was Zimmermann, as much as Rousseau, who illustrated the tendencies of the ardent genius. And whereas Zimmermann called *De la santé* "my breviary," Tissot showered praise upon all the books of his late friend in his final eulogy, which he began with this epigraph: "He lived long enough for his glory, but not long enough for humanity."[95]

Chapter 2

The Ardor for Study: Inwardness and the Zealous Cerebralist

Approaching *Gens de lettres*

When viewed in terms of cultural visibility, intellectual life in Enlightenment Europe can appear spectacular. Some of the period's biggest stars—Isaac Newton, Voltaire, Rousseau—were famous because of their ideas, and many authors went to considerable lengths to cultivate their public personae, whether as urbane wits or moral leaders of the nation. Those efforts were fostered by the tendency to glorify celebrated thinkers and writers both in print and in art: their life stories were recounted in academic *éloges* and biographical dictionaries, and their faces were immortalized through busts, statues, and the growing market in inexpensive portraits. Of course, as Antoine Lilti has emphasized, celebrity culture affected not just those who were lionized as intellectual and literary heroes but also entertainers, artistic virtuosi, and political leaders.[1] Still, it helped to create an exceptional amount of interest in the traits and habits of *gens de lettres*.

The term *gens de lettres* was broad and somewhat nebulous in meaning during the eighteenth century.[2] Just as the canon of "great Frenchmen" covered a range that included statesmen and soldiers as well as writers, scientists, and philosophers, the title of *gens de lettres* was applied to many sorts of people who engaged in intellectual activity.[3] The plural term *gens de lettres* was relatively gender-neutral, in contrast to terms like *femmes savantes* and *femmes philosophes* (both of which were pejorative). It was also more ideologically neutral than *philosophe*, a figure often endowed with specific moral characteristics—like critical reason and civic responsibility, as pro-Enlightenment authors insisted, or impiety and cynical self-interest, as their *anti-philosophe* adversaries countered.[4]

The appellation of *gens de lettres* was not necessarily synonymous with *écrivains* or *auteurs*. After all, as Voltaire observed, one could belong to the former category without ever putting pen to paper: "There are many *gens de lettres* who are not authors, and they are probably the happiest; they are shielded from the weariness that the writerly profession sometimes brings, from the quarrels that rivalry engenders, from partisan animosities, and false judgments; they have more solidarity among themselves and take greater pleasure in society. They are the judges and the others are judged."[5] While Voltaire's remark was clearly intended to make a wry point about the persecutions suffered by some contemporary authors (himself included), it also highlights two traits that provided a group identity to *gens de lettres*: a certain solidarity among themselves, and a prudent distance from society.

For the medical authors we examined in Chapter 1, what bound this group together was a particular set of ailments and obsessions, which physicians like Tissot believed they could cure through stern and sound advice to all those who engaged in mental work. When they dwelled on the obsessional aspect of mental endeavor, those doctors reflected a more general cultural belief: namely, that those who belonged to the ranks of *gens de lettres* shared a common passion—the passion for learning—that differentiated them from the common herd. Because it entailed a mixture of rational, sensuous, and social qualities, that passion was regarded with a combination of admiration and suspicion.

This ambivalence is evident in the abbé Claude Yvon's *Encyclopédie* article "Amour des sciences et des lettres," a text taken (without explicit attribution) from Luc de Clapier Vauvenargues's *Introduction à la connaissance de l'esprit humain* (1747). After a melancholic reflection on the sense of emptiness and imperfection that underpinned the passion for learning, Yvon (citing Vauvenargues) declared that "one cannot have a great soul or a somewhat penetrating mind without some passion for Letters. Most men honor Letters as they do religion or virtue: that is, as something that they can neither know, nor practice, nor love."[6] Those lines sum up the period's double-edged attitude about scholarly pursuit: a passion for learning was essential to greatness of soul and intellect, but only the fit and few could truly feel or understand it. The text also expressed broader thinking by underscoring that people gripped with this passion were inclined to misdirect it or carry it to excess. Rigorous knowledge seeking, in this view, wasn't appropriate for everyone, and those who undertook it required guidance to avoid its dangers.

The notion that knowledge seeking is rooted in passion had, of course, existed prior to this period. The seventeenth-century philosophers René Descartes and Nicolas Malebranche were ambivalent about curiosity and wonder, the two emotions they associated with intellectual endeavor. What made these cognitive passions problematic, in their eyes, were the nonintellectual motives that sometimes drove the desire to learn. In *La Recherche de la vérité* (1641), Descartes commented that "the desire to know, which is common to all men, is an incurable malady" and characterized insatiable, blind curiosity as particularly unhealthy.[7] In *De la recherche de la vérité, où l'on traite de la nature de l'esprit de l'homme* (1674–75), Malebranche ridiculed "those so called studious persons" who, although lacking the capacity to meditate, were moved to read ambitiously either by excessive esteem for some author or by "the stupid vanity that makes us hope to be esteemed as scholars."[8] However, there is an important distinction between the excessive, unproductive desire for knowledge criticized by Descartes and the sort of wonder or "admiration" that he described elsewhere as compatible with knowledge—as, for example, when he spoke of intellectual joy in article XCI of the *Passions de l'âme* (1649).[9] Descartes was one of the theorists who elaborated what Susan James calls an "internally complex conception of knowledge . . . closely linked to emotion" and who emphasized the joy that is achieved when the mind "rejoices in the operations of its own understanding."[10] Moreover, as Lorraine Daston and Katharine Park contend, curiosity was revalued by 1750 as a positive spur to knowledge, a respectable motive underlying earnest application to intellectual inquiry.[11]

The changing status of the cognitive passions was tied to a larger reconfiguration of philosophy that rejected the Stoical antithesis between reason and affect, took a serious interest in the psychological and physical underpinnings of the emotions, and saw the passions not as vices or obstacles to reason, but, rather, as forces instrumental to maintaining human life, bringing happiness, and pushing people to improve their condition.[12] Proponents of this view regarded the wish to improve and expand one's mind as an urge inherent to human nature—one that, with proper discipline and direction, could both extend knowledge and enable the individual to live a good and virtuous life. As part of their effort to integrate mathematics and the scientific disciplines into the quest for noble self-cultivation, Descartes,

Pascal, and Leibniz developed methods for training and perfecting the intellect that took account of the role played by the emotions in knowledge seeking.¹³ These views, along with John Locke's sense-based philosophy of mind, were adapted and expanded by various eighteenth-century French authors, ranging from sensationist epistemologists like Etienne Bonnot de Condillac to libertine writers like Boyer d'Argens.¹⁴

Overzealous or misdirected indulgence in learning was nonetheless an ongoing concern in eighteenth-century discussions of scholarship, and that worry was accentuated by medical warnings about the health risks of mental application. The association of study with work and strain suited both the polemics of the day and the newly revalorized myth of the suffering scholar. Whereas Rousseau emphasized the collective social and moral weakness produced by the advancement of the arts and sciences, Voltaire underscored the personal debility caused by intellectual effort, drawing attention throughout his correspondence to his ardent, exhausting stints of reading, meditating, and writing.

All of these factors fostered a perception of *gens de lettres* as a group that was temperamentally distinct from the larger cultural establishment. An aura of mystery as well as difference surrounded this group: whereas gregariousness was commonly viewed as a defining trait of the contemporary French social elite, serious intellectuals operated, according to some of their observers, in an affective register of intense inwardness and separateness from the world.

Curiously, aside from being mentioned occasionally in historical discussions of genius, this particular image of eighteenth-century and nineteenth-century *gens de lettres* has not received much attention—despite the fact that emotions have become a popular object of study in the past two decades.¹⁵ This may be due to the preoccupation with sentimentalism among scholars interested in emotions in Old Regime or Revolutionary-era France. Sentimentalism has inspired a range of interpretations, negative as well as positive. One of the sharpest critiques is that of William Reddy, who associates sentimentalism with "effusive, lachrymose emotives" that externalized extreme feeling via tears, sighs, trembling, falling on one's knees, and so on; he argues that those "emotives" were suffocating for those who weren't inclined to go along with such affectation.¹⁶ Taking a different view, David Denby and Sara Maza emphasize the socially transformative powers of literary sentimentalism: its dramatic verbal and bodily languages acted, as Maza puts it, as "a solvent of class differences."¹⁷ Building on that perspective,

Lynn Hunt contends that sentimentalism popularized an empathetic, emotionally intense style of reading, which contributed to the emergence of human rights as a sociopolitical principle.[18] Others have credited sentimentalism with such developments as the ascendancy of women in elite culture, the rise of a warmer and less authoritarian ideal of paternity, and the value placed by natural philosophers on empirical modes of scientific inquiry.[19]

My intent here is not to join the debate on sentimentalism's social effects, good or bad. Rather, it is to stress that the effusive style of emotional expression typically associated with sentimentalism coexisted with very different affective styles.[20] For example, Denis Diderot and other *philosophes* used sentimentalism as a tool: they aimed to reform theater, the novel, and the visual arts by making them vehicles for strong, even terrifying emotions that would literally jolt their audiences (it is worth pointing out the resemblance between this aesthetic project and the therapeutics of perturbation advocated by some contemporary biomedical theorists, particularly those who were experimenting with medical electricity).[21] However, these same authors lauded the mastery over feeling, which they held to be characteristic of the sages of the world. It was, as Diderot argued in the *Paradoxe sur le comédien* (1769), *sangfroid* that allowed certain people to be clearheaded observers of the workings of the moral and physical world, including the histrionic blathering of the more impressionable souls in their midst. The persona of the knowledge lover was sometimes endowed with that cool temperament, but not always: he or she could also be portrayed as an enthusiast, with all of the negative as well as positive connotations that enthusiasm held at the time.[22] In any case, this persona's detached aura makes it difficult to assimilate into the sentimentalist paradigm, which was by definition outward-turning and socially directed.

The knowledge-lover persona also illustrates the limits of the historical narrative that views sociability as the main structuring value of the eighteenth-century Republic of Letters.[23] Such a narrative unquestionably fits certain works of this era, like the *Considérations sur les moeurs de ce siècle* (1751), where Charles Duclos described modern-day *gens de lettres* as convivial sorts who enjoyed a mutually beneficial relationship with the better educated species of *gens du monde* that had formed in their enlightened century.[24] *Gens de lettres* certainly had greater social prominence in the Enlightenment era, a development aided by the emergence of what Geoffrey Turnovsky has called "a self-consciously new social elite, which appropriated 'literary' writing forms—along with their writers—in assertions of its cohesiveness, brilliance, indeed, its modernity."[25] However, as Lilti points out, eighteenth-century Parisian salons were not necessarily literary or intellectual venues: they were, above all, "the social spaces of elite leisure . . . deeply rooted in court society," and the writers who frequented these social spaces were keenly aware of the asymmetrical relationship between themselves and the *Grands* who received them.[26] Moreover, the image of the scholar as seamlessly integrated into fashionable society competed with the counterimage of the intellectual as yearning for solitude. Take, for example, these lines from Voltaire's "Discours en vers sur l'homme" (1738):

> God of thinking beings, God of fortunate hearts,
> Conserve the desires you have given me,
> This taste for friendship, this ardor for study,
> This love of fine arts and solitude:
> Those are my passions, my soul has at all times
> Tasted consoling pleasures from their attractions.[27]

The tidy balance struck by Voltaire's hemistichs—particularly in the line "This taste for friendship, this ardor for study"—suggests an equally tidy balance between the pleasures associated with sociability and intellectual endeavor. It also brings to mind the fluidity that existed between the "learned" versus "conversible" worlds in some aspects of salon culture.[28] There were, however, other contexts in which the boundaries between those worlds were firmly upheld, along with the otherness of the learned vis-à-vis the nonlearned elite. One such context was the period's debates on the inward-turning passions of the learned, a discussion that involved moral philosophers, physicians, pedagogical theorists, and *gens de lettres* themselves.

Pleasures and Dangers of the Love of Learning

In his *Encyclopédie* article "Étude," the Chevalier de Jaucourt drew on a long humanist tradition that regarded the pleasures of study as the highest, most universally rewarding source of human contentment.[29] Citing Cicero for support, he declared that the contemplative life was fully compatible with the values and duties of active life—adding that, rather than clinging to old stereotypes and treating scholars with mocking disdain, the social elite of his day should themselves engage in study, both for its private "charms" and for the benefits it brought to the nation and to humanity at large. Jaucourt's definition of study as a means of personal and collective refinement was clearly designed to appeal to worldly readers who placed a premium on polished language and manner. At the same time, he aimed to correct the pejorative view of scholars as boorish, low-born pedants, which had been common among seventeenth-century aristocrats—for whom refinement was tied not to book learning but to qualities like the keen social discernment, good taste, and *politesse* exercised by the *honnête homme* in courtly settings.[30]

Eighteenth-century moralists and pedagogues adapted and transformed the ideals of *honnêteté*: they invested study with broad edifying qualities and included both mental acuity and the capacity for deep feeling among the traits of the truly refined individual.[31] This period expanded the categories by which people could be labeled as more or less refined, and more or less intelligent: it produced a remarkable number of histories of the human mind, typologies of sentiment and intelligence, and narratives describing the progress (sometimes negative) that had been brought about through learning and the ongoing march of civilization.[32] Last but not least, it made the love of study more legitimate for women, despite the aura of ridicule that lingered in the wake of Molière's famous satires of intellectually pretentious *précieuses*.

The moral effects that Jaucourt attributed to study—admiration for true glory, zealous love of country, and enhanced sentiments of humanity, generosity, and justice—illustrate the century's general shift toward a more personal, feeling-based view of intellectual endeavor. The moral vocabulary of sensibility built upon a preexisting moralist rhetoric of *finesse* and *délicatesse*. Borrowing (without attribution) from Madame de Lambert, Jaucourt defined it in his short *Encyclopédie* entry "Sensibilité (morale)" as "a tender and delicate disposition of the soul that makes it easily moved or touched. . . . Sensitive souls have more existence than others: good things and bad are multiplied in them."[33] Sensibility was thus first and foremost a *heightening* quality—a trait that magnified feeling and made the sensitive more humane, more empathetic, and also more intelligent.

Magnification was not, however, perceived positively in regard to all affective experiences. In articles like "Digestion" and "Vapeurs," for example, medical encyclopedists attributed intensified feeling mainly to people who constantly and fretfully observed their feelings and sensations, a group that included *gens de lettres* along with aristocrats, ecclesiastics, *dévots*, women of leisure, and people worn out from debauchery.[34] And in the medical entry on sensibility, the Montpellier-trained physician Henri Fouquet equated heightened sensitivity in one body part with disruption of the overall animal economy.

Although Fouquet later dismissed this article as the "work of an *écolier*," his reflections capture the suggestive range of connotations that sensibility held at the mid-eighteenth century, a range made possible by two premises: the vitalist notion that physiological sensibility and contractility were diffused throughout the body, and the assumption that the physical and moral realms of human existence were deeply interdependent.[35] He began "Sensibilité, Sentiment (*Médecine*)" by characterizing the property as a "physical or material passion" common to all animals, which allowed individual organs to perceive and respond to the impressions made by external objects.[36] He then evoked the theory of vital centers, which Dr. Louis de Lacaze had popularized in his *Idée de l'homme physique et moral* (1755), according to which the epigastric region acts as a sort of fulcrum or rallying center for many, if not all, of these organic passions (40). Next, he described organic sensibility as a "taste" or tact that could turn it in either of two opposing directions: an expansive "intumescence" that was triggered by positive, pleasing stimuli, or a compression incited by negative ones (41–42). A compression was a crisis, in the medical sense of a process that moved from irritation, to climactic reaction, to resolution: an organ reacting to an unpleasant stimulus would recoil until its sensitive principle came back to "consciousness" and expelled the humors that it had concentrated within itself—affecting, for good or bad, all the organs in its vicinity. Sensibility's overall physiological scheme thus entailed a complex interplay between the particular organs or vital centers within the body, each of which felt its own passions and expanded or compressed in reaction to them. Vital departments were more or less lively, depending on how much stimulation they got—that is, on how much sensibility was "transported" to them—as a result of habit, age, sex, climate, and other factors (51).

As Fouquet's text illustrates, the medical vocabulary used to explain sensibility was suffused with psychological metaphors, a rhetorical technique that lent an air of dynamic agency to the workings of the body's organs. Human beings were, in this view, teeming with passions, pleasures, and pains deep within themselves, whether they realized it or not; and the more they stimulated certain vital centers—the brain, the heart, the stomach, and so on—the more those parts developed their own tastes, needs, and sensitivities. Out of this theory, theorists spun a functional anthropology that categorized people according to the organ or vital center that dominated their existence.

The tendency to set *gens de lettres* apart as a group was tied to this effort to typologize human beings along differential lines.[37] It was also connected to the period's veneration for great thinkers, which produced an abundance of eulogistic and biographical literature on France's most eminent philosophers, scientists, and literary writers. That sort of writing unquestionably had a sociable thread running through it: academic eulogists commonly styled their subjects as national heroes because of their devotion to publicly useful knowledge and the exemplary civic-mindedness they showed in their private lives.[38] Scholars themselves stressed certain social values as essential to good citizens of the Republic of Letters; examples of these values were modesty, civility, and trust toward other intellectuals; deference toward those at the top of the scholarly hierarchy; and a collaborative spirit (the last was deemed especially important for those engaged in the new, empirical style of natural philosophical experience).[39] However, the collegial sociability that regulated behavior within the scholarly world coexisted with a topos that emphasized detachment from the larger social world. The tension between the two worlds was, as we shall see in Chapter 3, often dramatized in the period's imaginative and biographical literature.

Another focus of dramatization was the moment of intellectual inspiration, standardly scripted as playing out far away from *le monde*. Fascination with that moment underpinned the notion (frequently mentioned in biographical notices) that true geniuses possessed a special, brain-centered constitution. In some cases, brain-centeredness was equated with tepidness in other affective realms. As Madame de Tencin put it, while pointing at the chest of Bernard Le Bovier de Fontenelle, "what you've got there is all brain," thereby implying that Fontenelle was a cold fish—an impression expressed in more elegant terms by Mme de Lambert, who described him as the embodiment of dispassionate reason.[40] More typically, however, this constitution was endowed with its own kind of emotional intensity. Fontenelle recounted that Malebranche was seized at the age of twenty-six with a life-changing passion for reading Descartes when he stumbled upon the *Traité de l'Homme* in a Parisian bookstore.[41] Descartes himself had a famous moment of enthusiastic illumination—as would Jean-Jacques Rousseau, even more famously, while walking on the route to Vincennes (to visit the imprisoned Diderot) a century later.[42] Such emotional intensity was central to the foundational story that biographers often told of a great thinker's discovery of his or her intellectual vocation. So, too, was the related theme of disdain for health and neglect of the body.

Ardor for learning also went hand in hand with a penchant for seclusion, like in this 1735 description of Baruch de Spinoza: "He was so ardent in his quest for truth that, although he had very weak health and needed a break [from his studies], he took so little respite that he once went for three entire months without leaving the house."[43] As Dinah Ribard emphasizes, biographers did not use the theme of retreat to suggest that eminent thinkers like Spinoza (or Pierre Bayle, Descartes, Malebranche, and, later, Rousseau) were reclusive out of a vainglorious desire to thumb their nose at the world. Rather, the theme served to signal the autonomy of the thinker vis-à-vis conventional categories of social or professional activity: academic eulogists often emphasized that a given scholar's social withdrawal was episodic rather than permanent, serving, for example, as a prelude to a life spent in proximity to princes.[44] Studious solitude nonetheless marked the cerebralist as a type who dwelled in a world apart from the rest of humanity, both spatially and psychologically.

Partial retreat from the world was central to the group habitus that developed when fifteenth-century northern European scholars first moved from university or monastic settings into urban family households, creating cloisterlike spaces within them that functioned, as Gadi Algazi has put it, as a "shield for a scholar's vulnerable self."[45] What the eighteenth century added was an updated list of the dangers to which the scholarly self was vulnerable, as well as an emphasis on the dangers associated with study itself.

One risk associated with study was its tendency to cut scholars off from useful and necessary contact with the wider world. This was particularly anathema to those who placed a premium on the socially utilitarian aspects of learning. Even as they defended and celebrated learned endeavor, these writers cautioned intellectuals about the deleterious effects of spending too much time confined in their studies or libraries. Louis-Sébastian Mercier, for example, waxed lyrical in *Le Bonheur des gens de lettres* (1766) about the delights enjoyed by cerebralists, whom nature had endowed with "that expanded, active mind that is aroused by all sensations, and that avidly grasps their connections."[46] Yet he also warned in his *Discours sur la lecture* (1764) that the attraction of reading was liable to turn some into "solitary misanthropes, when we should be active citizens."[47]

Although traditionally associated with male intellectuals, the principle of willed detachment from social and domestic obligations was embraced by some elite women who engaged in intellectual pursuits. Mme Du Châtelet displayed it at Cirey and at the court of Sceaux, where she and Voltaire worked so incessantly and kept such odd hours that they offended their more sociable companions. As the exasperated Baronne de Staal (Mme de Staal-Delaunay, protégée of the Duchesse du Maine, who held court at Sceaux) complained in a letter to the Marquise du Deffand, the renowned thinkers were like "two specters, with an odor of embalmed corpses that they seemed to have brought from their tombs. . . . Our ghosts don't show themselves during the day; they appeared yesterday at ten at night, and I don't think we'll see them any earlier today. One is busy describing great events, the other commenting Newton. They want neither to gamble nor to go for a stroll: they are, indeed, two non-values in a society where their erudite writings have no pertinence."[48]

This was, of course, just one of many images of Châtelet and Voltaire that circulated in the eighteenth century.[49] What makes it striking is the emphasis that Staal-Delaunay placed on the socially inappropriate, literally unworldly quality of their zeal for scholarship. Voltaire took pains to counter that portrayal in his "Éloge historique de Madame du Châtelet" (1752) where he simultaneously lauded his late mistress's quest for intellectual glory and praised her ladylike ability to hide her erudition from everyone except her fellow geometers and Newton specialists.[50] His effort to shape Châtelet's posthumous reputation may have been prompted by the smear campaign launched by Staal-Delaunay's correspondent, Mme du Deffand, who wrote an extremely nasty portrait of Châtelet after her death.[51] Both Staal-Delaunay and Deffand styled themselves as the upholders of worldly *politesse* and its imperatives, an aristocratic ethos that had little place for the unconventional behavior of those with intense scholarly inclinations.

Another set of imperatives emanated from the bourgeois ideology of family life. One of the more curious contributions to this sort of discourse was the anticelibacy competition held by the Académie Française during the 1770s, which inspired the otherwise unnotable bards Doigny du Ponceau and Jean-François Ducis to write epistles urging bachelor-scholars to marry, have children, and embrace the touching pleasures of domesticity and active civic involvement.[52]

The very existence of such a poetry competition might lead us to conclude that, as the century progressed, the ideal of sociability won out over the defense of solitude in portrayals of the intellectual. I would argue, however, that discussions of the temperament and role of *gens de lettres* oscillated between two opposing poles. The first was the ideology of active sociability and fellow-feeling, and the second was the topos of contemplative detachment from the social realm. Because the first was so firmly embedded in the ethos of the intellectual persona known as the *philosophe*, it was more loudly trumpeted than the latter. It did not, however, override the more established motif of speculative retreat, which was perhaps the most persistent element of the group habitus embraced by early modern scholars. Rather, the two coexisted, somewhat uneasily, in the images of intellectuals that circulated in the period's letters, memoirs, eulogies, and fictional works. The taste for studious retreat was particularly pronounced among learned women: as Mme Du Châtelet wrote regarding the quiet existence she shared with Voltaire at Cirey, "My taste for solitude in good company does nothing but grow and become more attractive."[53] Speaking more generally, Jean le Rond d'Alembert commented: "When torn away from their solitude, *gens de lettres* find themselves swept up into a new whirlwind.... It is an experience that I have had, and which can be useful, as long as one doesn't do it for too long."[54]

The Archimedes Syndrome: Meditative Absorption

For many commentators, both the pleasures and dangers of solitary meditation were personified by Archimedes, the ancient mathematician who was too lost in thought during the Roman siege of Syracuse in 212 BC to notice that his life was in danger. Plutarch's *Lives* (widely admired by eighteenth-century readers, as Rousseau's autobiographical works attest) included two stories about Archimedes in contemplative oblivion, both of which appeared in the life of Marcellus. The first was the tale that "the charm of his familiar and domestic Siren made him forget his food and neglect his person . . . being in a state of entire preoccupation, and, in the truest sense, divine possession with his love and delight in science." The second was the story of Archimedes' demise, when he was so "intent upon working out some problem by a diagram, and having fixed his mind alike and his eyes upon the subject of his speculation" that he either failed to notice or ignored the Roman soldier who had been sent to take him to appear before General Marcellus—so enraging the soldier that he killed Archimedes instantly.[55]

These anecdotes inspired diverse applications. Montesquieu mentioned the first story while commenting that pleasure and chance sometimes played a greater part in the discovery of truth than deliberate, laborious mental effort: "Archimedes found, in the delights of a bath, the famous problem that his long meditations has missed a thousand times."[56] Condillac used the same anecdote to support his thesis that deep thinkers were the group most liable to lose touch with the real world under the sway of the imagination, "whose characteristic is to arrest the impressions of the senses in order to substitute for them a feeling independent of the action of external objects."[57] Julien Offray de La Mettrie used the second story in his dedication to *L'Homme machine* (1747), to paint an erotically tinged picture of knowledge seeking: "It is a catalepsy or immobility of the mind, which is so deliciously intoxicated by the object that arrests and enchants it, that it seems to be detached, through abstraction, from its own body and everything that surrounds it, to be completely devoted to what it is pursuing. It feels nothing, by dint of feeling so intensely. Such is the pleasure that one feels both in seeking and in finding truth. Judge the power of its charms by considering the ecstasy of Archimedes; you know that it cost him his life."[58] The same tale got a more sanitized spin in the *Encyclopédie* article "Attention," where Yvon praised Archimedes' extraordinary powers of intellectual attention, so great that he ignored the fact that the world around him was being sacked.[59] So, too, did Louis-Jean Levesque de Pouilly in his *Théorie des sentiments agréables* (1748), where—leaving out the story's tragic ending—he cited Archimedes' "charmed" state of mind/body detachment as an example of perfect philosophical happiness.[60]

By contrast, the medical encyclopedist Henri Fouquet cited Archimedes along with the mathematician François Viète to point out that the sensory oblivion observed in some deep thinkers had pathological repercussions akin to those seen in melancholics and maniacs: "a man absorbed in a deep meditation lives only in the head, so to speak."[61] A tandem citation of Archimedes and Viète also appeared in Johann-Georg Zimmermann's discussion of the effects of excessive mental exertion in *Von der Erfahrung in der Arzneikunst* (1763).[62] His friend and colleague Tissot also mentioned Archimedes and Viète together in his *Traité des nerfs et de leurs maladies* while warning about the dangerous detachment of mind from body, which doctors had observed in deeply absorbed *gens de lettres*, people with exalted imaginations, and the *convulsionnaires* of Saint-Médard.[63]

These authors obviously held different theories on what happened to thinkers in the state of deep mental concentration. For some, Archimedian attention exemplified optimal mental concentration, the state achieved by those rare souls capable of enjoying the sublime bliss of a meditative trance. This was the view of Yvon, in "Attention," who favored blocking out sensations as much as possible to focus the mind on the quest for truth. It was also the view of the Swiss naturalist Charles Bonnet, who erected a veritable cult around painstaking focus on single objects of study—like the aphids to which he became sympathetically attached.[64] For others, however, full intellectual absorption created a perplexing split between consciousness and other operations, which seemed to carry on in the absence of regulation and direction by the will.[65] Physicians like Zimmermann and Tissot tended to medicalize extreme absorptive states of mind, and they used arguments similar to those which Dr. Philippe Hecquet had employed in the 1730s to debunk the miraculous claims of the *convulsionnaires* by "naturalizing" them.[66]

Clearly, then, despite efforts by many in the Republic of Letters to bring scholarly and artistic life into closer alignment with polite society, a distinctly different, asocial image of the knowledge seeker persisted. This was not simply because some intellectuals remained willfully aloof from *le beau monde*, as d'Alembert recommended. It was also due to the pervasive sense that the true "deep thinkers" of the world were constituted differently from the nonintellectual cultural elite as well as from the rest of society. According to this view, those who devoted themselves fully and intently to learned and creative endeavor had unique ways of feeling and sensing. Willfully or otherwise, they dwelt in a world apart.

The Enduring Taste for Studious Solitude

Ominous as they sometimes were, warnings about the absorptive effects of deep thinking were not necessarily heeded. Moreover, sustained, solitary meditation was vigorously promoted in some contexts, including pedagogical works like *L'homme de lettres* (1764) by the antiquarian and Hebrew professor Jean-Jacques Garnier. Garnier urged his students to confine themselves as much as possible to their libraries and avoid everything that could distract them from their studies—including the tumult of worldly life, social visits, gambling, dissipation, and even passing romantic involvement. The true man of letters, he declared, was devoted exclusively to the cultivation of the mind: "His life is a continuous meditation, and retreat is his element."[67] Taking a dim view of the "mania for *bel esprit*" that he believed had seduced many contemporary writers, he declared that "by losing the taste for retreat one soon abandons the effort to cultivate one's mind, and through a necessary consequence one ceases to be a man of letters to become a man of society."[68] Invoking Pythagoras, the only social role that Garnier recommended to his students was that of spectator. He even went so far as to wish that contemporary men of letters would revive the old custom of wearing a pallium to set themselves clearly apart from the social world.

Counter-Enlightenment critics also weighed in on the issue as part of their broader critique of the overreaching tendencies of modern *gens de lettres*, who, in their minds, ventured too far into society—and too far beyond the disciplines they were qualified to pursue. This was a favorite argument of the conservative journalist Elie Fréron, who contended that the very nature of the scholar was corrupted by excessive social engagement: "*Gens de lettres* have lost more by frequenting social circles than by living among themselves as they did in the past. It is true that they have gained fortunes, positions, and pleasures, but they have denatured, weakened, and debased their talents by taking on the tone of others. If one can put it in such terms, they have undone the original character that nature had given them."[69] Although Fréron was certainly no friend to Rousseau, his depiction of the un-denatured, solitary, highly "original" man of letters bears a resemblance to the self-portraits that Rousseau sketched after his dramatic break with Diderot and other *philosophes* in the late 1750s. From that point on, Rousseau made solitude and unsullied naturalness the cornerstones of his public persona.

The tensions between social engagement versus solitude come into sharper relief when one compares two different articles that Voltaire, one of Fréron's biggest targets, wrote on the topic of *gens de lettres*. The first appeared in the seventh volume of the *Encyclopédie* (1757) and the second in his own *Dictionnaire philosophique* (1764). In the *Encyclopédie*, Voltaire praised contemporary intellectuals as superior to their predecessors because "the spirit of the century has made most of them as well-suited for society [*le monde*] as for the study [*cabinet*]."[70] His tone in the *Dictionnaire philosophique* was quite different: "The men of letters who have rendered the greatest service to the small number of thinking beings spread around the world are the isolated authors, the true scholars enclosed in their study, who have neither argued on university benches nor muttered pronouncements in the academies; and those of this sort have almost all been persecuted. Our miserable species is so made that those who walk the beaten path always throw stones at those who are opening up a new way."[71] Seclusion, in the latter scenario, was what best suited true scholars. It did not protect them from persecution, but it did allow them to uncover new, useful sorts of knowledge.

Even the most convivial intellectuals spoke of a deep love for prolonged periods of solitary writing and thinking. It was, for example, a prominent theme of the letters that Diderot wrote to his mistress, Sophie Volland, during the fall of 1765. As he wrote in October, "Tomorrow, it will be eight days since I last left my study. . . . I've taken such a keen liking for study, application, and life with myself, that I'm tempted to stick to them"; and, again in November, "My taste for solitude increases by the moment; yesterday, I went out in my dressing gown and nightcap to go dine at Damilaville's house. I've taken an aversion to dress clothes; my beard grows as much as it likes."[72] Diderot's self-description here echoed the portrait of the absorbed geometer he would soon sketch in the *Rêve de d'Alembert*: he portrayed himself as gripped with an intense penchant for study and "life with himself," exhibited externally by his neglected beard (reminiscent of the iconographic bearded philosopher of antiquity) along with the nightclothes he wore when venturing out for a social dinner.

To some degree, these letters confirm the precept of distance from society, which Lorraine Daston has called essential to the ideology of the *philosophes*.[73] Diderot's taste for scholarly retreat can also be tied to the admiration for Seneca that he developed in his later years—which, as Elena Russo argues, illustrates the inclination he shared with other *philosophes* for dwelling in "a sort of time-lag," a state of detachment from the present that allowed them to commune with the great men of antiquity and the appreciative audience that awaited their works in the future.[74]

However, we should also keep in mind that the intent of the letters Diderot wrote to Volland was often seductive, as is amply clear in this passage: "My friend, the truth is that we're not made for reading, meditation, letters, philosophy, or sedentary life. It's a depravation for which we pay with our health. . . . We shouldn't break altogether with the animal condition, especially since it offers both an infinite number of healthy occupations and some that are quite pleasant, and if I wasn't afraid of scandalizing Urania, I'd tell you frankly that I would be healthier if I had spent some of the time I've stayed hunched over my books spread out instead over a woman."[75] By playfully contrasting the delights of solitary literary/philosophical endeavor with more robust carnal pleasures, Diderot pointed toward the two rival topos that structured the group habitus of eighteenth-century *gens de lettres*: on the one hand, the insistence on social/civic engagement, and on the other hand, the promotion of retreat (whether meditative, or of a different variety).

Solitary retreat was a prominent theme in the vignettes Diderot sketched of the thinkers and creative artists he most admired. I will explore his use of those personae more fully in Chapter 4, but it is worth citing one particular case here: Leibniz, or, more properly speaking, Leibniz as Diderot depicted him in the *Réfutation suivie de l'ouvrage d'Helvétius intitulé "de l'Homme"* (1775). Drawing, perhaps, on Fontenelle's curious biographical portrait of Leibniz as a solitary (he was, in fact, a diplomat who led an active, worldly existence[76]), Diderot depicted the famous philosopher/mathematician as having spent thirty years in a serene meditative trance:

> When Leibniz holed himself up, at the age of twenty, and spent thirty years in his dressing gown, plunged in the depths of geometry or lost in the shadows of metaphysics, he gave no more thought to obtaining a position, sleeping with a woman, or filling an old chest with gold, than if he'd been at death's door. He was a reflecting machine, like a weaving loom or a machine for making stockings; he was a being who took pleasure in meditating; he was a sage or a madman, whichever you like, who placed infinite importance on the approval of his peers, who loved the sound of [intellectual] praise like a miser loves the sound of a coin.[77]

The point of this anecdote is twofold. Diderot sought, first of all, to refute the simplistic causal logic that Helvétius had applied to human nature, which posited physical sensibility as the universal impetus for all human actions. Bodily pleasure and pain may (as Diderot retorted in his imaginary conversation with the by-then deceased Helvétius) have been fundamental motives for the "voluptuous" Helvétius, but they simply didn't fit the case of Leibniz: "You're obsessed with Mlle Gaussin [the famous actress], but he is chasing Newton" (539). Second, Diderot was intent on underscoring the wide range of "species" of reason to be found in the human race: "human reason is an instrument that corresponds to all the varieties of human instinct . . . every man is led by his organization, his character, his temperament, his natural aptitude to combine such and such ideas preferentially, more than other ideas" (540). Leibniz, as Diderot characterized him, was a strange bird in that he was more interested in winning out over Newton than in spreading out over a woman; yet he was a uniquely human beast, with a mind propelled as much by its own well-developed habits as by the pleasures peculiar to his "species": that is, the species of the ardent cerebralist. He conjectures that Leibniz was so intensely focused on making a glorious mathematical discovery (and being recognized for it) that if someone had broken down his door and entered his study "with pistol in hand" saying "your money, or your discovery of the calculus," he would have handed over the key to his safe with a smile (539).

In addition to humor, Diderot infused his portrait of Leibniz with admiration for the great scholar's prodigious powers of mental concentration. That sentiment is conveyed through the very particular machine analogy he used to describe Leibniz plunged in meditation: the stocking-weaving loom—which, as Daniel Brewer emphasizes in his reading of Diderot's *Encyclopédie* article "Bas," was "the most complicated machine of the time."[78] Diderot ends "Bas" by citing Charles Perrault's wonder-struck observation on the stocking machine:

> Those who have enough genius, not to invent such things but to understand them, fall into a state of deep astonishment upon seeing the almost infinite mechanisms [*ressorts*] with which the stocking machine is composed, and the great number of its diverse, extraordinary movements. . . . How many little parts pull the silk toward them, and then let it go and pull it back again, and then pass it through a stitch in an inexplicable manner? . . . It is quite bothersome and unfair, adds M. Perrault, that we don't know the names of those who imagined such marvelous machines.[79]

In other words, far from reducing the stature of Leibniz's genius, Diderot does just the opposite by characterizing him in *Réfutation d'Helvétius* as a "reflecting machine, like a weaving loom or a machine for making stockings." That comparison elevates the venerable mathematician and philosopher into a special category of wondrous machine, one driven by a rare intelligence.

Diderot also used Leibniz to make another argument about the peculiarity of the passions that drove cerebralists, passions that had nothing to do with earthly pleasures like sex or money. Although he rejected Helvétius's notion that all human actions and emotions could be boiled down to physical pleasure or pain, he agreed with the Helvétian thesis that passion of a certain sort is a prerequisite for intellectual superiority—and that dispassionate people are generally incapable of understanding a genius's fiery enthusiasm for a certain field, art, or idea.[80] Those endowed with genius were, as Diderot put it in his *Salon de 1767*, "poetic beings": although nature usually doomed them to unhappiness, they were excellent to paint.[81]

Ultimately, Diderot considered mental absorption and mind-wandering to be productive states that allowed the creative mind to make the complex, unexpected, perhaps aberrant connections among ideas that led to the discovery of truth and beauty. Distraction, as he put it in his *Encyclopédie* article on the subject, was rooted in "an excellent quality of the understanding, by which one idea easily sparks another"; and although he cautioned that those capable of being productively distracted should take care not to lose all regard for the people and things around them, he also maintained that "a good mind must be capable of distractions."[82] Moreover, despite his frequent borrowings from medical discourse, he did not share the concern evident among some contemporary physicians with waking up the senses when they closed as the result of deep thinking. In fact, he insisted that he had done some of his own best deep thinking when he plugged up his ears (as in the *Lettre sur les sourds et muets* [1751]), lingered in a dream state (as in the *Salon de 1767*), or cloistered himself for days in his study.

Equally crucial to Diderot's conception of knowledge seeking was the notion that the flights of genius involve a felicitous alienation, a separation of the conscious mind from its bodily trappings. That sort of alienation was central to his aesthetic theory and to the eighteenth century's larger discourse on "poetic" enthusiasm.[83] Diderotian artist characters like the poet Dorval of the *Entretiens sur "le Fils naturel"* (1757) have fits of enthusiasm and lapse into trancelike oblivion while pondering some aspect of art or nature, but the condition is temporary and promptly followed by an outpouring of new, inspiring ideas. As Kineret Jaffe explains, "It is the peace that follows these emotional episodes that the artist's more rational faculties take over, and he is able to compose"—although in some texts, Diderot "placed the enthusiastic moment *after* the act of composing."[84]

Usbek "Frenchified": The Fate of Scholars in Montesquieu's *Lettres persanes*

Clearly, commentators of many different ideological persuasions perceived a considerable distance between the two types of *homme d'esprit* that Montesquieu identified in his "Essai sur les causes qui peuvent affecter les esprits et les caractères" (c. 1734–36), where he wrote "there is really just as much difference between what is called the man of *esprit* in the world and the man of *esprit* among the philosophers, as there is between a man of *esprit* and a stupid person. *Esprit* according to the worldly [*gens du monde*] consists in connecting the most distant ideas, whereas *esprit* according to philosophers means distinguishing them."[85] Prior to writing that essay, Montesquieu had already established this opposition in his novel *Les Lettres persanes* (1721), where various nameless French characters are enlisted to embody the qualities of worldly versus scholarly *esprit*: for instance, the two fellows who conspire to work together on witticisms they can utter in social gatherings so that each can maintain his reputation as a *bel esprit* (letter 54); the bookish monk who gives Rica a prolonged tour of the mostly useless books in the collection of his abbey's library (letters 133–37); and the pompous scholar who, as Rica relates in letter 144, declares that anything he has not said is not true "because I have not said it."[86]

However, the novel's most significant treatment of the gap between the two forms of *esprit* involves the character Usbek. Usbek is never as fully integrated into polite French society as his fellow traveler Rica, a difference that critics typically explain by citing Usbek's attachments to the seraglio back in Ispahan over which he reigns as despotic master—an identity that coexists paradoxically with Usbek's other face, that of enlightened philosophical observer.[87] It is nonetheless arguable that the distance Usbek maintains from worldly life has just as much to do with his sympathy toward a particular subset of French society: its scholars.

This is, to be sure, a rather lamentable group, as Usbek underscores in letter 145: "An *homme d'esprit* is usually rather difficult in social circles. He likes very few people; and he is bored with the great number of people he refers to as 'bad company.' His contempt is impossible to disguise, and then they all turn into his enemies. . . . He tends to criticize, because he notices more things than do other people, and senses them better" (357). Life is even harder for true scholars, who toil in poverty and obscurity, endure accusations of irreligion or heresy from common people, and face "a thousand persecutions" when they publish (359). To illustrate these points, Usbek cites a letter he'd read by an anonymous French *homme d'esprit* who lamented that he communicated only with like-minded men in distant places (Stockholm, Leipsick, London), whom he had never met in person (358). Unhappy as they are, the genuine scholars portrayed in letter 145 have a sense of solidarity born of mutual esteem and fellow suffering. Moreover, the traits Usbek evokes when summing up their condition—"an equivocal reputation, the sacrifice of pleasures, and the loss of health" (360)—are similar to his own, in the end.

It is important to note, in this regard, that letter 145 of *Les Lettres persanes* is dated "the 26th of the moon of Chahban, 1720": that is, in October 1720, at a time when Usbek has already learned about the collapse of the seraglio he left behind in Persia nine years earlier.[88] Usbek reports how he has been affected by that collapse in letter 155 to his friend Nessir, where he laments: "I am living in a barbarous climate, in the company of everything that vexes me, far removed [*absent*] from everything that interests me . . . it seems to me that I am destroying myself [*je m'anéantis*]" (367). Letter 155 has attracted significant critical attention, including this observation by Josué Harari: "Usbek realizes his helplessness and the tragic meaning of his existence."[89] That tragic interpretation is, indeed, supported by the end of the letter, where Usbek confides to Nessir that he plans to return to Persia to face his enemies and angry, unfaithful wives—and thus die. However, if we look closely at the chronology of the letters, we see that, although presented later than letter 145 in the novel, letter 155 is actually written a year earlier, in Chabhan, or October 1719.

What the final letters penned by Usbek make clear is that he does not return to Persia; rather, he stays in Paris and writes both letters 145 and 146, dated "the 11 of the moon of Rhamazan, 1720," or November 1720. Letter 146 is a philosophical commentary on the moral disorders into which France has been plunged by the financial crisis of the early 1720s— that is, the collapse of the banking system created by John Law. Usbek is not, therefore, reduced to silence or driven to leave France by the destruction of his old harem; it is he, not Roxane, who has the last word in terms of the dates of letter writing. One can, of course, argue that Montesquieu set up the timing of Roxane's letter 161 (dated "the 8th of the moon of Rebiab [May], 1720") so that it would reach Usbek shortly after he wrote his final letter. Still, Usbek's preoccupations both before and after he sends his wives his thunderously punitive letter 154 (dated "the 4th of the moon of Chahban 1719") are clearly not focused on the state of his harem. This suggests that what Usbek ultimately becomes is a French-style scholar of the sort that Montesquieu admired but lamented. He is obscure and misunderstood by many in the "barbarous" climate in which he lives, but he continues to write and philosophize nonetheless. Usbek's fate is sad, but it may not be tragic; and judging from Montesquieu's comments here and elsewhere, he has plenty of company in France.[90]

Chapter 3

Passions and the *Philosophe*

Defining the *Philosophe*

The meanings and implications of the term *philosophe* changed a good deal between the seventeenth and eighteenth centuries, as the severe, disapproving, often pedantic figure of yore was supplanted by a more civil persona. No single text illustrates that transformation more clearly than "Le Philosophe," an essay first published anonymously in the *Nouvelles libertés de penser* of 1743.[1] Often attributed to César Chesnau Dumarsais, but widely circulated in edited form by Voltaire and others, "Le Philosophe" defined its subject as an even-tempered individual, "full of humanity . . . who knows how to divide his time between retreat and social engagement."[2] This new model of the *philosophe* did not go uncontested. For example, in *Progrès de l'éducation* (1743), René de Bonneval maintained that the sort of person popularly called a *philosophe* was a vain, showy character who affected *singularisme* in his ideas on everything—including religion, politics, and "common" sentiments.[3] More notoriously, Charles Palissot de Montenoy's satirical comedy *Les Philosophes* (1760) skewered Diderot, Rousseau, and Helvétius by painting them as con artists. For better or for worse, the new-style *philosophe* popularized during the eighteenth century was widely perceived as a very visible sort of intellectual.

The invention of this figure reflected a larger effort to balance intellectual work with engagement in public life. As J. B. Shank puts it, "The Siamese twins 'philosophe' and 'public' constitute arguably the core element of the French Enlightenment itself. The public was a necessary correlate of the philosophe persona because it served to locate him socially."[4] This often entailed grafting the figure onto more established "polite" personae like the *honnête homme*—as, for example, in the *Encyclopédie* article "Philosophe" (1765), an abridged version of the 1743 text, which stated, "Given that he loves society extremely, it is more important for him [the *philosophe*] than for the rest of men to use all of his mainsprings [*ressorts*] so as to produce nothing but the effects consistent with the idea of an *honnête homme*."[5] The *philosophe*'s temperament was clocklike in its reliability, ensuring that he could not possibly act in a manner inconsistent with reason, moral integrity, and the good of the public. As was often the case in *Encyclopédie* articles, "Philosophe" defined its subject by contrasting it to countermodels. The author thus opposed the *philosophe* to those who "are carried away by their passions, without reflecting before they act"—setting up an allusion, a few paragraphs later, to the hotheaded emotions fostered by religious fanaticism (509–10). Another countermodel was the unfeeling Stoic sage: in contrast to that figure, the *philosophe* "does not claim the chimerical honor of destroying the passions, because that is impossible; but he strives not to be tyrannized by them" (510). The true *philosophe* was, in short, both a master of self-control and a man of feeling—but only of the socially beneficial sort.

There are multiple fault lines hidden beneath the image presented in this text. Among other things, the principle of *honnêteté* it promoted left unresolved the tension between that principle's central notion, perfect adherence to society's rules and constraints, and the intellectual liberty claimed for the *philosophe*.[6] It also elided the essential incompatibility that many authors saw between rigorous truth seeking and the frivolous, vapid aspects of the worldly society in which the *philosophe* was supposed to be actively engaged. Also absent in "Philosophe" are three ideological strands that did much to shape the period's intellectual personae in other texts and contexts: the period's growing valorization of conjugality and paternity, a movement in which the *philosophe* was fully implicated;[7] the toiling aura that surrounded those who worked to expand knowledge; and the image of the *philosophe* as a person who could be moved to tears by compassion for the suffering of humanity's downtrodden. Whereas the first of those themes was prominent in theatrical representations of the *philosophe*, the others factored into debates over the state of the contemporary Republic of Letters—debates in which passions, and even a few manias, were front and center.

Society, Love, and Learned Life on the French Comic Stage

Theater was a key medium for commenting on the *philosophe* as a social figure from the beginning of the eighteenth century.[8] A few early plays featuring this character were written by Jesuit priests in order to be performed or seen by their pupils: for example, *Le Philosophe à la mode* (1720) was composed by Father Jean-Antoine du Cerceau to teach his students at the Collège de Louis Le Grand to beware of the "wickedness and corruption" of fashionable thinkers like his title character, symbolically named Narcisse.[9] Most playwrights, however, aimed less to preach about the dangers of the "new" *philosophe* than to poke fun at the personal peculiarities of intellectuals, variously defined.

According to Ira Wade's count, the eighteenth century produced approximately 225 plays in which a scholarly persona appeared, an estimate to which we can add greater precision thanks to the database "Calendrier électronique des spectacles sous l'ancien régime et sous la révolution," also known as CESAR.[10] Some intriguing patterns emerge when one peruses the sorts of characters who appeared before theater audiences in the guise of a *philosophe* or *savant*. First, judging from the dates on the CESAR lists, *philosophes* and *savants* were ambivalent stage personae from the very beginning of the century, their intellectual status sometimes cast into doubt through pejorative qualifiers like *faux, petit, soi-disant*, or *ridicule*. Second, male scholars or pseudo-scholars were the principal targets: although *femmes savantes* or *femmes philosophes* remained comic targets in the wake of Molière's famous satires, their virile counterparts were more frequently lampooned on the stage. Finally, love themes predominate in most of the plays that feature a *philosophe* or scholarly type, suggesting that even playwrights who sought to impute charlatanism or other dark ambitions to this type found sentiment to be the easiest mechanism for tripping up their target.

From Germain-François Poullain de Saint-Foix's *Le Philosophe dupe de l'amour* (1726) to Pierre-Antoine-Augustin de Piis's *Aristote amoureux, ou le philosophe bridé* (1780), the *philosophe* was regularly played for a fool by and in love—so foolish that, in the case of Piis's comic opera, the once haughty Aristote ends up allowing himself to be fitted with a bridle and hooked to the front of a cart carrying the gorgeous young Indian maiden with whom he has become smitten.[11] This illustrates the persistent tendency on the part of comic playwrights to associate the *philosophe* with romantic incompetence, a vestige of the pedant persona of centuries past. Given the degree to which some prominent intellectuals were integrated into worldly society, it may seem paradoxical that the stage persona of the *philosophe* retained this particular trait, but playwrights continued to exploit the entrenched idea that "philosophy," or the love of knowledge, was inherently incompatible with carnal love as well as *politesse*.

The notion of the *philosophe* as out of step with love and society was not, of course, unique to the eighteenth-century French stage: one version of it dates back to the medieval fabliau *Le Lai d'Aristote*, which inspired both Piis's *Aristote amoureux* and Saint-Foix's *Oracle* (1740).[12] The plot of *Le Lai d'Aristote* was also repeated in Jean-François Marmontel's "Le Philosophe soi-disant" (1759), a moral tale dramatized at least nine times between 1760 and 1790.[13]

Many of the comedic authors who satirized intellectuals did little more than recycle the devious tutor of *Le Pédant joué* by Savien de Cyrano de Bergerac (1654) or one of Molière's characters, like the hypocritical schemer Tartuffe of *Le Tartuffe, ou l'imposteur* (1664), the jealous Arnolphe of *L'École des femmes* (1662), and the pompous poet Trissotin and pretentious s*avante* Philaminte of *Les Femmes savantes* (1672). Other playwrights adapted the *docteur* character of Italian comedy and the Foire, a figure who, ridiculous by dint of his age, his pomposity, and his suspicious nature, invariably interfered in the efforts of two young lovers to achieve happiness via amorous contentment.[14] Still others used thinly veiled dramatizations of the tale of Socrates included in Marie-Catherine de Villedieu's short-story collection, *Les Amours des grands hommes* (1671)—itself an adaptation of biographical details gleaned from Plutarch's *Lives*—where Socrates is cast as a Stoic who falls in love with his young charge Timandra, claims to be interested only in making her a "philosophical" woman, and eventually loses her to his handsome, wily young disciple Alcibiade.

Of those various sources, Villedieu probably contributed the most to the more sympathetic view of the amorous *philosophe*, which came into favor among French theatergoers during the 1720s and 1730s. Villedieu's emphasis on the romantic motivations that drove antiquity's great philosophers was clearly tied to *préciosité*, a seventeenth-century cultural movement that sought to create greater respect for love and the tender feelings cultivated by women of refinement.[15] It was also connected to the emerging interest in the private lives of great thinkers and statesmen of the modern age. The basic plot of Villedieu's novella was not, in and of itself, favorable to the philosopher in love: her protagonist is an ugly fellow who preaches contempt for the passions while burning with desire for Timandre, the young beauty he has secreted away in the woods of Athens; and her Alcibiade has no more trouble in shaking Socrates' confidence in Stoic philosophy than in sweet-talking Timandre's gullible duenna, the "astrologess" Aglaonice, in order to gain access to Timandre's ear and heart.[16] Among the plays that appropriated elements of Villedieu's tale of Socrates, many did little more than mock the figure of the lovestruck pedant and/or a deluded *femme philosophe* modeled after her Aglaonice.[17] A notable exception to that rule is Pierre Carlet de Chamblain de Marivaux's *Le Triomphe de l'amour* (1732), which borrowed from Villedieu both in its plot line and in its nuanced view of a *philosophe* grappling with the eternal "surprise" of love.[18]

The Athenian philosopher Hermocrate of *Le Triomphe de l'amour* has not been seen as a legitimate *philosophe* by all modern-day critics: some view him as a narcissist and assume that Marivaux's sympathies lie with Léonide, a Spartan princess who, Alcibiade-like, falls in love with Hermocrate's handsome young charge Agis, masks her identity, and presents herself at the door to Hermocrate's garden in the guise of Phocion, a young man ostensibly drawn there only by the much-reputed wisdom of a great intellectual.[19] However, Léonide-Phocion is an ambiguous character: she fools Hermocrate and his spinster sister Léontine into believing that they, not Agis, are the objects of her ardor, and only one of her reasons is unequivocally just. That is her equitable wish to right the wrongs committed by her uncle, who had usurped the throne from Cléomène, by restoring Agis, Cléomène's son, to power.[20] Léonide's other reason is amorous obsession: she will spare no one to win the heart of Agis, a young man who has every reason to hate her. Moreover, Hermocrate is not a sinister figure: far from being the heavy of the play, as is the case in most amorous pedant comedies of the period, he comes across as a hapless victim of a con artist. His temperament and comportment are close to those exhibited by Villedieu's philosophers. He falls in love while at the height of his justly earned fame as a sage, and he undergoes his amorous adventure in the midst of a political situation that has life-and-death repercussions for his young charge Agis—whom Hermocrate and his sister bravely rescued as an infant, and whom they also seek to restore to the throne of Sparta.

Love does not so much reduce Hermocrate as redeem him, transforming his formerly "savage" wisdom into a more sociable virtue. Although he does not end up marrying, both he and his sister Léontine exuberantly embrace the possibility of marriage and full social engagement, as is poignantly illustrated by the comic scene between the love-besotted siblings that ends act II. Hermocrate and Léontine, both giddy at the thought of eloping with Phocion/Léonide but unaware of her real identity (or of their sibling's plans), gallantly recognize each other's lovable qualities and admit the shortcomings of the austere mode of life they have followed (176–77). This dual confession of discontent with a purely philosophical existence emboldens both siblings to hint that they intend to give it up in favor of marriage. However, Hermocrate ends the scene with a lucid aside in which he recognizes that he and his sister are both in a silly state, a condition he describes as the destiny of all humans (177).

Ultimately, therefore, Hermocrate the philosopher is true to his name: he is the play's chief spokesman for Marivaux's vision of love, life, and authentic wisdom. Wisdom, this play suggests, must be sociable, but it must also be compassionate, generous, and humble (qualities lacking in Princess Léonide).[21] Although the solitary *sagesse* in which Hermocrate and his entourage live is, as the valet Arlequin puts it, "uncivil for love" (138), one could just as easily invert the phrase to say that love proves distinctly uncivil toward philosophy in this comedy. *Le Triomphe de l'amour* makes it hard to say whether the punishment meted out to Hermocrate and his sister is justifiable, not just because the two recluses are simultaneously sympathetic and laughable, but because Léonide is such a mixed character. The Parisian audiences who saw this comedy when it was performed in 1732 seem to have viewed her as a scandalous trickster—and Hermocrate as her undeserving, mistreated victim. As Antoine-Jean-Baptiste-Abraham d'Origny reported in his *Annales du théâtre italien* (1788), "People found it unseemly that a Princess of Sparta disguised herself to go find a young man of whom she was not certain to be loved, and abused a Philosophe through a trickery unpardonable to anyone but Scapin."[22]

Five years before *Le Triomphe de l'amour*, another play featuring a *philosophe* fared much better at the box office: Philippe Néricault Destouches's *Le Philosophe marié, ou Le Mari honteux de l'être* (1727), the most frequently performed and well-attended French comedy of the first half of the century.[23] The subtitle expresses the comedy's central dilemma: Ariste, a well-born, bookish fellow, has secretly married Mélite, who is beautiful and refined but has no dowry. It is not Mélite's pennilessness that causes Ariste's shame about being married; rather, he regards love as a weakness and married life as a threat to the freedom he savors when alone with his muses in his *cabinet* (he is also susceptible to the teasing of his bachelor friends and annoyed by his new sister-in-law Céliante, an indiscreet chatterbox).[24] Act I begins with him surrounded by his books, pens, mathematical instruments and globe, exulting in the solitary pleasures of his study until he remembers that a very different existence awaits him in the next room:

> My retreat is my Louvre, and I command here like a king.
> But it is only here that I exercise supreme power;
> Outside of my study, I am no longer the same
> In the other apartment, I am always annoyed
> Here, I am a bachelor; there, I am married. (6)

Predictably, annoyance from the outside arrives early and often, in the form of the various women of the household who enter his study unexpectedly.

The most intriguing aspect of *Le Philosophe marié* is Ariste's transformation: he begins by viewing the "philosophical" and married modes of life as mutually incompatible, but ends by regarding marriage as the ultimate proof of a *philosophe*'s character and moral fortitude. The initial attitude is made abundantly clear in act I: Ariste, alone in his study, tries to read but is repeatedly interrupted, first by his friend Damon and then by the soubrette Finette. In scene 4, Finette barges in and mutters a dismissive "always reading!" and then loudly announces that "Madame your wife" wishes to speak with him (11). When Ariste rejects this request, the exasperated Finette makes a wisecrack regarding his procreative capacity: "They say that people don't have all gifts at the same time, / And that great minds, otherwise very estimable, / Have very little talent for producing offspring" (16). Although Ariste is piqued by this insult, he says nothing much to counter it. Instead, he simply begs Finette to keep Mélite from bothering him for an hour or two so that he can philosophize in peace.

Finette's salty intimation that Ariste may not be able to rise to his conjugal duties, if he ever fully accepts them, would go on to provide grist for the mill of the "cerebro-genital pole" theory popularized by the nineteenth-century medical author Julien-Joseph Virey, who cited Finette's wisecrack to support his thesis that great intellectuals were tepid lovers and poor sires because their vital fluids were channeled toward the brain.[25] Although *Le Philosophe marié* contains no more references to Ariste's possible physical inadequacy as a husband, Finette's remark evokes a persistent theme in both the biographical and medical representations of superior male minds: the notion that the trade-off for their intellectual creativity was a lack of interest in or capacity for social interaction, including sex and procreation.

Destouches, however, proposed other reasons for Ariste's ambivalence toward the state of marriage: his *philosophe* character values his independence, disdains women's idle chit-chat, and sees himself as a Stoic who must keep his distance from the passions. Events conspire to cure this character of his reluctance to accept the public and private duties of a married man. First, Ariste gradually moves out of his study, the space he initially regards as a sanctum to be shared only with like-minded men such as Damon and the Marquis de Laurens. Second, his philosophical mettle is tested against characters like his uncle Géronte, a venal, ill-mannered fellow who takes a dim view of the contemplative mode of life, but who possesses the fortune on which Ariste's future depends—and who, not knowing that his nephew is already married, wants him to marry his stepdaughter. In act IV, scene 3, to counter Géronte's portrait of intellectuals as socially useless prattlers, Ariste praises the ideal *philosophe* as a man of action rather than words, a true, fair, and compassionate person whose greatness shines in adversity (91–92). Ariste's conversion to this ideal is not complete until Géronte discovers his marriage to Mélite and threatens to break it up, putting Mélite's honor in peril and prompting Ariste to defend her before his powerful, quarrelsome uncle (123–29). Even then, his philosophical fortitude does not suffice to bring about a happy ending. That is accomplished by the Marquis's noble offer to marry Géronte's stepdaughter without accepting her dowry, thereby allowing Ariste to keep his uncle's fortune and stay married to Mélite (129–32).

Ultimately, therefore, *Le Philosophe marié* aims not to lampoon *philosophes* but to socialize them, while also drawing attention to the ways in which the so-called polite society that ridicules them has been corrupted by greed, aristocratic idleness, and anti-intellectualism. True to the tradition of the "comédie de moeurs," it offers a corrective to *philosophes* who don't live up to the name, along with edifying instructions for everyone on how to be a good spouse and citizen. Anticipating the slightly later text "Le Philosophe," it locates virtue and wisdom not in Stoic disdain for society, but in social engagement, with all of its complexities.

When we consider that Destouches's comedy was packing the Comédie Française at the same time that Marivaux's was getting a tepid public response, we might conclude that Parisian theater audiences in 1732 no longer wanted to see a *philosophe* played for a fool on the stage. And when we note that, two years later, Barthélemy-Christophe Fagan's comedy *La Pupille* won acclaim and popularity by reversing the standard "duped philosopher" plot line and depicting a lovely young heroine who pines away passionately for her forty-five-year-old tutor, we catch a glimpse at an interesting mutation in public opinion.[26] Although mocking satires of the amorous pedant continued to appear in French theaters until the end of the century, they were generally produced for the Foire or Opéra Comique, whereas more serious troupes offered dramas like Michel-Jean Sedaine's *Le Philosophe sans le savoir* (1765). Sedaine's play depicted the *philosophe* not as an intellectual, but as an exemplary family man devoted to protecting those around him from the often turbulent passions of the contemporary world.[27]

Passions and Manias in the Republic of Letters

> Whether one leafs through the annals of the world or supplements uncertain chronicles with philosophical research, one will not find that human learning has an origin corresponding to the idea we like to have of it. Astronomy was born from superstition; Eloquence from ambition, hate, flattery, and falsehood; Geometry from avarice; Physics from vain curiosity; all, even Moral philosophy, from human pride. Thus the Sciences and Arts owe their birth to our vices; we would be less doubtful of their advantages if they owed it to our virtues.
> —Rousseau, Discours sur les sciences et les arts, *17;*
> First Discourse *(translation slightly modified), 12*

According to Rousseau's polemical *First Discourse*, conventional thinking about the arts and sciences masked an ugly basic truth: far from arising from a natural, laudable desire to expand one's mind or improve the human condition, every existing field of knowledge owed its existence to an unsavory passion. Happiness and tranquility, he argued, were to be found solely in the state of ignorance, whereas the arts and sciences were mired in the artificial, agitating emotions that dominated life in civilized society. Making matters worse, laborers and soldiers were now outnumbered by *philosophes* churning out useless books. If, he declared, Socrates were to come back to life, "he would not help to enlarge that mass of books by which we are flooded from all sides."[28]

Extreme as it was, Rousseau's diatribe crystallized the era's ambivalence about the value and morality of knowledge seeking; by applying metaphors like "debility," "poison," and "remedy" to the practice and institutions of learning, he popularized the pathologizing language that was already present in discussions of civilization in general.[29] Disease rhetoric was particularly prominent in debates between the *philosophes* and their adversaries: whereas conservative journalists and critics bemoaned the corrosive effects that the "disease" of *philosophie* was exerting on society, pro-Enlightenment authors described those writers as poisoned by the plague of envy that was afflicting the contemporary Republic of Letters. The unhealthy pursuit of recognition as an author was also a well-established subject of satire: Alexis Piron made a splash with his 1738 comedy *La Métromanie ou le Poète*, where he poked fun at writers afflicted with the penchant for versifying and inflicting readings of their works on their houseguests. That play may have targeted Voltaire.[30]

Métromanie, a word that caught on quickly enough to be featured in a short *Encyclopédie* entry, was just one of the many "manias" invented to diagnose the excesses of the modern intelligentsia. As Jean-François Féraud observed in his *Dictionnaire critique de la langue française* (1787–88), mania meant mental derangement in a medical sense, but it also had the meaning of "passion carried to excess." Féraud added: "For some time now, it has entered into the composition of several words: *Anglomanie, bibliomanie*, etc. Someone has even said *Voltairomanie*. . . . All of these words, and those that can be forged via imitation, belong to the joking or satirical style." Mocking humor was, indeed, the context of many of the "manic" words that were composed to characterize activities or people associated with scholarship, like "Jordanomania," which Frederick of Prussia coined to complain that his learned friend Charles-Etienne Jordan was neglecting Potsdam for his library, where he was "always buried under a dusty pile of books" that no one else knew or cared about.[31] However, even when used in jest, mania words often reflected a more serious underlying debate.

Take, for example, the most personal term in Féraud's dictionary entry list, "Voltairomania," which entered the French cultural lexicon in 1738 through an exchange of venomous pamphlets between Voltaire and Desfontaines. Desfontaines targeted two specific defects when he dubbed Voltaire a maniac: first, the "insane," hateful fury that Voltaire had unleashed on him in *Le Préservatif*, which Voltaire had written in reaction to the journalist's dismissive review of his *Eléments de la philosophie de Newton*; and, second, his "stupid pride," which Desfontaines held responsible for Voltaire's sensitivity to criticism and delusional belief that he could excel not just as a poet but also as a scientist and philosopher.[32] The dispute that gave rise to *La Voltairomanie* illustrates that the use of mania as a smear word was tied to a larger struggle between the *philosophes* and their adversaries for control over print culture—and, more broadly, over the power to dictate the tastes, interests, and beliefs of the reading public.[33]

Anti-philosophes were particularly fond of imputing manias to certain types or tendencies within the Republic of Letters. In his *Essai critique sur l'état de la République des Lettres* (1744), Jean-Jacques Le Franc de Pompignan, Bishop of Puy, identified "the mania for being an author" as one of the causes underlying the "decadence" of contemporary *belles lettres*.[34] Sounding a similar theme in the *Lettres sur quelques écrits de ce temps* of 1753, Élie Fréron decried "the itch to write and the multiplicity of Books," adding that "this mania has never been carried to the extremes of which we are the witnesses and the victims."[35] Seven years later in the *Année littéraire*, he coined the term *Editiomanie* to poke fun at a related ailment: "Editionmania is one of the maladies afflicting our gens de lettres; they imagine that it is by the number of editions that posterity will calculate their successes, and they are only too pleased to impose them on it. But will posterity be their dupe?"[36] And in *Le Fanatisme des philosophes* (1764), Simon-Nicolas-Henri Linguet declared that the *philosophes* were afflicted with an incurable "chattering mania" that made them obsessed with publishing their opinions, out of the "fanatical ardor" to gain renown in the eyes of the public.[37]

Those in the opposing camp, the *philosophes*, also wielded mania words to draw attention to writerly excesses that called out for a cure. Taking aim at his critics in "Les Honnêtetés littéraires" (1767), Voltaire decried the pretension to *bel esprit* that had spread like an epidemic disease among minor authors, "either ex-jesuits or convulsionists," who maniacally attacked "the premier men of literature."[38] He also created a metromaniac of his own, in the form of the narrator of his anonymous poem "Le Pauvre Diable" (1758): fit for no other profession, this wretched character made a living writing for Fréron's weekly journal until Fréron started stealing his work. The poem portrays Fréron himself as a worm born from the ass of Desfontaines.[39]

Of course, the most established mania connected to the world of learning was bibliomania, a condition whose history reached back to the fifteenth century. The term itself did not appear in French until the seventeenth century, when commentators like Gabriel Naudé, Jean de La Bruyère, and the physician Guy Patin remarked a tendency among those seeking high social status to collect books and assemble private libraries for ostentatious purposes.[40] In the *Encyclopédie*, Jean le Rond d'Alembert defined bibliomania as a furor for possessing books as objects to display rather than as sources of intellectual enjoyment and edification.[41] Commenting that "the love of books, when not guided by Philosophy and an enlightened mind, is one of the most ridiculous passions," he proposed two remedies. First, one should learn to read "philosophically" in order to discern what is useful in a given book versus what is not; second, one should strive to possess books as much for others as for oneself. This utilitarian, public-spirited perspective was, of course, an ideal often evoked throughout the *Encyclopédie*, yet d'Alembert saw it as the exception rather than the rule in contemporary society. The mad passion for accumulating books was, he stressed, all the more ridiculous in that it rarely brought genuine pleasure, any more than the passion for accumulating paintings, curios, or houses.

Not all commentators on bibliomania considered it devoid of pleasure: some saw a kinship between the love of luxurious, rare books and the love of beautiful female bodies.[42] For those authors, bibliomania had an erotic side not mentioned by d'Alembert. Louis Bollioud-Mermet, perpetual secretary of the Academy of Lyon and author of the 1761 treatise *De la bibliomanie*, admitted that he himself had felt the seductive pull of this "strange and libertine taste."[43] Whereas the *Encyclopédie* offered its readers a collective exercise in the judicious triage of useful things to know, Bollioud-Mermet drew on personal experience to urge his fellow bibliomaniacs to take a healthier approach to books: "let us use books with discretion if we want to enjoy them fruitfully. Let their use be for us not a source of vanity, but a means of instruction. . . . Armed with these precautions, anyone who loves study will find in the elite company of a few good books a noble occupation and inexpressible satisfaction."[44]

Bibliomania thus belonged to a somewhat different category of passions from the ideologically driven manias that were evoked as part of the battle between *philosophes* and *anti-philosophes*. It was perceived as a genuine syndrome—perhaps a delusion, or perhaps a guilty pleasure—that affected certain individuals in a social climate in which books, but not necessarily good sense, abounded. This made bibliomania a cousin to the recklessly bad reading habits that Dr. Tissot attributed to "this love of knowledge [*les sciences*], which has been the reigning mania for the last century" (*SGL*, 185).

Let us make a brief detour back to Tissot to consider that remark in context. Although his chief aim in *De la santé des gens de lettres* was to warn scholars about the effects of learning mania on their own health, he also devoted some attention to its other victims: the readers of the excessive number of books that the mania had produced. Tissot was particularly concerned about women, who had been seized with a ruinous passion for consuming novels: "So many authors give rise to a great number of readers, and continuous reading produces all the nervous disorders; perhaps of all the causes that have harmed the health of women, the main one is the infinite multiplication of novels for the past hundred years. From the earliest infancy to the most advanced old age, they read them with such eagerness that they are apprehensive of a moment's distraction, take no exercise, and often sit up very late to satisfy this passion; by which their health is entirely destroyed" (*SGL*, 186). This immoderate novel reading was rendering women and girls unfit for their natural domestic functions: "A girl at ten years old who sits down to read, when she ought to be running about, will be an hysteric at twenty years and not a good nurse." It was also creating a growing number of women authors, which Tissot considered equally worrisome. A few years later in his *Traité des nerfs et de leurs maladies* (1778–80), he bemoaned the fact that the "furor" for reading had trickled down to artisans' workshops and country hamlets. Here, he cited as proof the case of a seamstress who had been found reading the Baron d'Holbach's "tedious" book *Système de la nature* (1770), perhaps out of the mistaken belief that it was a book of devotion.[45]

Both medical and imaginative writers would continue to associate intellectual pursuit with manias and other modes of excess well into the next century. Whereas Jean Baptiste Félix Descuret included a chapter on the "mania" for study in his 1841 treatise *La Médecine des passions*, Gustave Flaubert embraced book-mania and identified as a male hysteric.[46] Flaubert's example illustrates that such pathologization was not necessarily negative: nervous or mental disorders were often a mark of prestige for nineteenth-century authors. In any case, the eighteenth century tended to take a less solemn view of its manias than would the Romantic period. As d'Alembert quipped while referring to the fleeting fad that had made geometers highly sought out in worldly society, "no mania lasts in our nation."[47]

The Quest for Glory, the Pathologies of Envy

The Enlightenment may have taken its manias lightly, but it was earnest about the quest for intellectual glory. This was an age in which grand cerebral striving was celebrated and publicized with exuberance: famous thinkers like Newton were held up as benefactors of humanity, theater and poetry were glorified as fields of honor, and Antoine-Léonard Thomas extolled the service that intellectuals rendered to the nation in the *Discours de réception* he delivered at the Académie Française in 1767, on the subject of "L'homme de lettres citoyen."[48] In this era before the advent of the "hatred for great men," the effort to stir up admiration for the great minds of the scholarly and artistic pantheon was central to the rhetoric of the Enlightenment movement.[49] So, too, was the attempt to rid the Republic of Letters of what some saw as its most fearsome passions: the envy and jealousy that prompted some intellectuals to attack those who had achieved greater success.

In 1716, to commemorate his entry into the Bordeaux Académie des Sciences (founded just four years earlier), Montesquieu gave a speech in which he praised the gentlemen of the academy for ushering in a sea change in attitudes toward learning and the learned:

> Yes, gentlemen, there was a time when those who were devoted to study were regarded as bizarre persons [*singuliers*], not made like other men. There was a time when there was ridicule and affectation associated with freeing oneself from the prejudices of the people. . . . In such a critical time for scholars, being more enlightened than others did not come with impunity. If someone undertook to venture beyond the narrow sphere that marks the boundary of human knowledge, a mass of insects would immediately rise to form a cloud to obscure his path. Even those who esteemed him in secret rebelled against him in public and could not forgive him for the affront of not resembling them.[50]

The Bordeaux academicians had, he proclaimed, dispelled the antiintellectualism and the clouds of "insects" that had formerly pestered scholars; they had also helped to free the nation from the tyranny of ignorance. Now that the bad old days of ridicule and resentment were over, scholars the world over could look forward to receiving laurels from the fertile grounds of such academies, the glorious institutions that were destined to perfect all fields of knowledge.

Montesquieu's optimism about the prospects for glory in France also found its way into *Les Lettres persanes*: in letter 89, his character Usbek praises the French people's love of glory and respect for the "noble emulation" it inspired, qualities that attested to their liberty, sense of honor, and capacity for patriotic self-sacrifice.[51] That confident view was not, however, shared by all of his contemporaries; in fact, the century's failure to do justice to Montesquieu was a common theme among the encyclopedists.[52] In his "Éloge de Montesquieu," which appeared at the outset of volume 5 of the *Encyclopédie* (1755), d'Alembert lamented the fact that, despite the great acclaim that had greeted *De l'Esprit des lois* upon its publication, this masterpiece was being attacked by "the public and secret enemies of Letters and Philosophy."[53] A few years later, d'Alembert expanded his thoughts about those enemies in his unpublished "Réflexions sur l'état présent de la République des Lettres écrites en 1760, et par conséquent relatives à cette époque."

The year 1760 was, we should recall, exceptionally difficult for intellectuals affiliated with the philosophic movement. Coming right after Rousseau's noisy defection from the movement and the revocation of the *Encyclopédie*'s *privilège* in 1759, this was the year when Palissot's satire *Les Philosophes* appeared and when, on the occasion of his election to the Académie Française, the poet and devout Catholic Jean-Jacques Le Franc de Pompignan made a speech denouncing his century as "drunk with the philosophical spirit . . . the scorn of religion, and the hatred of all authority."[54] D'Alembert clearly wrote his "Réflexions" in reaction to those events, particularly the power struggle that was taking place between the pro- versus *anti-philosophe* factions of the Académie Française.[55]

The central question of "Réflexions" was why intellectuals were so often despised and denied the glory that should be "the patrimony proper to their state" (361–62). D'Alembert's answer departed somewhat from the stance he had taken in his 1753 "Essai sur la société des gens de lettres et des grands," when he criticized the deference that *gens de lettres* seeking attention in worldly society had to show toward those of higher social status.[56] In 1760, he placed intellectuals a notch above aristocrats because of the unique cultural power they wielded.[57] That power incited jealousy and hatred on the part of the nonintellectual elite, who depended on *gens de lettres* to have their talents celebrated, their mediocrity covered up, and their stupidities toned down—and who resented them for it (362). In "a large kingdom where so many fools want to have an existence, and where there are far more pretensions than titles," this created plenty of enemies for *gens de lettres* (363–64). Other enemies came from the ranks of those who belonged to "the lower chamber of literature" (363). Out of malice and envy, such writers unfairly branded the *philosophes* as a dangerous sect and trafficked shamefully in false eulogies and satires to tear apart "the best among us" (365–66). D'Alembert ended by offering some words of encouragement: "You who do honor to letters through your talents and comportment, you who represent the nation in the eyes of foreigners, you who uphold its glory during troubled times, do not let some passing storms discourage you; and refrain from lowering the nobility of the state you have embraced by engaging in flattery or satire" (365–66).The sounder judgment of Europe would, he assured them, eventually silence and shame their enemies.

D'Alembert's text typifies the rhetoric used by the *philosophes* to defend themselves and respond to their opponents. They often compared the sort of glory one might achieve in the realm of intellectual and literary production with the more traditional brand that arose from military prowess.[58] Their tone was simultaneously combative and suffering: illustrious *gens de lettres* were both courageous warriors striving for glory and victims persecuted by the lowly, jealous *pauvres diables* of the literary world. Generally speaking, the *philosophes* fretted more about envy than did their adversaries—although at least one *anti-philosophe*, Charles-Georges Leroy, turned the tables against the *philosophes* by depicting their most famous member, Voltaire, as little more than an envious hack himself.[59] To fight envy, the *philosophes* used the same sort of pathologizing language as that which they employed to combat the "infection" and "contagion" of religious fanaticism and persecution.[60]

It is useful to note here that the social context within which envy and related passions were examined changed somewhat from the seventeenth to the eighteenth centuries: high culture's centers of gravity shifted to include urbane salons as well as royal courts, and glory turned into a quality associated with intellectual or artistic renown. Both developments helped to remake envy into a vice associated particularly with *gens de lettres*.

Theories of envy followed the same conceptual trajectory as the rest of the passions, which went from being a topic of dogmatic morality to a subject of secular ethics after 1650 and then became a matter of profession- or temperament-specific ethics and medical therapy in the eighteenth century. The first shift is illustrated by René Descartes' *Traité des passions de l'âme* (1649), where he emphasized envy's social repercussions as well as its psycho-physiological effects on the envious.[61] According to Descartes' classification of the passions, envy was a species of sadness intermingled with a degree of hate, "a vice that consists in a perversity of nature," which made certain people angry when they saw something good happen to people who they believed were unworthy of it.[62] Adhering to his general principle that the passions were useful as long as they were not excessive or misdirected, he insisted that envy was not always vicious: it was justified when the possession a person envied was something that "could be converted into evil" when mishandled, like the glory of a high public office—glory being, in his estimation, the possession least communicable to a large number of people, and thus most generally envied (781–82). Yet he also warned about envy's damaging effects: those "tainted" with this passion disrupted the felicity of others while also destroying their own health and tranquility; and the damage was readily apparent on their faces. The envious typically had a livid, pale complexion mixed with shades of yellow and black, as if their faces were bruised. This, he maintained, was the result of "bruised blood": that is, blood tinged with yellow bile from the liver and black bile from the pancreas, a combination that cooled the venous blood and slowed its circulation (783).

A few decades later, the moralist François, duc de La Rochefoucauld, analyzed envy in his *Maximes* (fifth ed., 1678) by situating its function within the system of aristocratic rivalry and status seeking. He called it a chronic, shameful, secret desire to see those in favor humiliated—a "fury" distinct from jealousy because it sought not to preserve something one possessed, but to destroy what belonged to another.[63] Although La Rochefoucauld decried envy, he saw it as integral to the treacherous, constantly shifting universe of the social elite. A person's approval of those who were just making their debut in that world was, he observed, quite often based upon "a secret envy toward those already established"; moreover, the aristocratic pride that fueled envy also served frequently to moderate it.[64]

Envy's eighteenth-century commentators drew liberally on the explicative models proposed by their predecessors. In his short *Encyclopédie* entry "Envieux," for example, d'Alembert paraphrased La Rochefoucauld's distinction between envy and jealousy; the anonymous medical article "Envie" approached the passion in the jointly psycho-physiological manner of Descartes.[65] After characterizing envy as a malignant form of melancholic delirium, this author listed such debilitating symptoms as severe thinness; muscle atrophy; a propensity for dark, obsessive thoughts and horrible bouts of ennui; continuous agitation and insomnia; loss of appetite; and, finally, a deep languor usually accompanied by a slow fever. Some relief for this "base and vile passion" could be obtained from the therapeutic measures standardly used to treat hypochondria, like baths, mineral waters, and *laitages*. Those methods should, however, be combined with "the moral remedies provided by philosophy and religion, to try to cure the mind while also undertaking to change the disposition of the body."[66]

Nonmedical commentators proposed various moral cures for envy. Destouches, for example, wrote a one-act play entitled *L'Envieux ou la critique du Philosophe marié* (1727) as a coda to his famous comedy.[67] Its protagonist, Lycandre, bristles so intensely at the success of any literary rival that he goes to extreme lengths to disparage him and his work. His envy is directed at the author of *Le Philosophe marié*, which has just enjoyed a glorious premiere. The play's sympathetic characters are well aware that Lycandre will do anything to make a rival miserable, so they exploit his obsessive envy in such a way that he unwittingly sacrifices his chance to marry pretty, kindhearted Angélique and ends up stuck with her shrewish sister Bélise. Lycandre's character traits anticipate those of the *antiphilosophe* persona soon to be constructed by Voltaire, d'Alembert, and others: furious hostility toward a work that has both pleased and instructed its audience; despair over another writer's fame and happiness; and indignation when someone else wins the seat in the Académie that he thinks should go to him. In this play, Destouches defuses envy's potential dangers by making the *envieux* a comic dupe, a man so blinded by his ruling passion that it ruins his life. This forbearing attitude was, apparently, characteristic of an author who had many firsthand brushes with jealous sorts, at least according to the account that d'Alembert provided in his "Éloge de Destouches," delivered at the Académie Française in 1776.[68]

Another approach was to promote emulation as a counterweight to envy, a strategy based on the principle of countervailing passions—one of the most significant developments in early-modern theories of human nature. As Albert O. Hirschman explains, this principle consisted in pitting one passion against another as a means of keeping in check those that were most socially harmful: "the idea of engineering social progress by cleverly setting up one passion to fight another became a fairly common intellectual pastime in the course of the eighteenth century."[69] The countervailing passion principle is evident in the *Encyclopédie* article "Émulation," where Jaucourt characterized emulation as a "noble, generous passion that, out of admiration for merit, beautiful things, and the actions of another person, tries to imitate or even surpass them, striving to do so according to honorable and virtuous principles"; those qualities made emulation the exact opposite of "inordinate ambition, jealousy, and envy."[70] Whereas jealousy was a "violent," cold, sterile passion that did nothing to improve the situation of the envious individual, emulation was voluntary, productive, and ardent. Emulation was thus capable of bringing order and progress to the scholarly and artistic realm, the sphere Jaucourt emphasized in his conclusion.

Other writers despaired of finding a remedy for envy. Voltaire, for example, described it in his *Discours sur l'homme* (1738) as both the soul and the hangman of high culture in contemporary France—a dangerous, cowardly vice that menaced the reception of new plays, guided the satirist's poison pen, inspired the desecration of paintings, and slithered, like a venomous snake, at the feet of all the great creative geniuses.[71] Germaine de Staël made envy a central theme of her youthful tribute to the work and character of Rousseau, where she called on the great men of the present day to rise up in defense of this misunderstood genius and form a "league" against envy.[72] Her tone was distinctly melancholic.

Envy seemed to preoccupy Diderot throughout his career. In *De L'interprétation de la nature* (1754), he called envy and superstition the major obstacles facing those who resolved to take up the philosophical study of nature.[73] In the *Éloge de Richardson* (1762), he exclaimed: "What a passion envy is! It is the most cruel of the Furies: it follows the man of merit right up to his tomb, and there, it disappears, and the justice of the centuries settles down in its place"; and in *l'Essai sur la vie de Sénèque* (1778), he defiantly declared that "there are men whose hatred is a source of glory; the torment of envy is always a form of praise."[74] The last remark sums up one of the central themes of Diderot's late masterpiece *Le Neveu de Rameau*, where he forced the *philosophe* persona to confront the jungle of hateful, envious sorts lurking in contemporary Paris.

The title character of *Le Neveu de Rameau*, LUI, belongs to a particular species: the ankle-biting denigrators of the *philosophes*, a category also represented by Palissot, Fréron, and other critics named at various points in this dialogue. Yet LUI is more complex and multifaceted than his fellows: he is an extraordinary actor who can mimic everything from a fawning minister, to a girl being seduced, to an entire orchestra; he is a musician endowed with a fine ear and a Stentorian voice; he is a hedonist for whom the appetite reigns supreme; and he is a clown—or, more specifically, the former clown of the financier Bertin and Mlle Hus, a position he enjoyed until he was chased from their household for being just a bit too impertinent. What his interlocutor, the *philosophe* character MOI, finds useful about conversing with LUI is his unsettling bluntness: "he stirs things up, shakes them about, provokes approval or blame; he makes the truth come out; he reveals who's genuinely good, he unmasks villains; and that's when a man of good sense pricks up his ears and sees the world for what it is."[75] All of that combines to make him the perfect guide for MOI through the unsavory world of fashionable French society, where reputations are made and unmade around elegant dinner tables.

Envy and calumny drive the entertainment that LUI and his fellow lowlifes provide to dissipated Parisians like the Bertin-Hus, and the menagerie they form is particularly ferocious in denigrating the prominent intellectuals of the day: "You've never seen so many miserable, embittered, spiteful and ferocious beasts all in one place. You hear nothing but the names Buffon, Duclos, Montesquieu, Rousseau, Voltaire, d'Alembert, Diderot, along with God knows what epithets. None shall have wit unless he be as foolish as thee and me" (*Neveu*, 134; *Nephew*, 49). It was at such a gathering, LUI explains, that the plan for writing *Les Philosophes* was conceived; during a typical meal, after "the great beasts" are sacrificed, the troupe moves on to slaughtering other people.

However, envy also drives LUI more personally. This comes up early in the text, when LUI and MOI debate the pros and cons of genius (a quality whose "fiber" LUI lacks, along with the fiber responsible for moral sensitivity and empathy). LUI's opening attack targets his renowned uncle, the composer and music theorist Jean-Philippe Rameau. Embittered by his uncle's indifference toward him, the nephew derides him as a "philosopher of a certain species" and complains that his uncle is so fixated on the quest to perfect his theory of the fundamental bass that he is oblivious to the existence of his family (*Neveu*, 76; *Nephew*, 11). LUI then generalizes the accusation, applying it to all geniuses: "They are only good for one thing. Apart from that, nothing at all. They don't have the least idea what it is to be a citizen, father, mother, brother, relation, friend. . . . We need men, but as for men of genius, no thanks." MOI has no good counterargument: he sticks to a "high culture" defense, arguing that some geniuses may well be nasty (like Racine, "not supposed to have been a particularly nice man" [*Neveu*, 80; *Nephew*, 13]), but that the temporary effects of their meanness are a small price to pay for the lasting benefits that their works give to humanity. The debate is left unresolved, leaving us hanging between the moral shortcomings of some recognized geniuses and the aesthetic posterity of great art.

Despite his critique, LUI regrets not being born a genius himself, and his envy makes him enraged when geniuses are praised, while he delights when they are degraded. LUI also yearns for the privileges that come with being a "great man": a nice house, fine wine, and beautiful women to sleep with. Imagining himself as his famous uncle, recognized as the author of the *Indes galantes*, *Profondes abîmes du Ténaire*, and *Nuit, éternelle Nuit*, he acts out these various pleasures, punctuating his words with evocatively pantomimed gestures (*Neveu*, 85). When he returns to the fantasy of himself as a wealthy man later in the dialogue, LUI introduces a cast of insipid adulators, all taken from the ranks of the critics who had tormented Diderot in print. Here, LUI envisions himself as rich enough to command a troupe of cads to entertain him by belittling the great, upstanding minds of the day: "It'll be fabulous. We'll prove that Voltaire has no genius; that Buffon is nothing more than a sermonizing old windbag; that Montesquieu is merely a wit; we'll send d'Alembert back to his sums; we'll give all you little Catos a good thrashing for looking down on us when *really all you are is envious*, your modesty merely a mask for pride, and your sobriety simply the dictate of necessity" (*Neveu*, 113; *Nephew*, 35; my emphasis).

Illustrating one of the dialogue's many lexical mutations, envy migrates in this passage from one interlocutor to the other: LUI insinuates that MOI and his fellow *philosophes* are the true *envieux*, jealous of the power their critics possess to influence public opinion. He goes on to warn "Mister Philosopher" that "at this moment I represent the majority in town and at court." He then dismisses as futile all of the virtues promoted by the *philosophes*—devotion to country and friends, the duties of one's social position, the education of one's children—and derides the "wise and philosophical universe" they dream of creating as "miserable as hell" (*Neveu*, 114–15; *Nephew*, 35–36).

MOI does his best to defend his position: he insists that he, too, enjoys sensory pleasures (good food, fine wine, a pretty woman) but finds it infinitely more delightful "to come to the aid of someone in need, to bring a fraught situation to an end, to give a piece of advice, to read something pleasant, go for a walk with a man or woman dear to my heart, spend a couple of instructive hours with my children, write a good page, fulfil the duties of my position, say some tender loving words to the one I love" (*Neveu*, 116–17; *Nephew*, 37–38). Growing more and more impassioned, he mentions the inspiring example of Voltaire clearing the name of the persecuted Calas family. He then tells the story of the friend of his who had fled to Carthagena after being harshly treated by his parents, but who, upon hearing that they are languishing in poverty, returns to France to restore them to their home: "as I tell you this story, I can feel my heart fill with joy, and it gives me such pleasure I can hardly speak" (*Neveu*, 117; *Nephew*, 38). LUI simply takes this as one more proof that, far from setting the tone of public opinion, MOI and his fellow *philosophes* are a strange lot ("des êtres bien singuliers"; *Neveu*, 118). What the public wants, he insists, is not to admire acts of virtue, but to laugh at the foolishness of others.

As MOI's defense of virtue's pleasures makes clear, emulation is not entirely absent from *Le Neveu de Rameau*. However, its power to countervail the nasty passions that dominate contemporary society is sabotaged—not just by LUI's consistently sarcastic reactions to MOI's earnestness, but also by the topsy-turvy ethical system LUI espouses. A perverse kind of emulation underpins that system: LUI strives to be perceived as belonging in a "long line of glorious good-for-nothings," the rare elite formed by the completely unscrupulous, cleverly malicious people of the world (*Neveu*, 156; *Nephew*, 63).[76] Two characters occupy the top spots in this hierarchy: the farmer-general Bouret, who devised a brilliant scheme for social advancement that involved using a disguise to trick his faithful little dog into attaching itself to a powerful official who'd taken a liking to the animal (*Neveu*, 127); and the Renegade of Avignon, who won the confidence of a wealthy Jew only to persuade him that they were both about to be handed over to the Holy Inquisition, and who then denounced his gullible friend and made off with his fortune. These are the characters whom LUI considers worthy models for those who aspire to perfection in the craft of flawlessly executed duplicity.

The darkest of these examples is the tale of the hideous crime committed by the Renegade, which LUI presents like "a connoisseur of painting or poetry would examine the beauties of a work of art" (*Neveu*, 156; *Nephew*, 63). As an expert in the art of duping people, he considers the Renegade's atrocious action to be sublime in both design and execution. Yet admiration is not the only reason that LUI tells this story: he seeks above all to reduce MOI to speechlessness. After listening to this story, which ends with the Jew being burned in "a nice big bonfire," MOI's mind is so filled with horror (especially when LUI starts singing a triumphal march) that he feels physically ill and can think of nothing but to change the subject to music (*Neveu*, 157).

However painful, this episode reveals some essential truths. It proves that some refined sensibilities can admire the "art" of a brigand and remain unmoved by human suffering. It also shows the evil face that genius can take. As LUI puts it, "If there is one genre it's worth being sublime in, it's evil. We'll spit in the face of a petty thief, but can't help admiring a great criminal" (*Neveu*, 151; *Nephew*, 60).[77] This remark sums up one of the most complex questions raised by the dialogue: namely, the presence of great criminals next to great creative minds in the class of "sublime" beings. Sublime scoundrels, as MOI is forced to admit, belong to a distinct class—an idea that bears an eerie resemblance to the reflection Diderot made about great artists in the *Salon de 1767* when he observed that there may be "a morality unique to artists, or to art, which may well run counter to ordinary morality."[78]

In their anthropological dimensions, these realizations anticipate what happens between MOI and LUI at the end of *Le Neveu de Rameau*, which occurs on the safer terrain of the comically satirical. Here, as MOI evokes the various sorts of flatterers, courtiers, valets, and beggars who tirelessly dance the "vile mime" that drives social life, the nephew brilliantly mimes "the positions of the people as I mentioned them" (*Neveu*, 191; *Nephew*, 85). Working in tandem, LUI and MOI effectively distribute these people into the various "species" or laughable social types they represent. In the end, MOI is able to smile alongside his perturbing interlocutor and see him as a source of inspiration for a new way of perceiving the various figures that dominate public life: "The follies of this man, the stories of the Abbé Galiani, and the wild imaginings of Rabelais have at times sent me into deep reverie. These three storehouses supply me with ridiculous masks to put on the faces of the most serious of personages; and so I see a prelate as Pantalon, a high court judge as a satyr, a cenobite as a piglet, a minister as an ostrich, his private secretary as a goose" (*Neveu*, 190; *Nephew*, 84–85).

Placing distorting or exaggerating masks on the faces of the "most serious of personages" allows MOI to see them for what they really are, by discerning the animal instinct that drives their behavior.[79] What he embraces by the end of this encounter is a theatrical, caricatural perspective on the world. Ultimately, therefore, LUI is much more than just an *envieux* who rubs shoulders with the *philosophes*' worst critics: he is a source of inspiration for the grotesque—an artistic mode that turns out to be an excellent means of carrying out the philosophical function of uncovering the true face of both the genuinely good and the villains. In his way, LUI is as much of a *philosophe* as MOI, although he would never lay claim to the name.

Chapter 4

Corporality and the Life of the Mind in Voltaire and Diderot

"I dare you to explain anything without the body": so declared Denis Diderot in his *Éléments de physiologie* (1778).[1] The corporeal side of human life was indeed vital to eighteenth-century French thought and culture, for reasons that went beyond the philosophical materialism that found supporters in certain quarters (including Diderot). These include the emphasis placed on somatic expression in theories of painting, acting, music, and language; the expanded market for consumer goods, which increased the possibilities for physical pleasure and contentment; and the philosophical current known as sensationalism, which gave a fundamental role to the impressions the mind received through the senses. Building on Locke's empirically based, phenomenological approach toward the formation of human knowledge, Diderot and other French-language philosophers proposed metaphysical "anatomies" of the external senses, designed around the idea of "decomposing a man, so to speak, and considering what he gets from each of the senses he possesses."[2] Theorists in various fields also speculated about the part played by more internalized sensations in the workings of the human psyche: that is, the organic processes that act upon the mind but unfold beyond the purview of consciousness and will.

Such questions keenly interested Voltaire. In 1727, upon arriving in London for the first time, he marveled at the power of climate to lift or drop one's mood: "how much we are machines, and how much our minds [*âmes*] depend on the action of our bodies!"; and in the *Dictionnaire philosophique* (1764), he endorsed Condillac's idea that "sensation envelopes all of our faculties."[3] Voltaire gave equal emphasis to the effects of lower bodily functions on the mind. As he asked polemically in the article "Passions" of the *Questions sur l'Encyclopédie* (1774), "Tell me what secret connection nature has created between an idea and a bowel movement?"[4] That question was directed at a hypothetical theologian who, insisting on the mind's immateriality, would never understand a thing about "this incomprehensible mechanism by which the eternal architect directs your ideas, your desires, your actions." Voltaire's countermodel was a medical doctor, "who knows something, who has examined at length the curves of the cerebellum, investigated whether the nerves have a circulating fluid, probed in vain into uteruses to see how a thinking being is formed there, and knows everything we can know about our machine."[5] Beyond ridiculing the theologian (a "fat automaton" who stammers jargon he doesn't understand), his larger aim was to underscore the connection between mental operations and their material substrate—a connection he deemed crucial, even if no one, as yet, understood it fully. That echoed a remark he'd made decades earlier in the *Lettres philosophiques*: "I am a body and I think; I don't know anything more about it."[6]

Although Voltaire was not a materialist, he nonetheless reflected what Daniel Cottom has called the eighteenth century's visceral turn, which reoriented epistemological inquiry "away from conjectural innate ideas and toward the palpable, dissectable, scrutable organs of the body."[7] For Voltaire the man, the visceral turn entailed quite literally scrutinizing his own entrails, which he regarded as delicate and disease-prone from an early age. His voluminous personal correspondence is full of remarks on his "bad stomach" and the remedies he employed to cope with it. Those letters show that one of the most eminent Enlightenment authors earnestly embraced contemporary medical notions about the abdomen's centrality in the health and illness of *gens de lettres*; at the same time, they illustrate the playful use Voltaire made of visceral matters as part of the image he projected to his correspondents and visitors. Visceralism was also threaded through his satires: he devoted one of his final tales, *Les Oreilles du comte de Chesterfield* (1775), to a tongue-in-cheek exploration of the determining powers of digestion over intellectual capacity, moral character, and the fate of nations.

Corporality was equally important to Diderot's conception of the life of the mind. Unlike Voltaire, he expressed some skepticism about the syndrome known as *maladies des gens de lettres*. For example, he rejected the causal link it assumed between study and melancholy: "Melancholy is a habit of temperament with which some people are born, and which doesn't come from study. If it came from study, all studious people would suffer from it, which isn't true."⁸ He did, however, take a resolutely body-based approach to thinking and feeling. His early work *La Lettre sur les aveugles* (1749) contained this intriguing materialist twist on the notion that thinking requires bodily exertion: "If ever a philosopher, blind and deaf from his birth, were to construct a man after the fashion of Descartes, I can assure you, madam, that he would put the seat of the soul at the fingers' ends, for thence the greater part of the sensations and all of his knowledge are derived. Who would tell him that his head is the seat of his thoughts? . . . I should not be surprised if, after a profound meditation, his fingers were as wearied as our heads."⁹ Diderot's views became overtly psychophysiological around 1765, when he was reading a score of biomedical works and taking the notes that formed the basis of his *Éléments de physiologie*.¹⁰ Inspired by that reading, he rejected both philosophical dualism and iatromechanistic theories of physiology (which described the animal body as a hydraulic machine), in favor of the vitalism popularized by medical theorists of the Montpellier school, who stressed the holistic interaction of the various levels of function in human beings.¹¹

Diderot rejected the unnaturalness that some, like his erstwhile friend Rousseau, imputed to the cultivation of the arts and sciences. He did make this Rousseauistic-sounding remark: "nothing is more contrary to nature than habitual meditation, or the state of the scholar. . . . The man of nature is made to think very little and act a good deal; to the contrary, knowledge-seeking [*science*], involves thinking a good deal and moving very little."¹² That was not, however, a condemnation of learning as morally corrupting: Diderot's comment referred to the sedentariness typical of studious persons, a trait he attributed to their tendency to forget "all of the animal things." Remembering "animal things" was a point on which he insisted when discussing the mechanisms involved in thinking and feeling.

Diderot was especially interested in how the mind/body relation worked in people of genius; and those reflections interwove three major threads of his thought. The first was his conviction that the "higher" aspects of human nature are inseparably connected to its "lower" aspects through a complex network of dynamic, sympathetic interaction; this idea was central to his portrayals of cerebralists absorbed in thought, like the d'Alembert character of the *Rêve de d'Alembert*. The second was his interest in sophisticated machines: the heuristic models he used to depict superior minds included not just the famous "spider in its web" metaphor but also moving mechanical devices like the automaton, the stocking loom, and the *tableau mouvant*. The third thread was perfectibility, which Diderot defined as a uniquely human, brain-based capacity to transform oneself and the world. It was here that he most clearly joined Voltaire's perspective on human nature. Both championed the capacity of reason—the properly "human," as they defined it—to transcend the animal, at least under some circumstances.

Voltaire's Views on Digestion, Suffering, and Intellectual Life

Voltaire's provocative remark "The stomach governs the brain" could be applied to several aspects of eighteenth-century high culture. Nowhere did the French love of food and the equally French passion for ideas converge more harmoniously than in the mythic *repas philosophique*, the imaginary gathering of Voltaire and other famous talking heads painted by Jean Huber, which would become one of the century's iconic images.[13] However, even in this supposed golden age of intellectual sociability, the connection between eating and mental/moral function was far from simple. Some prominent intellectuals were avid gourmands who disavowed the ascetic image of the scholar that had prevailed in the past;[14] but others took a dim view of the gastronomic refinements of the day. These included Rousseau, who devoted considerable attention to diet in *L'Émile* and in *La Nouvelle Héloïse*, and Jaucourt, who wrote on culinary matters in the *Encyclopédie*.[15] Both warned against gourmandise, disapproved of rich dishes and exotic foods, and preached the virtues of a simple regimen.

The simple regimen was considered especially crucial for scholars. A fashionable Parisian doctor, Anne-Charles Lorry, declared that cautious eating and proper digestion were of paramount importance for those in this group: "A Philosophe's first attention must be not to work nor meditate while his stomach is digesting."[16] Study, Lorry contended, dried out the viscera, made the humors fester, kept the body bent over, and diminished circulation, thus leading to poor digestion, constipation, and shortened life spans. Warnings about weak stomachs abounded in health manuals directed at scholars, but their authors also tended to flatter their readers by repeating the age-old notion that there was an inverse relation between high intelligence and good health. That perspective, evident in Tissot's *Santé des gens de lettres*, was also expressed in the *Encyclopédie* article "Santé," whose author contended that robust people were rarely *gens d'esprit*—and vice versa.[17]

The close link perceived between the mind and the abdomen was not, of course, unique to this period. Humanists like Montaigne and Rabelais had already woven a rich web of interrelations between the intellectual and the alimentary, and eighteenth-century British physicians frequently depicted the genteel stomachs and delicate nerves of the upper crust as teetering together on the brink of disaster.[18] Multiple factors nonetheless gave the viscera special significance in eighteenth-century France: the sensual ethos ushered in during the Regency, which championed both culinary and sexual pleasure-seeking; the pervasiveness of the vapors (a digestively related nervous ailment) among aristocrats; and the invention of the restaurant, a development connected to the expansion of both gastronomy and food science.[19]

Another factor was the influential doctrine of vitalism elaborated by physicians associated with the Montpellier medical faculty. One of their trademark ideas was a "triadic conception" of the body, according to which the human organism was dominated by three centers: the brain, the abdomen, and a third organ (the designated third center was sometimes the chest, and sometimes the "exterior organ"—roughly speaking, the skin).[20] Although these theorists often spoke of sympathies when describing intraorganic influences, they used the term "antagonism" to explain how the three centers interacted. Louis de Lacaze, for example, argued that the animal economy was driven by contrary currents of oscillation within the ethereal fluid, some emanating from the brain, others from the exterior organ, and still others from the phrenic region, which he defined as encompassing the stomach, the entrails, and the diaphragm. Because every force in the living body presupposed what Lacaze called a "power of *ressort*" (that is, a capacity to react to stimuli), each vital center worked to maintain or renew its own *ressort* while also resisting the actions of the other centers.[21] Digestion was a key physiological function because "the alimentary mass acts as a sort of ballast or counterpoint that serves to rewind, so to speak, the entire machine by renewing the *ressort* of the stomach" (140). The act of reflection, by contrast, greatly increased the *ressort* of the brain and reduced that of the phrenic region, thus suspending the ordinary laws of action and reaction necessary for good health (380).

The stomach was also assigned great importance by Lacaze's nephew Théophile de Bordeu, one of the most influential vitalist physicians of the 1750s through the 1770s. Bordeu regarded the stomach as a dynamic organ endowed with a sort of animal intuition, its own distinct tastes and distastes, and an influence in most illnesses.[22] Although he did not focus specifically on the weak stomachs of *gens de lettres*, he did criticize the "poorly directed" regimens, unhealthy foodstuffs, and perpetual moral agitation of the urban elite.[23] The vitalists' emphasis on the stomach endured in French medical doctrine for decades. Early psychiatrists located the seat of many psychic illnesses in the viscera, arguing that such disorders were often caused by the passions (the passions, they contended, belonged to the realm of organic life).[24] The most radical proponent of this perspective was the Restoration medical theorist François-Joseph-Victor Broussais, who contended that virtually all mental disorders arose from gastric irritation.[25]

Voltaire's relationship to medicine was, of course, that of a patient: he was famous not only for "doing his body" every morning via vigorous purging, but also for writing volumes of letters about his fragile health, bad stomach, and preference for cassia over rhubarb as a home remedy (he often fretted over whether he could obtain enough cassia to maintain his heavy purgative regimen).[26] That was not, however, the context in which he said that "the stomach governs the brain," a line from a 1748 epistle dedicated to his niece and mistress Madame Denis:

Man the machine, the mind that depends on the body,
By eating well rewinds its springs [*ressorts*]:
With the blood the soul is renewed
And the stomach governs the brain.[27]

Read in isolation, that stanza might sound like a verse adaptation of La Mettrie's man-a-machine treatise. However, Voltaire entitled the epistle "La vie de Paris et de Versailles," and the machinelike eaters to which he referred belonged to the "absurd and frivolous troupe" constituted by the French upper crust—people less concerned with savoring their food than with thinking up weak jibes and witticisms to utter at the next elegant dinner.[28] This particular observation on the mechanical effects that eating exerted on the brain was thus aimed not at serious thinkers but at idle aristocrats, about whom Voltaire was highly ambivalent.

Voltaire often used the stomach to pass judgment on the intellectual or moral aspects of other people, friends as well as foes. In a 1744 epistle, he linked the hospitality and affable character of Président Charles-Jean-François Hénaut to his good stomach, and then proceeded to deride his enemy Pierre Desfontaines as a fat, greasy goat who ate and slept happily among his rat-infested books while those of genuinely "good company" suffered unfairly from indigestion.[29] He also employed the stomach to establish or reinforce certain social bonds, tailoring his digestive references to convey the nature of his relationship with a particular correspondent. In 1724—not long after his almost fatal bout of smallpox—he flattered his mistress of the moment, Mme de Bernières, by praising her generosity in loving him even though he was burdened with "a bad stomach and a mind discouraged by illness."[30] Writing five decades later to his friend and fellow invalid Mme du Deffand, Voltaire offered both advice on particular remedies and the consoling thought that the lady's indigestion proved her superior wit and breeding (Deffand herself subscribed to that idea, and made recounting her ailments a central component of her letter writing).[31]

Voltaire sometimes linked his dyspepsia to power as well as friendship. In 1751, he solidified his ties to Frederick of Prussia by commiserating in verse form over the colic that afflicted them both. While praising Frederick as the "King of beautiful verse and of warriors," he urged him not to overdue his literary efforts, for fear of aggravating his stomach weakness:

Your debilitated stomach / Is not worthy of your head.
Kings are men like us; / The human machine is quite fragile:
Great king, the stomach is for you / What the heel is for Achilles.[32]

In another text, Voltaire artfully interwove the enduring nature of his chronic bad health with the equally enduring nature of his devotion to Frederick (a devotion considerably shaken when Frederick's agents incarcerated Voltaire and Mme Denis in 1753).[33] That curious analogy is found in a letter Voltaire wrote in 1738, when he was a relatively youthful forty-four and Frederick was still Crown Prince of Prussia: "If it is allowable to compare an evil with a good, I have been persuaded for some time now that my illness is, like my attachment to your person, a life-long affair."[34]

Illness truly did seem to be a lifelong affair for Voltaire; it was certainly a prominent element in his public as well as private persona. As René Vaillot notes, Voltaire complained of his health in nearly half of the approximately one hundred letters that he wrote to Mme Denis.[35] In her analysis of those letters, Deidre Dawson remarks, "Like his desire, Voltaire's illness is, paradoxically, a reliable presence in his life, a constant factor that manifests itself in different ways but never dies out."[36] Geoffrey Murray draws a related conclusion out of his study of Voltaire's general correspondence from 1754 to 1762: "Voltaire *malade* . . . is one of the most constant representations we find"—adding that Voltaire's self-styling as "le malade" frequently appeared with other Voltairian stage names such as "le jardinier" or "le suisse" (as when he described himself to the countess Bentinck as "the ailing Swiss man, surrounded by snow").[37] Citing the accounts of Cosimo Alessandro Collini and Jean-Louis Wagnière, Voltaire's secretaries, Murray shows that Voltaire slipped easily into the *malade* personage and played it with verve.[38] Nicholas Cronk finds a similar theatricality in the anecdote recounted by the Prince de Ligne of a very loud fart Voltaire made during the young officer's visit to Ferney in 1763—a burlesque episode worthy of inclusion in the tradition of "flatulent" literature that was popular in some eighteenth-century worldly circles.[39]

The stomach loomed large in Voltaire's self-portraits as *malade*: in addition to signing letters with piquant epithets like "the sickly person [*le malingre*] of Délices" and "the old patient of Ferney," he compared his physique to that of a mummy or a skeleton with a bad stomach attached to it.[40] Digestion also contributed to the ways in which he connected his bodily frailty to his intense mental application. Take, for example, the letter he wrote to Stanislas Leszczynski, the king of Poland, while staying at the king's palace at Lunéville: "His Majesty knows that I am very sick, and that continuous intellectual labors keep me in my apartment, as much as my ailments do."[41] Voltaire's specific purpose here was to get the king's steward, Alliot, to serve him his meals in his apartment so that he would not have to attend meals served in the general dining room.

Clearly, Voltaire used the role of the suffering but good-humored invalid to advance his relations with high-born patrons, and sometimes to get rid of unwelcome visitors. Yet being dyspeptic wasn't just a game or playacting for him: he truly believed that nature had cursed him with a frail machine and weak stomach that might carry him to the grave at any moment, and he expressed that conviction repeatedly in his letters, from the 1720s until his death in 1778. To prevent this, Voltaire adhered to an activist system of hygiene and dietetics loosely based on the recommendations of his personal physician, the renowned Genevan doctor Théodore Tronchin. An energetic self-purger, he employed some of Tronchin's remedies and diligently reported on his health. In a July 1764 letter, Voltaire reminded Tronchin that he had been taking his prescribed "marmelade" four times a week for ten years, adding plaintively: "It has conserved my life, but under very uncomfortable and hard conditions. I cannot go out, and my weakness, which increases every day, makes me incapable both of carrying out my duties and of indulging in pleasures."[42] In practice, the regimen that Voltaire adopted seems inspired as much by his own notions of health and the mind/body relation as by advice he received from Tronchin, a medical and moral conservative who regarded Voltaire's obsession with purging and his constant worries over his body with a mixture of skepticism, humor, and annoyance.[43]

Voltaire claimed that he had read "more medical books than Don Quixote had read books on chivalry."[44] He also treated the servants and local peasants of Ferney when they fell ill. He had a mixed attitude toward his own ailments, wavering between stoical resignation, anger, and humor. This fluctuation is illustrated by two letters written on the same day: March 7, 1760. In the first, addressed to Marquis Francesco Capacelli, Voltaire echoed the reasoning of his fictional optimist Pangloss, declaring that he had forgiven nature for endowing his soul with such a frail machine "since that would necessarily be part of the plan for the best of all possible worlds." In the second, written to Count Francesco Algarotti, he raged against his bad health—but then went on to say: "I enjoy despite my bodily ailments the consolations that your book provides to my mind; that is worth more than Tronchin's pills."[45]

Voltaire may not have been entirely serious when he exclaimed to Mme du Deffand that "the way in which we digest almost always determines our way of thinking,"[46] but he did adhere to the practice of keeping his entrails as empty as possible in order to keep his mind clear. One could compare his personal hygienic philosophy with the doctrine promoted by the famous English "hyp" doctor George Cheyne: "Crudely put, he posited an inverse relationship between weight and spirituality: the less matter, the more spirit."[47]

One could also say that Voltaire embodied Michelet's remark that "men of letters always suffer, but live nonetheless."[48] Although he lamented for years that he was dying, Voltaire came to regard his bad stomach as the key to both his physical longevity and his prolific literary life. What kept Voltaire going may have been the life of retirement that he adopted partly to accommodate his stomach and partly to avoid trouble from the authorities over his writings. Not until the 1760s did he overtly declare that he owed his continued existence to regimen and to retreat; yet even in his early letters, he described his frail health as inseparable from his zealous devotion to intellectual work. In other words, although living in perpetual retreat from the elite social whirl did not always suit Voltaire's temperament, it clearly advanced his mission as a writer and *philosophe*—and his stomach contributed to both.

Visceralism in Voltaire's Satires

Voltaire's use of visceralism in his satirical writings echoed the mixture of facetiousness and deeper philosophical reflection found in his correspondence. He used alimentary humor to lampoon everything from the belief in vampires to the Jesuits.[49] As he aged, he was increasingly inclined to evoke the brute facts of digestion and excretion for polemical ends—like in the tongue-in-cheek article "Ventres paresseux" (1772), where he defended the residents of Crete against Saint Paul's accusation in the Epistle to Titus that their "lazy" abdomens made them liars and nasty beasts.[50] Yet even in texts such as this, one detects a note of pathos: underneath the scatological jokes, Voltaire made melancholic reflections on the power of lower bodily functions to shape human existence. His article "Déjection," for example, is a paean to nature's art in designing the mechanism of excretion, but it also describes man as an abject being who "is born between fecal matter and urine"—a condition that "decides his character and most of his actions in life."[51]

Voltaire's most darkly humorous treatment of visceral matters is his philosophical tale *Les Oreilles du comte de Chesterfield* (1775), which recounts the philosophical education of a talented but impoverished young Anglican clergyman named Goudman. References to the belly abound in this text, certainly compared to his more famous *Candide, ou l'optimisme* (1759), where they are limited largely to a few meals (including the one at which the Oreillons prepare to eat Candide and Cacambo while exclaiming, "Let's eat some Jesuit!") and four mentions of a "slit abdomen" that belongs either to Cunégonde or to her brother. In *Les Oreilles*, Voltaire returned to one of his favorite themes: the notion that fatality implacably rules everything in this world. Here, however, the arbitrary nature of destiny is embodied not by wars or earthquakes or scheming Parisians (as in *Candide*), but by the bodily conditions of poor hearing, an irrepressible sex drive, and constipation.

Les Oreilles du comte de Chesterfield can, of course, be read as a story about sex, that is, the amorous misadventures of Goudman and the beautiful Miss Fielding; it can also be read as a tale about the ears of Goudman's kindly but hard-of-hearing benefactor, evoked in the title. Roger Pearson emphasizes both of those elements in his reading of the text, venturing the idea that they come down to the same thing: "the "*oreilles* themselves may have the slang sense of 'testicles.' "[52] There are, however, equal grounds for emphasizing the link between the ears and the belly in this tale: listening and digestion converge in its climactic scene, echoing the connection Voltaire made between them in other contexts. As he declared in a particularly anxious letter to Dr. Tronchin, "When the stomach is free, the organ of hearing is, too, because everything is connected in nature."[53]

From this point of view, the decisive moment of *Les Oreilles* occurs in chapter 7: after enjoying a fine meal with Goudman and a well-traveled doctor named Grou, the character Sidrac (described as an "excellent anatomist"[54]) takes over their conversation on the miseries, stupidities, and horrors that afflict humankind by reducing all the great dramas in political history to the bowel movements of the leaders involved. Constipation, Sidrac argues, has produced some of the bloodiest scenes known to man, including Oliver Cromwell's beheading of Charles the First and the Saint Bartholomew's Massacre, authorized by France's Charles IX, whom Sidrac describes as "the most constipated man in his kingdom" (183). Sidrac mentions these examples to prove his decidedly bizarre theory that wandering fecal matter determines moral character:

> What happens to a constipated man? The finest, most delicate elements of his excrement intermingle with the chyle in the veins of Azellius, and go to the portal vein and the reservoir of Paquet. They pass into the sub-clavicular region and enter the heart of the most gallant man, the most coquettish woman. It is like a mist of dried turd coursing through his body. If this mist inundates the inner organs and vessels of an atrabilious person, his bad humor turns into ferocity; and if he is a Minister of State, one should take care *not* to present him with any request before discreetly asking his favorite valet if his grace has emptied his bowels that morning. (182)

Sidrac insists that digestion and excretion form the secret engine to the passions on both the grand and the private scales. History, he contends, would be better served if historians stopped stuffing their chronicles with platitudes about moral causes and instead paid closer attention to the influence of bodily functions upon the course of human events (184).

Clearly, Voltaire invented Sidrac's visceral fatalism in order to poke fun at the high and mighty, while also injecting a note of farce into reflection on the human condition. Sidrac's scatological worldview is tied to his metaphysics: in chapter 4 of *Les Oreilles*, he dismisses the notion of the immaterial, immortal soul as inconceivable, given the realities of biological generation. However, this tale also includes elements that temper the notion that lower bodily functions inexorably determine our intellectual capacity and moral character. First, Sidrac himself acknowledges that good moral and physical hygiene can do wonders to weaken the "empire" of the toilet (184). Second, young Goudman realizes that other, nonsomatic forces help to determine the destiny of an individual; as he remarks in chapter 8, "I see that digestion alone doesn't decide everything in this world, and that love, ambition, and money also play a major role" (187). Armed with this personal philosophy—and the hundred and fifty guineas he has just received from another of Miss Fielding's suitors, who wants to rid himself of a rival to her hand—Goudman goes on to win a position as curate and to enjoy Miss Fielding's favors in secret. In short, although the physicians of the story influence Goudman's philosophical perspective, their reductive materialism is not endorsed by its hero, who ends up as "one of the most zealous priests of England"—still persuaded, in principle, of the implacable powers of fatality, but living in a manner that affirms the powers of self-determination (187–88).

However facetious, the visceralist philosophy espoused in *Les Oreilles* may have had a personal edge for the author. That is, Voltaire's intense purgative regimen may well have been the means by which he strove to resemble what his character Sidrac calls "those people favored by nature [who] are sweet, affable, gracious, thoughtful, and compassionate" because they "defecate as easily as they spit" (184). Voltaire's letters suggest that he regarded purgation as a method of redeeming his abject, sickly body by keeping his temper sociable and his intellect sharp, just as he enlisted his stomach ailments to a higher purpose by deflecting the pleasures of the table into literature and conversation.[55] His lifelong stomach care may also have helped him to keep "Lisette"—the nickname he gave to his soul in 1764—in good humor, despite the sorry condition of the "doddering body" in which she was lodged.[56]

Corporality and the Myth of Voltaire

Although it did not get as much press as Rousseau's sufferings, the image that Voltaire fashioned of his ailing body had an interesting legacy. It was not merely a strategic construct: quite the contrary, Voltaire's poor stomach and general frail health did much to shape his humor, his views on mental endeavor, and his emphasis on the hidden, often humble forces at play in human life. His dyspepsia also shows the role played by invalidism in intellectual celebrity: fueled both by the disease syndrome of *maladies des gens de lettres* and the Enlightenment's "great man" cult, the ailments of famous writers took their place among the intimate traits that critics as well as physicians used to size them up.

In Voltaire's case, the measurement was sometimes less than charitable: at least two of his contemporaries turned his dyspepsia against him to take aim at his character and ideology. One was Voltaire's own "Esculape," Théodore Tronchin, who, early in his treatment of Voltaire, diagnosed his ills as emanating from "a constantly irritating bile and constantly irritated nerves," and who later described the effects of Voltaire's anticlerical persiflage as equivalent to the "wars, plagues, and famines that have depopulated the earth in recent years."[57] Another was the Benedictine monk Louis-Mayeul Chaudon, who, in his *Dictionnaire anti-philosophe* (1767), dismissed Voltaire's critiques of the Bible as the product of bad digestion:

> M. de Voltaire is the universal man, and so universal that he has explained Newton without understanding him, and who argues every day with the pastors of Geneva about the inadequacies of Hebrew without understanding that language. Some of these pastors . . . take part in M de V.'s suppers, and they provide him with arguments over dessert that he uses right away to turn into chapters of his *Dictionnaire philosophique*. Because he works while digesting, and because his digestion is laborious, it is not surprising to find a lot of bile in everything he has produced.[58]

Guillaume François Berthier also used lower body rhetoric to denounce *La Pucelle d'Orléans* (1762) in the *Journal de Trévoux*: "Never has hell vomited up a more deadly plague."[59] Berthier, Chaudon, and (to a lesser extent) Tronchin obviously disliked Voltaire, but they also imitated him by exploiting the metaphoric potential of visceralism to denounce his irreverent wit.

In that sense, these critics attested not simply to the celebrity enjoyed by Voltaire's bad stomach, but also to his emerging status as a "cultural unit"—an individual who, like the Revolutionary leaders Maximilien Robespierre and Georges Danton, was the object of an evolving series of representations that drew very explicitly on his physical aspects.[60] Beliefs about the body and disease played a fundamental role in making Voltaire a cultural unit; so, too, did ideas and debates about civilization, civility, Frenchness, the philosophic movement, and the state of the contemporary Republic of Letters. Voltaire personified many of those ideas and debates—and his famously thin and ailing physical form helped to accomplish that.

The evocative power of Voltaire's body was extraordinarily enduring. The nineteenth-century physician Joseph-Henri Réveillé-Parise called him the epitome of the "poetically organized" man, a being whose "heroic souls" had almost stripped him of all carnality.[61] Speaking at the Sorbonne in 1944, Paul Valéry exclaimed, "This man is a physiological marvel. He is the essence of vitality, using and abusing a fragile body."[62] And in 2012, Franck Nouchi published *Le Cerveau de Voltaire,* an ironic detective story built around the fantasy that Voltaire's brain had been stolen by an obsessive fan hoping to clone him and bring the Enlightenment back to life.[63]

Lost in Thought: Mental Absorption and Animality in Diderot

Diderot, too, was sometimes on the receiving end of sarcastic visceralist critiques: Jean-François de la Harpe compared his mind to "those hot, avid stomachs that devour everything and digest nothing, and those are not the stomachs of healthy men."[64] However, distraction was a more prominent theme in the myth-making that surrounded Diderot's mind. He seemed to identify with the proverbial absentmindedness of the cerebralist, even to the point of embracing the legend created during his lifetime (by friends and enemies alike) that he was a "naïve dreamer . . . whimsical, casual, but above all distracted."[65] There may, therefore, be a self-referential aspect to the remark Diderot made about intense thinking in the *Éléments de physiologie*: "There are no deep thinkers, no ardent imaginations that are not subject to momentary catalepsies. A singular idea comes to mind, a strange connection distracts us, and our heads are lost. We come back from that state as from a dream, asking those around us, 'where was I? What was I saying?' "⁶⁶ That passage also shows the double, inside/outside perspective Diderot took to mental operations, a perspective rooted in his materialist ideology. Intent on externalizing the secrets of nature and demolishing the notion of an immaterial soul, he undertook to objectify everything from generation to the faculties of the mind and envision them all as processes that arise out of natural organization.⁶⁷

Like contemporary authors who drew on anecdotes of Archimedes to describe contemplative oblivion (examined in Chapter 2), Diderot was intrigued by the strange state that occurred when a person lost consciousness of everything beyond a single idea. He found it aesthetically appealing: oblivion was, as Michael Fried puts it, an "extreme instance or limiting case" of the interest in absorptive activities evident in the art criticism produced by Diderot and other midcentury theorists.⁶⁸ The same interest is apparent in his literary theory, which invested depictions of characters engrossed in reverie with a special power to interest and touch their readers. His major venture into the novel of sensibility, *La Religieuse* (1770/1780–82), contains a striking example of this idea: at the moment when the heroine Suzanne Simonin is forced against her will to take monastic vows, she turns into an "automaton" out of deep dejection and dread for the existence that awaits her—a tableau designed to elicit horror and pity from the novel's inscribed reader, the Marquis de Croismare.⁶⁹ Yet Diderot also found considerable philosophical appeal in mental absorption, especially when the ideas responsible for triggering the state involved abstract thinking.

One of his earliest discussions of absorption is found in the *Encyclopédie* article "Animal" (1751), composed as a series of annotated excerpts from the second volume of Buffon's *Histoire naturelle générale et particulière* (the excerpts were selected by Buffon's collaborator Louis-Jean-Marie Daubenton and drawn particularly from the chapter "De la nature de l'Homme").⁷⁰ Diderot turned the article into an imagined dialogue with Buffon over the qualities that distinguish humans from animals, and, at one point, he paused to reflect on Buffon's claim that the difference is spiritual. Animals, Buffon contended, may possess "something similar to our first apprehensions and our brute, most mechanical sensations," but they are incapable of the complex association of ideas that produces reflection, because all they have is the material substrate necessary for thinking, not the divinely granted power of reflection. As for humans, Buffon took a stance that was both dualistic and philosophically skeptical: he argued that the order of ideas we form in our minds is completely independent of the material body, but he declared that "we exist without knowing how, and we think without knowing why."[71] Diderot countered the first claim by insisting that the material body exerts a prodigious influence over the order of our thoughts. Then, addressing the second point, he argued that it isn't so difficult to envision how thinking works, particularly if we consider states like sleep or deep meditation. During those states, the mind goes into a sort of "inertia" in which it stays stuck on the same thought unless jolted back into action by something exterior to itself. The deep thinker who moves from one object of reflection to another may appear to be exercising his will, but he is not: what carries his mind along are the connections that exist among the objects themselves. This, Diderot concluded, showed that thinking is at bottom a mechanical process: "I don't know anything as mechanical [*machinal*] as a man absorbed in profound meditation, other than a man plunged in a deep sleep."[72]

That comment provides an early example of Diderot's use of the idea of obscure or "un-thought" thoughts, which belonged to a philosophical tradition associated with Leibniz.[73] It also offers a glimpse into his developing interest in the bodily processes that unfold when the mind is unhinged from the conscious will. Although he did not venture a physiological theory in "Animal" to explain the mechanical, self-propelling nature of idea formation in the dreamer or the meditator lost in thought, he located that process in the animal part of the human being. That becomes clearer when we consider the adjective *machinal* in the phrase "I don't know anything as mechanical as a man absorbed in profound meditation." Jean-Luc Martine notes that *machinal* was used at the time to refer to jerky, reflexive, involuntary body movements; and whereas Buffon used *machinal* to grant animals nothing more than a crude resemblance to humans in the realm of perceptions and sensations, Diderot applied it to the human at the highest end of the intelligence spectrum.[74] Deep thinking, he implied, was something deeply rooted in the body, quite distinct from willful, orderly reflection.

Although it shocked some conservative commentators (like Abraham Chaumeix),[75] Diderot's vision of the absorbed thinker as a not-quite-conscious animal machine echoed aspects of contemporary medical discourse. As we saw earlier, physicians often used mechanical images to portray scholars plunged in meditation. Some evoked musical instruments: the notion of the resonant human body was popular among both physicians and music theorists, who used it to account for a range of phenomena, from the effects of music to the workings of intersubjective moral sympathy.[76] Diderot, too, borrowed images from the realm of music: he employed the harpsichord metaphor in the *Lettre sur les sourds et muets*, to support an acoustical model of mental activity, and again in the *Rêve de d'Alembert*, to explain the process by which sensory impressions are transmitted, received, and interpreted by the mind (with the mind understood as both part of the instrument being played and part of the musician playing the instrument).

Diderot shared the widespread medical opinion that deep meditation concentrates vital activity in the head so fully that the whole body is affected. This is one of the phenomena discussed in *Le Rêve de d'Alembert*, a trio of dialogues whose cast of characters includes a medical authority loosely based on the real-life Théophile de Bordeu. The text's fictional interlocutors employ a number of metaphors—the sensitive harpsichord, the bee swarm, the spider in its web, the polyp—to explore the implications of the vitalist-materialist cosmogony that is introduced in the opening dialogue, "L'Entretien entre d'Alembert et Diderot," which conceives of the world in general and human beings in particular in terms of sensible matter in motion.[77] Because the overall function and progression of those metaphors have been well explored by others, I will focus specifically on those that are applied to the state of being lost in thought, a condition portrayed as similar but not identical to the full-fledged dream in which the character d'Alembert spends a good part of the central dialogue.

The absorbed thinker is first mentioned during a discussion of the brain. According to the text's main heuristic metaphor, the brain's relations with the rest of the body resemble those of a spider vis-à-vis its feet and the threads that it has spun out to form a web (the threads are conceived as maintaining a vital, sensitive connection to the body of the spider, as much as its feet). As Dr. Bordeu explains to Mlle de l'Espinasse, intense mental exertion concentrates the thinker's sphere of conscious sensibility in a single point, so fully that it wipes out sensorial awareness of anything else.[78] In metaphorical terms, the meditator's mind is the equivalent of a spider so fixated on what is happening at its center that it loses contact with its peripheral parts (its feet and threads). Dr. Bordeu describes this shutting out of sensations as a case of the system working backward, comparable to what happens in delirious fanatics, ecstatic savages, and madmen (171). Yet he also points out that the phenomenon is not without its advantages: some savvy scholars concentrate their minds on a difficult question as a means of blocking out bodily pain like chronic earache (173). Such voluntary suppression of physical sensation is, however, only temporary, and the *philosophe* in Dr. Bordeu's story ends up paying with horrible pain for the trick he'd tried to play on his sensory system (174).

More typical is the involuntary oblivion to which cerebralists of the highest order are susceptible. Dr. Bordeu mentions this in response to a question raised by his second interlocutor, the geometer d'Alembert, who awakens partway through the central dialogue from his long, often agitated dream. When d'Alembert asks Dr. Bordeu to explain the difference between free will in a dreamer versus a man awake, Dr. Bordeu exclaims, "You of all people ask me this question! You are a fellow much given to deep speculation, and you have spent two-thirds of your life dreaming with your eyes wide open. In that state, you do all sorts of involuntary things—yes, involuntary—much less deliberately than when you are asleep" (184–85).[79] As Dr. Bordeu insists, an odd separation occurs between the mind and the conscious will in both the state of full mental absorption and the dream state: the d'Alembert engaged in mathematical speculation is no more aware of his body's actions than is the dreaming d'Alembert. Although he carried out an impressive number of seemingly willful acts while deep in sleep, d'Alembert was not willfully conscious. Nor is he, Dr. Bordeu contends, when his mind is buried in complex calculations:

> In the midst of your meditations, your eyes are scarcely open in the morning before you are deep in the idea that was on your mind the previous evening. You get dressed, you sit down at the table, you keep on meditating, tracing figures on the cloth; all day long you pursue your calculations; you sit down to dinner; afterwards you pick up your combinations again; sometimes you even get up and leave the table to verify them. You speak with other people, you give orders to your servants, you have a bite of supper, you go to bed and you drop off to sleep without having done a single act of your own free will the whole livelong day. (*Dream*, 160; *Rêve*, 185)

Commenting on this passage, Aram Vartanian declares that there is something anomalous about Diderot's robotlike representation of the geometer actively engaged in thinking, given that "the ability to think mathematically is anything but automatic."[80] Vartanian argues that the effect of the passage—conveyed rhetorically through the "lulling," repetitious structure of the passage—is to "defeat our expectation of interiority."[81] That, however, depends on what expectation we bring to the text. The interiority at play here is not psychological in the modern sense: rather, as Jacot Grapa explains, what Diderot is describing is "something subjacent to self-mastery . . . which involves a definition of man steeped in the animality that determines his will, his movements."[82] One of the most insistent themes of the dialogue is that nothing in the "higher" realms of human existence fully transcends the basic, animal level of sentient existence—not individual consciousness, nor the self, nor any God of which one might conceive (*Rêve*, 143).

The character d'Alembert does, indeed, behave rather like an automaton in Dr. Bordeu's portrait of him observed in wakeful intellectual reverie. In fact, the automaton analogy is even more pronounced in the version of the same anecdote that appears in the *Éléments de physiologie*, where Diderot compares the lack of free will in a geometer preoccupied with a math problem to that of "a wooden automaton who carried out the same things as he did" (485–86). However, the absorbed geometer is fully interior in the terms that Mlle de l'Espinasse uses elsewhere in the *Rêve de d'Alembert* to describe the muting of her bodily sensations when her mind is completely absorbed by an idea: "I seem to be reduced to a single point in space; my body almost seems insubstantial, and I am aware only of my thoughts. I am unconscious of location, movement, solidity, distance and space. The universe is annihilated as far as I am concerned, and I am nothing in relation to it" (*Dream*, 139; *Rêve*, 157). Like Mlle de L'Espinasse as she imagines herself in the absorbed state, the meditating d'Alembert is suspended in space and time, focused so entirely on a particular thought or problem that he can feel nothing else.

These passages are, of course, meant to disconcert, and the characters of the *Rêve de d'Alembert* express some fears regarding the loss of voluntary, conscious thinking and feeling. The central dialogue begins, we will remember, with Mlle de l'Espinasse explaining that she has called Dr. Bordeu to d'Alembert's bedside because she was alarmed and worried by the strange, disconnected ideas he was uttering in his sleep. Yet, as Kate Tunstall stresses, Diderot deliberately "refuses any sense of [psychological] interiority by having d'Alembert's body also express his ideas"—as when d'Alembert masturbates in his sleep after dreaming about different forms of possible human generation, thus externalizing in a sexual way the ideas that are agitating his mind.[83] Moreover, even though Dr. Bordeu injects the occasional note of pathos into the anecdotes he relates about individuals who, through illness or injury, lose the unified sensibility necessary to have an enduring and coherent sense of self, he and Mlle de L'Espinasse are positively gleeful when conducting anatomical thought experiments to envision carrying out that loss—as, for example, when they imagine reducing the great genius Newton to a "unorganized pulp" endowed with nothing but vitality and sensitivity (*Rêve*, 189).

In short, the *Rêve de d'Alembert* pushes us, like its fictional interlocutors, to take an externalist perspective and consider deep thinkers as living machines with integrated but detachable parts. Viewed from that perspective, consciousness and the other higher faculties of the mind are materially rooted, contingent phenomena whose organic foundation shows most clearly when those faculties are shut down or temporarily disrupted.[84] Diderot uses the d'Alembert character to demonstrate both sides of the comparison he'd made in his comments in the *Encyclopédie* article "Animal": the man absorbed in a deep meditation, and the man plunged in sleep. D'Alembert is just as *machinal* in the meditating state as in the dream state; what differentiates the two is that his body is more active and efficient during wakeful mental absorption. To refer once again to the details of the geometer's day vignette in the *Rêve*: even when d'Alembert's mind is completely wrapped up in a math problem, other parts of his organism—his arms, legs, and stomach—get him up, dressed, fed, and finally back to bed at the end of the day; and they have done so habitually, as the repeated use of the French imperfect past tense in the passage underscores ("vous vous vêtiez, . . . vous soupiez, vous vous couchiez, vous vous endormiez" [*Rêve*, 185]).

The body parts of the conscious automaton in the *Rêve* thereby demonstrate their own particular "life," a local sensitivity, appetite, and judgment —just like the eye that, in the *Éléments de physiologie*, helpfully guides an absentminded "nous" through the streets of Paris:

> How is it that we manage to cross Paris through all sorts of obstacles, when we're deeply preoccupied by an idea? . . . The eye guides us; we're the blind man. The eye is the dog that guides us; and if the eye weren't really an animal reacting to the diversity of sensations, how would it guide us? For this isn't a matter of habit. The obstacles it avoids are at every moment new to it. The eye sees, the eye lives,

> the eye feels, the eye guides us on, the eye avoids the obstacles, the eye guides us, and guides us surely. . . . The eye is an animal within an animal, carrying out its functions very well, and on its own. The same is true of other organs.[85]

Consciousness in this anecdote is a fleeting, unreliable state. However, the eye and other organs compensate for mental distraction because they have their own sort of awareness or attentiveness to their surroundings, along with a capacity for discernment that ensures both the self-preservation and the preservation of the whole.

One more anecdote from the *Éléments*—related directly after the example of the helpful eye—bears mentioning because it highlights the role of useful physical automatism in another context: artistic production. Here, Diderot illustrates the phenomenon of distraction with the example of a well-trained musician who continues to play his part in a harpsichord concert after his mind becomes distracted by an interesting conversation he is having with his neighbor.[86] The vignette splits the musician's being in two parts: the *homme* (or conscious self) and the *animal* (represented here by his eyes, ear, and fingers). The musician's animal parts work together to keep playing the music: despite the mind's distraction, they are "nonetheless in agreement with each other; not a single chord is out of place, not a single silence is forgotten, not a single mistake is made in movement, taste, measure." When the conversation ends, the musician returns his attention to his music but "his head is lost, he doesn't know where he is." The *homme* is disconcerted, but the *animal* could have carried on playing if the *homme* had remained distracted—a phenomenon due, Diderot posits, to the mutual sympathy created among sensitive living parts when they acquire the habit of working together toward a common goal, "without the participation of the entire animal."

The focus of these vignettes is not the conceptual combinations formed in the mind of the absorbed thinker or artist, about which Diderot provides scant information. Instead, they dwell on the operations taking place elsewhere in the body, operations that are not purely a matter of habit. By shifting emphasis away from the ideas these personae are thinking, Diderot draws our attention to the dynamic powers that are activated at the organic level when the mind is too busy to notice.

We might be tempted to evoke the modern notion of the unconscious to characterize what Diderot was trying to get at when he depicted states of automatism brought on by deep mental concentration. However, the "other" of consciousness for its eighteenth-century theorists was something rather different from the entity that came to be called the unconscious in the later context of psychiatry and psychoanalysis.[87] Moreover, what Diderot sought to grasp was not just the inner workings of the mind: he wanted to explore the inner workings of the body as well, and he rejected any sort of dualistic philosophy that kept the two neatly separated. Rather than "unconscious," a more appropriate term for the body/mind state of Diderot's creatively absorbed automatons might be "dual consciousness." This is the term that Joseph Roach uses to describe the highly skilled, habitual automatism of the Diderotian theater genius, whose ability to perform intense emotions in a seemingly spontaneous yet technically flawless manner depends on a properly corporeal memory and "a consciousness heightened to the point at which activities outside the perimeter of attention are rendered unconscious, automatic, absorbed."[88] Seen from that perspective, the principal purpose of Diderot's "deep thinking" automatons—as opposed to his negative automatons, like Suzanne Simonin of *La Religieuse*, or the narrator of *Jacques le fataliste* expressing indignation with his impatient reader[89]—was to work through key aspects of his materialist conception of the human being, from the role of the body or "animal" in the thinking process, to the jointly physical and moral causes of geniality.

Mind, Brain, and Body in Diderot

Although Diderot is sometimes called a "radical" materialist, he was more of a mentalist on certain topics. As Jonathan Crary underscores in his analysis of the *Lettre sur les aveugles*, Diderot placed less emphasis on the "immediate subjective evidence of the body" than on the way in which the mind combines the ideas it receives from whatever sensory organs it possesses.[90] Moreover, departing from the sentimental moral philosophy he sometimes championed, he took a dispassionate, empirical approach to the mind's operations. Diderot relegated moral sensibility to a decidedly secondary status in some of his best-known portrayals of creative production, like those found in the *Paradoxe sur le comédien*. He did regard the brilliant as more "human" than the less intellectually endowed, but this was not a question of ethics: it was a matter of perfected intellect, a condition that a few, rare individuals attained by concentrating their energies entirely in their heads. As he put it in his last work, the *Essai sur Sénèque* (1778),

> Man, keep in mind that you owe the quality that distinguishes you from animals to the weakness of your organs. Do you aspire to the piercing view of the eagle? You would be staring endlessly. Do you wish to have a dog's sense of smell? You'd be sniffing around from morning to night. The organ of your judgment has remained predominant and the master; it would have been the slave of one of your senses if it had become too vigorous: that's the source of your perfectibility. If there is a fiber in your brain that is more energetic than the others, you are no longer good for anything but a single thing, you're a man of genius: the animal and the man of genius are alike in that way.[91]

He made a similar point in the *Réfutation suivie de l'ouvrage d'Helvétius intitulé "de l'Homme"*: "The man of genius and the animal are related because there is in both a predominant organ that leads them invincibly toward some sort of occupation, which they execute perfectly."[92] The predominant organ of superior minds was the brain—"from which emanate the astonishing differences among men, relative to the intellectual operations."[93] As he reasoned, geniuses were only good for one thing;[94] but they were so good at it that it made up for the socially odd behavior they sometimes displayed. What they also displayed was the "tyrannical drive of genius"—along with the corporeal, animal foundations of reason's perfectibility, in all of its variations: "Man is also an animal species, his reason is nothing but a perfectible and perfected sort of instinct; and the field of sciences and arts there are as many diverse instincts as there are dogs in a hunting pack."[95]

Diderot's views on the mind were shaped by the "distributive account of life and sensibility"—a decentralized model of the unity of the organism, which made the particular vital action of local parts crucial to the functioning of the whole—that became popular in multiple areas of European (and particularly French) thought and culture during the 1750s, 1760s, and 1770s.[96] So while it is true that Diderot often took a mentalist stance toward the phenomena of sight, touch, and language, his vitalist materialism led him to espouse a pan-corporeal view of the thinking process. He clearly emphasized the importance of the brain, proper, in some texts. In addition to singling it out in the *Réfutation d'Helvétius* and *Essai sur Sénèque*, he devoted a long section of the *Éléments de physiologie* to phenomena of the brain, and in the chapter of that section devoted to memory, he compared the brain to a "mass of sensitive, living wax" endowed with amazing powers to register and record sensations, and to a "book that reads itself."[97] However, he never ventured far into speculations on the brain's physio-anatomical makeup. Indeed, he called it "this soft cheese [*fromage mou*] that fills the capacity of your cranium and mine" in the *Salon de 1767*, where he argued that the brain was less important than the visceral organs in our reactions to the terrifying experiencing of sublime art: he compared the brain there to the body of a spider who sits passively while its feet and web do all the work, and he made the intestines, not the brain, the place where the aesthetic experience of the sublime was registered and recorded.[98] For Diderot, the brain was part of a larger dynamic: memory, imagination, and even reasoning involved the lower as well as "higher" parts of the human being.

Devices of Wonder: Diderot's Genius Personae

Like the fictional Dr. Bordeu of *Le Rêve de d'Alembert*, Diderot often pondered "the way in which great men are made"—that is, the particular ways in which natural attributes, training, and force of habit combined to allow certain individuals to excel in a given field, whether it be poetry, art, medicine, or government. That dialogue's depiction of the great mind as a self-possessed, dispassionate sage illustrates one of the central tenets of the conception of geniality that Diderot espoused from the 1760s on: the "great" were not simply made by nature, they made themselves. This process of self-making depended on what he called the moral causes that allow genius to emerge and flourish.[99] Those ideas also shaped his portraits of the greatest creative artists of his generation, from the novelist Samuel Richardson to the painters Jean-Baptiste-Siméon Chardin and Claude Joseph Vernet. He perceived certain gifts of nature at the root of their genius: they had *le secret*, a power that combined innate talent with a keen eye and fertile imagination. Yet he also emphasized the experiential aspect of their greatness, which derived from the years they devoted to studying nature and perfecting *le faire* or *le tact* necessary to capture its essence on the page or canvas.¹⁰⁰ When deployed with the proper combination of verve and judgment, those qualities made such individual "magicians" who could create entire worlds with their brushes or pens—a capacity that Diderot clearly regarded as worthy of assiduous study in itself.¹⁰¹

The tensions implicit in Diderot's musings on great men reflect larger tensions in this period's thinking about genius, which bore the traces of two distinct ancient notions: the conception of genius as inspiration from a divine or demonic source, a state involving delirium and enthusiasm; and the conception of genius as arising from natural disposition or talent.¹⁰² Diderot shifted back and forth between these two views when portraying visual artists in his *Salons* and other essays on art. Sometimes he dwelt upon the feverish, intoxicated state of artistic inspiration, but at other times he stressed the technical skill required to conceive and execute an outstanding work of art. In other words, he echoed the notion of genius as fleeting and ardent, and he made verve or the creative moment contingent on "animal" matters—like the "two drops of fluid" that, as he conjectured in the *Salon de 1767*, Vernet may have lost by caressing his wife one morning, instead of getting to work on what turned out to be a mediocre painting.¹⁰³ Yet he also emphasized the mastery that great artists exert over both their *faire* and their minds—evident both in Raphael's perfect, machinelike "repeatability," and in the ability of Chardin and Vernet to "see" their paintings twelve years before they painted them, and then bring them to life on the canvas.¹⁰⁴

As Herbert Dieckmann pointed out, the eighteenth century ushered in a "transition from the conception of genius as mere talent to the conception of *the* genius as an individual"—and Diderot played a fundamental role in that development.¹⁰⁵ Developing that idea, Darrin McMahon emphasizes that this period also introduced a new set of cultural practices for displaying "the prodigies of nature and mankind."¹⁰⁶ Diderot did not claim to be a genius himself: he believed he'd caught a few glimpses of the mysterious sphere in which the brilliant dwelled but relegated himself to a more modest rung on the great chain of intellectual being.¹⁰⁷ His works are, however, filled with displays of intellectual and artistic prodigies, from the experimental physicists of *De l'interprétation de la nature* to the great actors of the *Paradoxe sur le comédien*. Although he insisted on their individuality, he did not construct them as psychological beings—or, at least, not primarily. Rather, they serve the same function as the blind mathematician Saunderson of the *Lettre sur les aveugles*, whom Diderot used to project himself and his readers into an unfamiliar regimen of sensing, feeling, and thinking.[108] One can compare such characters to the specimens that he envisioned encountering in an ideal natural history cabinet: they are heuristic constructs, designed to provide the observer with a means of grasping and thinking through some aspect of nature.[109]

The particular puzzle at the heart of Diderot's speculative observations of geniuses had to do as much with the animal as with the cognitive side of their minds. How, he wondered, was the superior mind attached to the body? How did the interconnections of mind and body shape the mental, emotional, and moral experience of those who belonged to the first rank of human intelligence and creative ability? And what happens to the rest of us—the mediocre sorts, as he sometimes put it—when we enter into contact with the works created by such extraordinary human beings? To borrow an apt formulation from Daniel Brewer, Diderot sought not so much to resolve those questions as to *figure* them, in the sense of representing or staging the processes he was pondering.[110] Diderot occasionally tried to catch his own mind in the act of thinking, as he recounted in his 1751 "Lettre à Mlle de la Chaux" (a supplement to his *Lettre sur les sourds et muets*): "Several times, in an effort to examine what was happening in my head and to catch my mind in the act, I threw myself into the deepest meditation, retreating into myself with all the exertion I could; but these efforts didn't produce anything. It seemed to me that one would have to be entirely inside and outside oneself, and play the role both of observer and that of the machine observed."[111] Perhaps, he mused, this sort of examination would succeed for a *dicéphale* that could use one of its two heads to observe the mechanisms unfolding in its other head; however, nature had not yet produced such a two-headed monster. Lacking such a creature, he turned to projecting himself into the heads of geniuses—using heuristic metaphors to bridge the gap between what could be directly observed with the limited sensory experience of a one-headed person, and the ways in which he imagined superior minds operated.[112]

Seeing, or optical sensing, was fundamental to some of the models Diderot used to figure mental machinery. One was the *tableau mouvant* analogy he evoked in a frequently quoted passage from the *Lettre sur les sourds et muets*: "Our mind [*âme*] is a *tableau mouvant*, which we are perpetually copying [*peignons*]. We spend a good deal of time in rendering it faithfully; but the original exists as a complete whole, and all at once; for the mind does not proceed step by step, like expression. The brush takes time to represent what the artist's eye sees in an instant."¹¹³ Many critics who have discussed this passage focus on the word "tableau" and the verb "peindre" that follows right after, translating the first sentence as "our soul is a moving picture after which we are constantly painting."¹¹⁴ That rendering (inspired, perhaps, by the overt painterly metaphor Diderot used in the third sentence) is an imprecise and somewhat misleading translation, because it misses the specific meaning of the key term, *tableau mouvant*.

The expression *tableau mouvant* was a fixed term in Diderot's day, used to denote the sort of miniature, animated picture box that had entertained French audiences ever since the seventeenth-century technical genius Father Sébastien (Jean) Truchet invented it for Louis XIV and his children. Fontenelle described two of them in his 1729 *éloge* of Truchet:

> *His tableaux mouvants* were, moreover, one of the ornaments of Marly. The first, which the king called his little opera, changed decor five times at the call of a whistle, because these *tableaux* also had the property of being resonant or sonorous. . . . The second tableau [that he presented to the king], larger and even more ingenious, represented a landscape in which everything was animated. A river flowed through it; tritons, mermaids, and dolphins swam by occasionally in a sea that bordered the horizon; people were hunting, fishing; and soldiers were climbing up to the look-out tower in a citadel built into a mountain; ships were arriving in a port, and saluted the city with their canon; and Father Sébastien was there himself, leaving a church to go and thank the King for a recently acquired grace, because the King was passing by to hunt with his entourage.¹¹⁵

The *tableau mouvant* was, in other words, a dynamic, lifelike mechanical device, one of the many machines (clocks, automatons, garden waterworks, and so on) that provided entertainment to wealthy Europeans from the sixteenth century on.¹¹⁶ Two animated paintings created by the master watchmaker Jean-Baptiste de Saint-Jean can be viewed today at the Musée des Arts et Métiers de Paris. One of these, constructed in 1759 for Mme de Pompadour and then acquired by Marie Antoinette when she was the *dauphine* of France, is particularly intricate because it includes sonorous as well as visual action: set against the backdrop of Mme de Pompadour's château and estate at Saint-Ouen, it shows in the foreground an ornamental pond bustling with the activity of washerwomen, boatmen, and fishermen, while in the background a bunch of mooing cows, bleating sheep, and a cart pass by, making sounds produced by a bellows that is hidden, along with the other gears and parts, behind the canvas.[117]

This, in other words, was what Diderot envisioned when he used the *tableau mouvant* as an epistemological metaphor to describe the lively, fast-moving operations of the mind. Interestingly, he mentioned it shortly after proposing another mechanical analogy: that of a bell clock "furnished with little hammers attached to an infinite number of threads which are carried to all corners of the clockcase," which he evoked to explain unconscious perception.[118] In that passage, Diderot conjectured that, like such a clock, the head receives several sensations at once but does not examine them unless the pull of a certain "thread" is painful or pleasurable. The *tableau mouvant* analogy adds more complexity to the comparison between the mind and a mechanical device: it represents how the mind judges and compares, a process that combines perception, memory, and judgment. The passage of the *Lettre sur les sourds et muets* pertaining to the *tableau mouvant* could thus be paraphrased as follows: "our mind is like a *toy theater* filled with fast-moving scenes and figurines; and we, as thinking subjects, try constantly to render them faithfully." Diderot called such renderings "emblems" or "hieroglyphs": that is, traces of the ideas glimpsed in the mind that are inscribed onto words or some other conventional signs like brushstrokes on a canvas.[119] Jay Fellows sums up the key idea of the *tableau mouvant* analogy in these terms: "The information of the soul, its vision, calls for a technique that seems to aspire toward the condition of film."[120]

Diderot emphasized this notion of the inner vision of the soul or mind at several points in his aesthetic writings. One was the long opening section of the *Salon de 1767*, where he reflected upon what he called "the true ideal model of beauty . . . the true line."[121] The truth to which he referred in the term "true line" was not located in the phenomenal world but, rather, in the mind of the artist: that is, in the heads of grand masters like Raphael, Poussin, and Falconet; and even they never succeed in transmitting their inner model to their students as rigorously as they conceived it. However, those great artists held that vision in their minds with extraordinary precision, and they could render it faithfully for decades afterward, in whatever medium they had mastered.

Diderot generalized this model in his unpublished fragment "Sur le Génie" (probably written around 1774), where he sought to pinpoint the qualities shared by great minds, whether they were poets, philosophers, painters, orators, or musicians. After ruling out several traits commonly cited to explain what they had in common—imagination, judgment, wit, *chaleur*, liveliness, sensibility, and taste—he settled on "a certain conformation of the head and viscera," combined with what he calls *l'esprit observateur*: "The observing mind [*l'esprit observateur*] to which I refer is exercised without effort, without exertion; it does not look, it sees; it learns, it extends itself without studying; it has no phenomenon present, but they have all affected it and what this mind retains from them is a sort of sense that others don't possess; it is a rare machine that says: 'this will work' . . . and it works; 'this will not work,' and it doesn't work; 'this is true or this is false' . . . and it turns out to be as such a person has predicted."[122] He took pains to distinguish this quality from the everyday sort of discernment, at which (as he put it) women excel: *l'esprit observateur* in the intellectual and the creative realms was more akin to prophetic intuition. By using the term "rare machine" to describe this sort of mind, Diderot repeated the language he used to speak of master artists in the *Salons* and great actors in the *Paradoxe sur le comédien*.[123]

Such was the mind of his late friend Nicolas-Antoine Boulanger, an erudite linguist, engineer, scientist, and philosophical historian. Boulanger died in 1759 at the age of thirty-seven, after contributing a handful of articles to the *Encyclopédie* and writing the manuscripts of the controversial books *Recherches sur l'origine du despotisme oriental* and *L'Antiquité dévoilée par ses usages*. He is known today as a radical *philosophe* for arguing that religion and despotism originated in natural disasters like the universal flood.[124] Diderot acknowledged elsewhere that the police took vigorous measures to smother Boulanger's *Despotisme oriental*—a work that belonged to the "new anti-Christian library" that Diderot and d'Holbach were secretly editing.[125] He did not, however, dwell on Boulanger's radicality in his posthumous tribute "Sur la Vie et les ouvrages de Boulanger," which appeared as an anonymous preface to the 1765 edition of *L'Antiquité dévoilée*. Although he alluded in this essay to the fury Boulanger would have faced if he had lived to see how "intolerant people" reacted to his ideas about religion, he was more intent on conveying a sense of the special workings of his late friend's masterful mind.

Boulanger was, as Diderot depicted him, an odd-looking but lively fellow, most at ease when conversing with his intellectual friends about philosophy, history, and erudition.[126] After inauspicious beginnings at the

Jansenist college of Beauvais, where his pedantic instructors almost ruined his naturally good intellect through their inept teaching, Boulanger turned to studying mathematics, where he acquired "a clear and just mind," and architecture, which taught him "simple, good taste" (447). He then became an engineer charged with the construction of bridges and roads in the provinces, which allowed him to examine nature while also observing the inhumanity with which royal officials treated poor peasants through practices like "la corvée" (448). Inspired by his conjectures about the earth's deep history, he threw himself into the study of dozens of ancient and modern languages (452). "If ever a man showed in his progress the true traits of genius, it was this one" (450).

Such were the underpinnings of Boulanger's inner eye, which allowed him to perceive the hundred past worlds that lay hidden in the layers of the earth—worlds that had been buried by the cataclysms of nature, which, he theorized, were the root causes that gave rise to primitive societies, governments, and religions (451). What made it possible for him to "see" in this way was his spiderlike intellect, an analogy Diderot first applied to Boulanger's capacity for absorptive introspection: "I have rarely seen a man who retreated more suddenly into himself when he was struck with some new idea . . . the change evident in his eyes was so obvious that one could have said his mind had left him to go hide in a fold of his brain" (449). He then extended the metaphor to describe Boulanger's extraordinary talent for analogical thinking: "Sometimes I compared him to that solitary insect covered with eyes who pulls out of its intestines a silk that it manages to attach to a point in the most vast apartment to another, distant point, and who, using that first thread as the basis of its marvelous and subtle work, casts an infinity of other threads, left and right, to fill up the entire space with its web. The comparison did not offend him" (450). The space in which Boulanger "spun" his threads was the gap between the ancient world and the present day, which he bridged thanks to his "powerful imagination," extensive and diverse learning, and an "uncommon subtlety" in perceiving fine links and points of analogy between distant objects (449–50). The works he composed were so rich that one would think, while paging through them, that he had lived for more than a century—when in fact, "he saw, lived, looked, reflected, meditated, wrote and lived only for a moment" (450).

In short, before he used the spider metaphor in the *Rêve de d'Alembert* and the *Salon de 1767*, Diderot deployed it in "Sur la Vie de Boulanger" to pay homage to an exceptionally fine mind, possessed by a thinker who died too young. Diderot marveled at the workings of Boulanger's mind, just as he marveled elsewhere at the workings of Leibniz's mind and at the genius who had invented the stocking-weaving loom. Multiple factors were at play in Diderot's use of such compositional metaphors to describe the human mind at its highest level of operation. One, clearly, was his philosophical materialism: insisting on the mechanical aspects of deep meditation and artistic production was his way of giving the body—the animal—its due in human existence. Another was ideological: this was also a way of taking a stand in favor of civilization and the sophisticated machines it produced. By using mechanistic analogies to describe mental processes, Diderot expressed his admiration for complexity and dynamism both in nature and in the productions of human technology. If, as Angelica Goodden has put it, Diderot was "unequivocally opposed to the machine pessimism" of his former friend Rousseau, nowhere was that more apparent than in his reflections on masterminds: they were, in his eyes, the ultimate devices of wonder, as intricate and surprising as one of Truchet's *tableaux mouvants*.[127]

Chapter 5

Melancholy, Genius, and Intellectual Identity: The Cases of Rousseau and Staël

Jean-Jacques Rousseau and Germaine de Staël were both celebrated as singular geniuses in their day, a status tinged with suffering as well as glory. Rousseau overtly sought "a fame for naturalness, a fame for inner qualities," and that fame earned him godlike status in the eyes of some fans—particularly those enthused by his best-selling sentimental novel *La Nouvelle Héloïse*.[1] Although he encouraged the intense emotional identification those readers felt with him and his works, Rousseau disliked the unwanted attention it attracted. He thus embraced solitude, the state he considered most compatible with his love for liberty and distaste for the duties associated with civil life.[2] He also refused to be seen as a man of letters in the conventional sense: he denounced the frenetic, ambition-driven lifestyle he considered typical of that type and championed reverie in pointed opposition to more deliberate modes of mental application.[3] However, despite his efforts to fashion a singular identity, Rousseau was commonly diagnosed as a melancholiac, one of the typical attributes of the intellectual according to many contemporary accounts.

Staël, for her part, was widely declared a "superior" being. "From childhood on, her family and entourage constantly asserted Mme de Staël's genius"—even though her mother, Suzanne Necker, was cold toward her, and her father, the powerful Swiss banker and French statesman Jacques Necker, "did not like what he called her scribbling."[4] Staël's public identity was merged with that of the fictional woman genius she created in *Corinne, ou l'Italie* (1807), as is attested by Vigée Le Brun's well-known portrait of Staël as Corinne; and she was considered "intellectually the greatest woman that ever lived" for almost a century.⁵ Maintaining respect as a woman of intellectual renown was nonetheless far from easy during Staël's lifetime, a dilemma she addressed in the chapter "Des Femmes qui cultivent les lettres" in *De la littérature* (1800): "As soon as a woman has been noted as a distinguished person, the public in general is biased against her."⁶ Staël lived this plight very personally: after weathering the storms of the Revolution, which forced her to retreat from Paris to her family château at Coppet, she spent many years in exile because of Napoleon's hostility toward her. Those experiences clearly shaped her worldview, which combined a steadfast belief in the perfectibility of the human race with a tragic perspective on the situation of "superior beings" in the contemporary era. As she lamented in her journal, "Genius in the midst of society is a pain, an intermittent fever that one would have to have treated like a malady, if the compensations of glory didn't ease its sorrows."⁷

Considered in tandem, Rousseau and Staël illustrate the complex interrelationship that existed between melancholy and genius during a period when both conditions were undergoing a major theoretical reappraisal, along with an upsurge in cultural prestige. Those developments were tied to a range of factors, including the rise of new forms of life writing, the popularity of nerve theory as a causative explanation for psychological suffering, the emergence of mental medicine as a distinct discipline, and changes in thinking about the "nature" of the sexes.

Melancholy and the "Vapors" from the Enlightenment to the Revolution

As Jane Darcy points out, there was a close connection between the literary biographies that flourished during the eighteenth century and the self-labeling of their authors as melancholiacs or "hypocondriacks"—the term that James Boswell, an admirer of Rousseau, applied to himself.⁸ Thanks to transformations introduced by writers like Samuel Johnson, the focus of literary biography shifted away from the achievements of illustrious subjects (the point of emphasis in Plutarchian biography, much admired and imitated in the early modern period) toward their personal suffering. Moreover, acute sensibility was widely held to be a sign of intellectual and social refinement on both sides of the English Channel. This was so well before the rise of the brooding Romantic/Byronic type, "the writer whose creative genius springs from the depths of melancholy."[9]

Whereas melancholy is understood today in psychoanalytic terms (rooted in a tradition that runs from Freud to Kristeva), Enlightenment Europe associated it with a variety of factors, physical as well as moral.[10] The best-known type of melancholic disorder in the eighteenth century was the "English malady," which Dr. George Cheyne (author of the well-known 1733 treatise by that name) described as a cluster of ailments that included poor digestion, lethargy and listlessness, "autumnal intermittent fever," vertigo, and feeling "jumbled and turbid."[11] Like melancholy in general, the English malady had ethical as well as bodily components. For the individual, it could function as "a silent protest against that society in which one is anxious to participate," but it was also identified by some social theorists (including Staël) as a "precondition and result of political freedom."[12] Even in those more morally directed formulations of melancholy, the body was not abstracted out: quite the contrary, melancholy was a vehicle for reflecting on the moral-material unity of the human being.[13]

Melancholy lost some, but certainly not all, of its age-old religious orientation during this period. As Jeremy Schmidt argues in regard to the British context, the religious understanding of melancholy as "godly sorrow" was largely displaced by a medicalized perspective that "located melancholy very concretely in the body as an organic condition of the nerves."[14] That displacement was arguably more radical in the French context, where religious melancholy was often discredited though association with superstition and fanaticism.

Across Europe, physicians treated the disorder with a mixture of moral and physical remedies, including several that involved diet and exercise. Echoing the old proverb "Le bon vin chasse la mélancolie"—"good wine chases away melancholy," cited in the definition of melancholy given in the 1762 *Dictionnaire de l'Académie française*—French doctors often prescribed wine as an antidote. Wine was "one of the great anti-melancholic remedies" in the estimation of the author of the *Encyclopédie* article "Mélancolie," who added, "In treating this illness, one can count a good deal on a change of air, the return of springtime, travel, horse-riding, frictions applied to the lower abdomen, venereal exercises (especially when their lack has brought on the malady), and even more from the enjoyment of a beloved object."[15]

Melancholy was sometimes associated with dramatic alterations in mental state and self-perception. The sufferers featured at the outset of the

Encyclopédie's medical article "imagine that they are kings, lords, gods; others believe they have been transformed into beasts, such as wolves, dogs, cats, rabbits, etc."[16] Patients who related their bouts of melancholy often mentioned physical symptoms like pain and heat due to hypersensitivity. As Micheline Louis-Courvoisier stresses in her study of the dozens of consultation letters that Samuel-Auguste Tissot received about this illness, melancholic patients sometimes located their symptoms in places that we, as modern readers, usually don't associate with the condition: for example, the skin, the blood, the stomach, the eyes, and the internal cavities of the body.[17]

To understand how the psychic and the somatic intermingled in eighteenth-century notions of melancholy, it is useful to consider its place within the larger syndrome popularly called "the vapors." In pre-Revolutionary Europe, this was an umbrella term for the cluster of jointly physical and mental ailments that doctors grouped together, with little clear demarcation, in a "mixed hystero-hypochondriasis concept."[18] Although melancholy had richer emotional and poetic resonances than hysteria and hypochondria, it was distinguished from those ailments in degree rather than in kind. Moreover, eighteenth-century doctors situated melancholy rather loosely between the humors (that is, the ancient notion of black bile) and the nerves: both explicative models were evoked, sometimes in combination. Anne-Charles Lorry, for example, identified two species of melancholy: humoral, which manifested itself through indigestion, versus nervous, a variety whose symptoms included convulsions. What he and like-minded physicians proposed to treat nervous melancholy was gentle stimulation of the nerves to restore homotony, "the judicious readjustment that brings the strings of this delicate, fragile instrument, the human organism, in tune once more."[19] As Jean Starobinski notes, some odd therapeutic procedures were suggested in the second half of the century, "at the moment of transition between the humoral interpretation and the nervous conception of melancholy": these included rotating chairs and swings that twirled patients about while also making them vomit.[20] Other methods devised to shake the mind out of a low emotional state involved immersion in cold water—either prolonged or sudden. More conventional therapies were travel, the music cure, taking the waters, and, for women, marriage.[21]

The vapors were, in the minds of many, a "polite" malady, peculiar to members of the upper crust. When the soubrette Suzanne of Pierre Augustin Caron de Beaumarchais's famous comedy *Le Mariage de Figaro*

(1784) asks to borrow the count's flask of ether to calm her mistress's vapors, and he suggests that she save some of it for herself, she replies, "You think women of my station get the vapours? It's an affliction of status; you catch it only in boudoirs."[22] Although moralists from Mme de Lambert to Louis-Sébastian Mercier ridiculed those who made a fashion of being vaporous, some doctors insisted that the vapors were a true illness—albeit one that was devilishly protean in nature.[23] Tissot's perspective on vapors sufferers was as ambivalent as his views on sickly intellectuals. He expressed irritation in his *Essai sur les maladies des gens du monde* (1770) with the "ridiculous name of vapors" and with people who were so hypersensitive that "the slightest impression becomes for them an intense sensation," making their tastes and desires as unstable as their nerves.[24] Yet he took a sympathetic approach in *Avis au peuple sur sa santé* (1761), where he described the vapors as an involuntary disorder brought about by a vice of the nerves, whose symptoms varied greatly because there were so many branches of nerves within the body.[25] The mutability or "bizarreness" of the vapors did not, he stressed, make them any less real. In his *Traité des nerfs et de leurs maladies* (1778–80), Tissot recommended either calming or stimulating remedies to treat the vapors, depending on the symptoms.[26] He added that, although rarely fatal, such nervous ailments tended to destroy the sufferer's happiness, warp his or her perception of life, and "transform" the patient, "always for the worse."[27]

Medical authors often tied the vapors to an ennui rooted either in an unwholesome lifestyle or in chagrin (violent chagrin, as Tissot maintained in the *Traité des nerfs*, could also lead to other nervous ailments, including catalepsy and epilepsy). The gender distinctions they made regarding this disorder usually targeted people of the upper class. Vaporous women were perceived as widespread in European aristocracy because of high living, a lifestyle associated with physical inaction as well as overindulgence in eating, gambling, theatergoing, and romantic dalliances. Elite men were held to contract the ailment through a somewhat broader range of passion-related causes that included ambition and overstudy. The author of the *Encyclopédie* article "Vapeurs" (1765) summed up both etiologies when assessing why the illness had become more prevalent: "This illness is more common today than it ever was, because the bad education of the fair sex disposes women to it quite a lot, and because young men indulge either in the passion for study or in some other passion just as furiously, without measure or judgment."[28]

Not everyone accepted the negative causal link between the vapors and mental or creative application. The cosmopolitan Isabelle de Charrière, for example, was diagnosed as vaporous at the age of sixteen, when she was known as Belle de Zuylen, and some in her social circle saw this as proof of her refinement and exceptional mind. As Philip Rieder has shown through his analysis of her correspondence, young Belle de Zuylen believed she had a strong constitution, thanks to the good "blood" she had inherited and her physical capacities; yet she worried about the liveliness of her imagination and her inability to master her body, and she was keenly aware of the pressures to adhere to social norms like marriage.[29] The future Mme de Charrière refused to accept the conventional medical opinion (echoed by some of her friends) that her poor health stemmed from her incessant intellectual activities. She argued just the opposite, insisting that the only way to combat her low moods was to keep her mind intensely occupied: "What people don't realize is that, susceptible as I am to dark melancholy, I have neither health nor, so to speak, life except through the means of continuous mental occupation."[30] The regular health bulletins she sent to her friends and acquaintances could be viewed as an illustration of the social advantages of suffering from "nerves": for some, the vapors were "a flexible means of self-fashioning, self-stylisation, and self-dramatisation."[31] However, they also attest to the personal battles that Zuylen/Charrière waged throughout her life: she was tormented by the effort to find an equilibrium between her intense emotional states, her active imagination, and her health.[32] Similar torments confront two of the most striking novelistic characters Charrière created: Mistriss Henley of *Lettres de Mistriss Henley publiées par son amie* (1784), who sinks into deep melancholy over the emotional distance between herself and her proper English husband; and the talented actress-musician heroine of *Caliste, ou Continuation des lettres écrites de Lausanne* (1787), who is forsaken by the man she loves but continues to receive public expressions of esteem, some addressed to Aspasie, as she lies mortally ill at the novel's end (her sobriquet alludes to Aspasia of Miletus, consort of the statesman Pericles, and a scholarly woman who exerted intellectual influence in Athenian culture).[33] Charrière gave a distinctly heroic quality to the acute sensitivity, exalted imagination, and refined intelligence of both characters.

Although the word *vapeurs* lingered on in European culture after the end of the Old Regime, it ceased to be an accepted nosological term among physicians. Historians have attributed this shift to two developments: the demolition of the aristocratic life that had provided the overarching social frame for the vapors, and the emergence of new conceptions of the nerves. Some pro-Revolutionary political writers imbued nervousness with a positive value by associating it with a combative masculine vigor, and doctors who frequented aristocratic circles reported a marked decrease in the number of fits of vapors, which they attributed to fear of the guillotine.[34] Expanding on both ideas—and drawing on reports made by Benjamin Rush that hysteria had disappeared in the American colonies during their struggle for independence—Dr. Marc-Antoine Petit of Lyon declared in 1796 that the French Revolution had "destroyed through its salutary shocks the hysterical and hypochondriacal diathesis. It has thus corrected this nervous idiosyncrasy, too mobile and too easily excited by the soft life of yore, by injecting more energy and spirit into mainsprings [*ressorts*] that were formerly too delicate and too weak."[35] Other physicians writing during the 1790s concurred that the Revolution had brought a swift and salutary end to the nervous and chronic ailments that had previously plagued the French nation. The pioneering alienist Philippe Pinel and the biomedical theorist Pierre-Jean-Georges Cabanis initially celebrated the Revolution's invigorating health effects, with Pinel declaring in a 1790 letter to the *Journal de Paris*, "People can be heard to say, 'I feel better since the Revolution.'"[36] Their confidence in the salutary jolts of the Revolution was, however, short-lived: within a decade, alienists were declaring that nervous/mental illness was afflicting more people than ever in the new French nation.

Melancholy continued to be a culturally saturated term, one that still carried some of its Old Regime connotations of upper-class ennui, or of the "sweet," tender languor associated with love or pity in sentimental literature. It was also involved in the complex gender realignment of nervous pathologies that took place during and after the Revolution (a topic to which I will return in Chapter 6, while discussing the separation of hypochondria from hysteria). Melancholy's national associations persisted, too, as Staël illustrated in her literary-historical essay *De la littérature* (1800), where—building on the pre-Revolutionary topos of "English spleen"—she attributed the melancholic imagination of English poets to that nation's penchant for meditation as well as its political liberty.[37] Staël did not, however, confine this mode of imagination to a particular national culture: rather, she saw it as a trait shared by intellectually superior persons in general—including her literary idol, Jean-Jacques Rousseau.

The Vapors, Reading, and the Making of "Jean-Jacques"

No thinker embodied the ambiguities of singularity more fully than Jean-Jacques Rousseau, who declared in "Mon portrait" that "I am not concerned with being noticed, but when I am, I don't mind if it is in a somewhat distinguished manner; and I would prefer to be forgotten by the entire human race than to be regarded as an ordinary man."[38] Rousseau always insisted that he had become a writer by accident: that is, through the feverish illumination he had while walking along the route to Vincennes in 1749, an experience that produced the *First Discourse*. He also contended that his temperament bore no resemblance to the jealous, hateful personality of the typical *homme de lettres*.[39] To cite his sharpest critique of that figure, "in all of mankind, people of wit [*gens d'esprit*] and especially men of letters are the ones who have the greatest intensity of self-love [*amour-propre*], and who are the least inclined to love and the most inclined to hate."[40] Hatred—and the wish to avoid it—clearly played a complex role in the personal myth of Rousseau, his intellectual identity, and his conception of literature.[41] So, too, did melancholy.

The diagnosis of Rousseau as a melancholiac started in 1761, when Chrétien-Guillaume de Lamoignon de Malesherbes, a French royal administrator sympathetic to Rousseau (and to the encyclopedists), wrote him a letter arguing that Rousseau's illumination had emanated from "an extreme sensitivity [*sensibilité*], a deep ingrained melancholy, and a great tendency to see things from the darkest angle."[42] It was this letter that prompted Rousseau's first autobiographical effort, the four letters he wrote to Malesherbes in 1762 (which were published in 1782, shortly after Rousseau's death in 1778). The diagnosis was reinforced by various contemporary physicians.

One was Johann-Georg Zimmermann, who referred to Rousseau while discussing the effects of excessive mental application in his treatise on experience in medicine (*Erfahrung in der Arzneikunst* [1763]; first French translation 1774). Rousseau appeared there as part of a series of biographical vignettes that also included Voltaire, whose "triangular" face was, in Zimmermann's opinion, an outward sign of the weak stomach, thin constitution, and overly mobile nerves found in many *gens de lettres*.[43] Rousseau, with his head perpetually bowed in reflection and sadness, typified what Zimmermann perceived as the great writer's constitutional tendency toward debilitating melancholy—a condition that always hovered on the edge of the pleasure savored by those who pursued a studious, contemplative existence. Rousseau's posture also illustrated the old adage that "all gens de lettres have a weak stomach"; intriguingly, on the same page, Zimmermann recounted the stomach ailments Tissot suffered in 1762. Zimmermann returned to Rousseau as a clinical case in his book on solitude, *Über die Einsamkeit* (1784–85), first translated into French by J. B. Mercier in 1788 as *La solitude considérée relativement à l'esprit et au coeur*. There, citing Rousseau's letters to Malesherbes, Zimmermann presented Rousseau as a melancholiac who was drawn to solitude because of his taste for the life of the imagination.[44] He aimed, in part, to counter the misanthropic image that had been circulated by Rousseau's detractors.

Other physicians discussed Rousseau's case at around the same time. In 1787, for instance, Pierre Fabre added a chapter to his *Essai sur les facultés de l'âme* (first ed., 1785) in which he examined the seminal moment of intellectual "effervescence" that Rousseau had experienced back in 1749.[45] Like Zimmermann, Fabre used Rousseau's letters to Malesherbes as the basis of his remarks—but for less sympathetic purposes. He described Rousseau's internal revolution as a "hypochondriacal frenzy" that made him believe "he had come into the world to reform the Universe," much like certain "fanatics," "convulsionnaires," and "magnetized" people, who thought they were divinely inspired when, in fact, they were in the grips of emotions produced by the constant irritation of their nerves by an "atrabilious humor.[46] What these case studies illustrate is that, despite Rousseau's effort in his letters to Malesherbes to disprove his friend's diagnosis of him as consumed by black bile, those letters provided armchair clinicians with a rich foundation for pathography. A similar pattern is apparent among the French alienists of the Revolutionary and Bonapartist eras who drew on Rousseau's autobiographical works to support their theories on melancholy or hypochondria.

But what did Rousseau himself have to say about the role of nervous ailments in his life? The most explicit answer, beyond the letters to Malesherbes, lies in book 6 of the *Confessions*, which describes a period when, despite his bodily sufferings, Rousseau felt more purely happy than at any other moment in his existence: the time he spent as a youth at Les Charmettes. The Charmettes episode is singularly important in relation to Rousseau's mission to explain and chronicle his emergence both as an author and as a self-described unique being: it is here that he recounts how he ended his youthful floating, describes his first experience of crippling illness, and relates the climax of his intense, ambiguous relationship with Mme de Warens. Book 6 also contains some of Rousseau's most lyrical reflections on the melancholic pleasure he derived both from reading—a prominent theme in the episode—and from the act of writing about his past moments of bliss.

The tale recounted in book 6 is a continuation of an illness narrative begun in book 5, concerning the years 1735–36: young Rousseau abruptly falls into a state of fragile health after a failed scientific experiment involving sympathetic ink, and he begins to suffer from chronic ringing in the ears, palpitations, arterial throbbing, and shortness of breath. He had been reading ardently prior to this attack, consuming "obscure" books on music by Rameau and reading the imaginary misfortunes of Prévost's hero Cleveland "with fury."[47] Forced into sedentariness by his poor health, he succumbs to melancholy, a term he uses interchangeably with "vapors" to describe his languor and sadness over what he takes to be his impending death (LC, 221). This crisis is, however, temporarily cured by increased intimacy with his beloved "Maman" (Mme de Warens), who undertakes to restore Jean-Jacques to full vigor by prescribing a milk regimen and taking him away to the country estate of Les Charmettes (223).

Once settled in this bucolic retreat, he finds himself drawn "irresistibly" to book learning, a compulsion triggered by his weakened physical state and growing acquaintance with Maman's Cartesian-minded physician M. Salomon, who encourages him to follow the orderly method of study recommended in Bernard Lamy's popular *Entretiens sur les sciences* (232). Although the young Jean-Jacques follows that advice, he is hardly methodical about it: he promptly "devours" Lamy's book and many others, alternating his time between readings of philosophy, geometry, Latin, and books that mix "devoutness with the sciences," and *fonctions champêtres* like turning the garden and taming pigeons (234). At several points in his narrative, Rousseau notes that he was ill-suited for the kind of prolonged mental application he pursued at Les Charmettes. However, he attaches a great, enduring personal value to this studious idyll: "Two or three months went by in this way testing the inclination of my mind and enjoying, in the most beautiful season of the year and in a place that it rendered enchanting, the charms of life whose value I felt so well, that of a society as free as it was sweet (if one can give the name of society to such a perfect union), and that of the fine knowledge that I proposed to acquire for myself; . . . the pleasure of learning contributed a great deal to my happiness" (LC, 235–36; TC, 197). Far from repudiating the pursuit of knowledge as unhealthful or denaturing (as he did so famously elsewhere), Rousseau describes his youthful attempts to cultivate his mind as "enjoyments, but too simple to be capable of being explained" (LC, 236; TC, 198). Study, as much as the bucolic setting and the presence of Mme de Warens, is integral to the happiness he enjoys at Les Charmettes; yet that happiness also involves illness.

Rousseau's conviction that he is gravely ill ensures the uniform quality of his daily existence, and it drives him to learn as much as possible with as much speed and diligence as he can muster: "I felt myself being carried away toward study with an irresistible force in spite of my condition, or rather because of my condition, and all the while looking at each day as the last one of my life, I studied with as much ardor as if I must live forever. . . . That application for which I was impassioned became so delightful to me that, no longer thinking of my illnesses, I was much less affected by them" (LC, 232; TC, 195). What is extraordinary about this passage is that the very same Rousseau who elsewhere heaped condemnation on book learning embraces here a conception of study that is more typically associated with *philosophes* like Voltaire and Diderot, who glorified intellectual endeavor as both exhausting work and as a "delightful" passion known only to true initiates. One could, of course, interpret the passage as a sort of morality tale about the dangerously absorbing charms of study, comparable to this declaration: "The charm of study soon renders any other attachment insipid . . . the cultivation of the sciences withdraws the heart of the philosopher from the crowd."[48] However, in the Charmettes episode, young Jean-Jacques's affection for Maman and devotion to his household duties do not wane as a result of his ardor for learning. Moreover, the mature Rousseau speaks affectionately of his adolescent efforts to combine reading, agricultural labor, veneration for the wonders of God and nature, and devotion to Mme de Warens in a single, harmonious system (LC, 235).

There is no mention of melancholy in this part of the story—although Jean-Jacques is filled with the "terror of Hell" by the harsh Jansenist theology preached in the writings of Port Royal and the Oratory, "the ones I read most frequently" (LC, 242; TC, 203). Those sad impressions are counterbalanced by the gentle morality of his Jesuit confessor, along with Maman's efforts to soothe his soul. Rather than melancholy, Jean-Jacques is dominated by an ardor for learning so intense that it reaches the point of "mania": he tries to read even while working the fields, thereby ruining a good number of his books; and he goes about in a stupor, "incessantly and totally occupied as I was with muttering something between my teeth" (LC, 242; TC, 202–3). Recounting the experience, Rousseau draws increasingly on medical vocabulary to describe the condition he was in: "I was as pallid as a dead man and thin as a skeleton. My beating of the arteries was terrible, my palpitations more frequent. I was continually oppressed, and my weakness finally became so great that I had trouble moving; I could not walk quickly without suffocating. I could not bend over without becoming dizzy, I could not lift up the lightest load; I was reduced to the most tormenting inaction for a man as restless as I am" (LC, 247; TC, 207). And then, very interestingly, he adds, "It is certain that the vapors were very much mixed up with all of this"—by which he means that he was suffering "the malady of happy people." Given that the other symptoms Rousseau describes here are unequivocally physical, this mention of the vapors comes as a surprise. He explains it by describing the vapors as "a boredom of well-being" (*ennui de bien être*) that makes the sufferer cry without reason, take fright at the sound of a leaf or a bird, and exhibit other symptoms of an "extravagant" sensibility of a sort felt only by those who are fully happy.

Happiness, of course, is an ephemeral state in Rousseau's philosophy, which is the register in which he concludes his remark on the vapors: "We are so little made to be happy here below that either the soul or the body must necessarily suffer when both of them are not suffering, and the good condition of one almost always injures the other" (LC, 247; TC, 207). What this reflection suggests is that, far from impeding his happiness, Rousseau's physical frailty during the Charmettes episode was the condition of possibility for his being fully happy: it allowed him to realize, albeit briefly, the dream of perfect happiness with Maman, which he had glimpsed seven or eight years earlier (LC, 245). The vapors, in other words, are a vehicle for poetic melancholy: Rousseau's youthful case of vapors prepared him to feel later, as he was writing the *Confessions*, an extraordinary "vigor and life in myself for suffering" (TC, 207).

Returning to his story, Rousseau relates what "finished him off" and made him truly sick: the books on physiology and anatomy that he added to his readings. In a passage that would go on to attract significant attention from turn-of-the century medical diagnosticians interested in hypochondria, he describes this as a "fatal study" (LC, 248; TC, 207) because those books persuade him that he has a heart polyp. Some critics have argued that Rousseau invented the heart polyp as a pretext to leave Les Charmettes to seek a cure in Montpellier, thereby extricating himself from a suffocating attachment to Maman.[49] However, the strange mixture of happiness and ennui that Rousseau associates with the vapors is tied to more than his amorous adventures: it also involves his youthful obsessive attachment to books and reading.

Pathography: Rousseau as Medical Prototype

Biographical vignettes of suffering scholars were common not just in books on the health of *gens de lettres*, but also in the works of the early French alienists. Rousseau was one of the case histories most often discussed by these physicians. This was due, in part, to his theories on education and the passions: as Jan Goldstein puts it, Rousseau reigned like a "crowning deity over the birth of French psychiatry" because of the "implicit and diffuse Rousseauism" of the theorists who founded alienism in France.[50] She particularly notes the parallels between Pinel's famous moral treatment and the principles of Rousseauean schooling, and the connection between Pinel's grand theory of insanity and Rousseau's idea that socially created *passions factices* have pathogenic tendencies. There was, however, another reason for the regular mentions these authors made of Rousseau: they viewed him, like the other famous thinkers on whose lives they drew, as a prototype of the diseases they were trying to define and classify. Claude Wacjman underscores that turn-of-the-century French physicians considered "mediate literary observations" to be more useful than immediate clinical observations for establishing nosological classifications of mental illness.[51] In other words, methodology was a factor in these doctors' interest in Rousseau's "autobiographical display of psychological suffering": they found it useful for their larger nosological enterprise.[52]

The alienists' methodological preoccupations were connected to the larger effort to reform the medical profession by bringing it more in line with *Idéologie*, the "science of ideas" that dominated Revolutionary-era philosophy and pedagogical theory.[53] To achieve the goals of linguistic precision and sound therapeutic practice, doctors specializing in mental pathologies undertook to establish clear-cut distinctions among the species they observed among their patients: mania, melancholy, hypochondria, hysteria, dementia, and idiotism. They drew their information from three sources: the extensive bank of clinical observations they were amassing at newly formed asylums like Bicêtre and Salpêtrière; patient histories gleaned from earlier works on nervous maladies; and famous literary or historical cases of mental alienation.

Rousseau's status as a leading psychiatric prototype may have been enhanced by the fact that he was singled out in *Nouveaux éléments de physiologie* (1801), an influential physiological textbook in which Anthelme-Balthasar Richerand described Rousseau as a "perfect" example of the melancholic temperament. Rousseau also proved, in Richerand's mind, the reciprocal influence of the mental on the physical and the physical on the mental: the mysteries of that interdependence could be solved if physicians paid closer attention to the ancient and modern biographies of illustrious men.[54]

The image or persona of Rousseau available to turn-of-the-century French readers had diverse, sometimes conflicting facets: it included the "friend of humanity" face, which he put forth in his political writings; the moral portraits of him written by Staël and other near contemporaries; the highly patriotic eulogies of Rousseau written for the 1791 Académie Française competition; and the post-Thermidor construction of Rousseau as a "sentimental champion of the disinherited and reformer of female morals."[55] Physicians of this period also viewed Rousseau through the lens of pre-Revolutionary doctors who did not wholeheartedly endorse his extreme ideas on the ills of civilization and the pursuit of learning.

Pinel's views on the health effects of intellectual work resembled those of his medical predecessors Tissot and Zimmermann. As he declared in the *Nosographie philosophique* (1797), "The cultivation of the sciences and arts, when undertaken without moderation, combined with deep meditations and prolonged late nights, is undoubtedly very conducive to developing the same nervous ailments [hypochondria and melancholy]. Indeed, if study is conducted without method, and exercises the judgement less than the imagination and the memory, these ailments can degenerate into mania."[56] He repeated that idea in his *Traité sur la manie*, where he cited the registers of the Bicêtre asylum as proof that literary writers, musicians, and painters were most at risk for mental illness because they exercised their imagination more intensely than those who worked in fields like mathematics or science.[57] In other words, imagination—rather than mental application per se—was to blame for the pathologies that most concerned him. Regarding Rousseau himself, Pinel cited his manifestations of melancholy in the last two parts of Rousseau's *Confessions* and in the *Rêveries*, which illustrated his conviction that "all men are his enemies," his tormenting "mistrust," and his continuous fears.[58]

Along with Rousseau's autobiographical writings, early French alienists cited Staël's *Lettres sur les ouvrages et le caractère de Jean-Jacques Rousseau*, an intellectual biography first published in 1788 and more widely diffused in a second edition that appeared in 1798. Written in the Enlightenment tradition of the laudatory "great-man" eulogy, this work began on a highly sentimental note.[59] It took on a more clinical tone in the sixth and final letter, "Sur le caractère de Rousseau," which opened with a physiognomic analysis close to that presented by Zimmermann: "He almost always had his head lowered, but it was not flattery or fear which had bowed it; meditation and melancholy had made it lean over like a flower bent by its own weight or by storms."[60] Staël also attached significance to Rousseau's pronounced eyebrows, which "seemed made to serve his unsociability [*sauvagerie*], to protect him from the sight of other men" (83). Staël then turned to the subject of his real or rumored moral transgressions, the most notorious being the reputed abandonment of his five children. That behavior, she argued, should be understood in the context of his exalted, "delirious" genius: "Rousseau was not mad, but one of his faculties, the imagination, was in a state of dementia; he had a great power of reason over abstract matters, over objects that have no reality except in thought, and an absolute extravagance regarding all objects whose measure is taken outside of ourselves; he had too great a dose of everything: by dint of being superior, he was close to being mad" (85).

Staël clearly sympathized with the moral pain that Rousseau endured as a result of his deep feeling but unsocial temperament. However, by dwelling at length on his "demented" imagination, she helped to transform the question of his genius into a properly medical issue. Although she described melancholy as the sentiment naturally felt by anyone who "considers at length the destiny of man," she depicted Rousseau's case as pathological in its intensity, its self-destructiveness, and the generalized mistrust it triggered in him: "Rousseau increased through reflection all of the ideas that afflicted him; soon a look, a gesture from a man he met, a child who ran away from him, seemed to him to be new proof of the universal hatred of which he thought himself the object . . . he believed himself destined to suffer, and did not act against his destiny" (94). Although she briefly entertained the fantasy that she might have saved Rousseau, had she been there to console him and steer his thoughts back to happier, more hopeful subjects (95), Staël regarded his melancholy as incurable: "Rousseau's despair was caused by that somber melancholy, that discouragement over living, that can seize all isolated men, whatever their destiny. His soul was withered by injustice; he was afraid of being alone, of not having a heart near to his own, of returning incessantly to himself, of neither inspiring nor feeling any interest, of being indifferent to his glory, tired of his genius, tormented by the need to love, and the unhappiness of not being loved" (96). This, she suggested, played a role in his death: "Rousseau may have allowed himself to commit suicide without remorse, he felt so insignificant in the immensity of the universe."[61] She ended letter 6 by shifting out of the clinical register and assuming a tone of lament more conventional in a eulogy: here, she exhorted all sensitive souls to cry with her over Rousseau's tomb and make a common cause of defending genius against the insidious forces of envy and mediocrity (97–98).

One of the earliest alienists to draw on Staël's portrait of Rousseau as a melancholiac was Jean-Baptiste Louyer-Villermay, an early affiliate of the Pinel circle, who cited the 1798 edition of Staël's *Lettres sur Rousseau* in his *Recherches historiques et médicales sur l'hypocondrie, isolée, par l'observation et l'analyse, de l'hystérie et de la mélancolie* (1802).[62] Villermay explicitly referred to Staël's theory that Rousseau's melancholy led to suicide, and he also alluded to Staël when he spoke of writers who had judged Rousseau with "fitting severity."

Villermay used a lengthy sketch of Rousseau's life to establish a clear distinction between hypochondria and melancholy: as he argued, "Jean-Jacques" was suffering from a pronounced case of moral melancholy with none of the digestive or nervous symptoms typical of hypochondria.[63] Rousseau's entire existence was, Villermay maintained, shaped by melancholy: the sad circumstances of his birth, when he lost his mother; the extraordinary development of his mental faculties as a young man, combined with the emergence of his touchy character, somber imagination, and "philosophical" vanity; the series of vexations experienced by Rousseau after he became famous, which aggravated his prideful, antisocial disdain for his fellow *philosophes*; his excessive reaction to the putative stoning at Motiers; his haughty behavior in London—a place where, Villermay pointed out, the splenetic Rousseau should have fit right in; the pathological terrors and suspicions that he exhibited in his later years; and, finally, the suicidal projects that may have caused Rousseau's death.[64] Moving away from the details of Rousseau's case, Villermay then addressed another consequence of the moral tendency toward melancholy: namely, the hateful passions and taste for tyranny evident in men like Nero, Louis XI, Cromwell, and the "bloodthirsty scoundrel" Robespierre.[65] Given that Villermay had himself suffered greatly during the Terror, there is nothing surprising about his denunciation of the radical Revolutionary Robespierre;[66] however, its juxtaposition with the Rousseau case is intriguing. Villermay ended by aligning Rousseau with melancholic but virtuous thinkers such as Socrates, Plato, Pascal, Tasso, and two eighteenth-century medical luminaries, Zimmermann and Bordeu.

Echoing many of Villermay's arguments, C. A. T. Charpentier devoted his 1803 thesis *Essai sur la mélancolie* to presenting the various causes that could trigger melancholy: climate, age, bad diet, suppressed evacuations, overstudy, idleness, celibacy, heredity, violent chagrin, religious or political terrors, unrequited love, superstition, and stormy social passions such as hate or ambition. In his case histories, Charpentier showed a clear preference for the special, "Aristotelian" class of melancholiacs who were predisposed to contract the disease because they possessed an "excessive and profound" sensibility and ardent imagination. It was, he added, these people who "feel the most intense moral affections, the most violent emotions, men of genius, whose vast conceptions are the fruit of the deepest meditations, men of letters, whose unrelenting work ends up producing mental exhaustion, those who cultivate the fine arts with enthusiasm, and whose overly exalted imagination is not counter-balanced by an adequate exercise of the other functions of the understanding."[67] Insisting that melancholy of this sort was specific to men, Charpentier cited a number of famous male thinkers who had fallen victim to the obsessive delirium characteristic of melancholy. His list included Huyghens, Pascal, Tasso, Zimmermann, the *anti-philosophe* poet Gilbert, and Jean-Jacques Rousseau.[68]

One could, of course, dismiss medical biographies of this sort as taking excessive liberties with Rousseau's autobiographical writings.[69] That argument was, in fact, made at the time by E. Frédéric Dubois d'Amiens, who, in his *Histoire philosophique de l'hypochondrie et de l'hystérie* (1833), refuted Villermay's diagnosis of Rousseau as a lifelong melancholiac.[70] Dubois also took a swipe at Jean-Guillaume Fourcade-Prunet, author of the 1826 treatise *Maladies nerveuses des auteurs*, for arguing that Rousseau was suffering from an "irritability of the brain" that, gradually and inevitably, increased to the point of darkest melancholy.[71] Dubois's own hypothesis was that there were two very distinct periods in Rousseau's life, "one in which he showed all the symptoms of hypochondria, and the other during which he sunk into the deepest melancholy."[72] To prove this, he gave a long transcription of book 6 of the *Confessions*, about which he observed that "no one else could trace in a truer, more vigorous, and more picturesque manner the symptoms of the first stage of hypochondria."[73] Dubois's conclusion was that Rousseau's reading of medical books while he was a young man living at Les Charmettes had made him hypochondriacal—but not melancholic, a condition that did not afflict him until much later in his life.[74]

Dubois's refutations illustrate a broader tendency among the alienists who referred to Rousseau's biography from a clinical perspective: generally speaking, they subjected their colleagues' anecdotes about Rousseau to more rigorous standards than those that circulated about more temporally distant celebrities like Pascal or Tasso. Moreover, they often used direct citation of Rousseau himself as a measure against which to judge each other's rewritings of his life story.[75] They also departed from the ideological Rousseauism of placing the blame for mental disorder at the door of society. Rather than attributing Rousseau's melancholy to his social circumstances, most diagnosed it as a temperamental condition exacerbated by excessive irritation of the nerves or the brain.

Rousseau thus embodied a disorder that, in these physicians' eyes, loomed over the health and happiness of intellectuals in general—not least the alienists themselves, many of whom included self-observations or the case histories of other physicians in their remarks on the illnesses to which thinkers were most prone. Villermay, for example, alluded to his own experience with nervous maladies in the preface to his 1816 treatise on the subject.[76] A particularly poignant biographical vignette appears on the title page of the edition of Maurice Roubaud-Luce's work available at Harvard University's Countway Medical Library: it features the sad handwritten comment "the author of this work hanged himself in Tours on August 4 1817," along with a quote said to come from Roubaud-Luce's suicide note: "Spleen is more or less the disease that has forced me to end my existence."[77] It may be, therefore, that the founders of mental medicine in France enlisted Rousseau as a model because they identified with him personally.

Sexual Dimorphism and the Dilemma of Learned Women: Staël's *Corinne*

Whatever their personal motives for citing certain literary writers, the early French alienists contributed to the practice of pathography that became widespread in nineteenth-century Europe, taking such forms as phrenology, "cerebral biographies," and the school of "physiological" literary criticism.[78] Pinel summed up the logic behind those endeavors when he asked rhetorically "Can the physician remain a stranger to the history of the most intense human passions, since these are the most frequent causes of mental alienation? And from that point on, shouldn't he study the lives of people who have been the most famous through their ambition for glory, their enthusiasm for the fine arts, the austerities of monastic life, the delirium of an unhappy love?"[79] Three out of four of those conditions (excluding monastic life) were integral to the existence of Germaine de Staël and her fictional woman genius Corinne—both of whom embodied the dilemma particular to women intellectuals in their era.

That was not an entirely new situation. During the Old Regime, learned women enjoyed greater social prominence than in centuries past, but they were still vulnerable to the biting ridicule made popular years earlier by Molière's satires of pretentiously intellectual *précieuses*. Despite efforts made by women moralists as well as certain male authors to refute the notion that learning could be nothing more than a vainglorious fad among women, that idea sometimes tainted the public image of learned women: for example, Émilie Du Châtelet, who was attacked after her death for having appeared too "singular" in both her scholarly aspirations and her love life.[80] The double bind that confronted learned women is evident in Voltaire's memorial tribute to Du Châtelet, where he underscored that "never was a woman more scholarly than she, and never did anyone deserve less that one say of her: 'she's a *femme savante*' . . . amidst a mass of projects that the most laborious scholar would scarcely have undertaken, who would have believed that she found time not just to fulfill all the duties of society but avidly seek out all of its amusements? She devoted herself to high society as she did to study."[81] In other words, a woman like Du Châtelet might be just as adept as a man at cultivating knowledge, but she had to counterbalance her scholarly achievements with dutiful attention to social obligations—obligations that were particularly extensive for Du Châtelet, given her status as an upper-class, wealthy woman (of course, that status also allowed her to pursue intellectual distinction with greater ease than those of more modest social standing).

This double bind became more acute in the wake of a theoretical development in a normative area of biomedical theory: namely, the effort to define the essential "nature" of the male versus female sex. Starting in the 1770s, vitalist physicians like Pierre Roussel began to argue that the female constitution was "soft," hypersensitive, and womb-centered. Praising Rousseau for drawing attention to the radical specificity of women's "nature" in book V of his famous pedagogical fiction *Émile* (1762), Roussel undertook in his *Système physique et moral de la femme* (1775) and the *Système physique et moral de l'homme* (unpublished before his death) to justify that idea in terms of physiology and anatomy.[82] He also sought to give greater precision to the contemporary theory of sensibility: he differentiated this property along gender lines by assigning a physiologically and morally heightened sensibility to women and a "higher," mentally concentrated sensibility to men, whose stronger physical constitution also made them less susceptible to nervous disorders. Women, as Roussel portrayed them, had a keen but volatile sensitive constitution, one that was highly conducive to empathy, maternal tenderness, and social sagacity, but incompatible with the "dangerous labors" involved in study.[83] Echoing Tissot's warnings, he argued that the acquisition of knowledge almost always came at the price of one's health, a truth familiar to men of letters, who tended to contract "vapors or hypochondriacism" if they engaged too much in deep meditation.[84] Any woman reckless enough to imitate such men would not only lose her natural beauty and graces, but also make herself sick. Roussel insisted that although women's sparkling, uncultivated natural intelligence was perfectly designed for the sort of refined social intercourse characteristic of the salon, it was altogether unsuited for the "sweeping views of politics," "great principles of ethics," and "scientific erudition" that occupied certain male minds.[85]

Roussel's ideas were taken up by other prominent medical thinkers such as Cabanis, who developed them in a memoir on the influence of sex on the character of ideas, which he included in his *Rapports du physique et du moral de l'homme* (1802)—where he branded women with serious intellectual aspirations "ambiguous beings [*des êtres incertains*] who are, properly speaking, of neither sex."[86] Because of the sexual dimorphism these theorists promoted, the intimations of monstrosity that had long been implicit to the literary tradition of *femme-savante* parodies burst into the open during the Revolution and the Bonapartist era, the period that ushered in a new medical doctrine of incommensurability between men and women, along with widespread attempts to exclude women from politics, education, and most other areas of the public sphere.[87] Biomedical justifications for the view of the mind as embodied, and of female intellect as "naturally" inferior to male, did not, of course, reshape the entire conceptual field surrounding women's role in cultural and intellectual production.[88] Champions of a woman's right to education and authorship continued to be vocal at the turn of the eighteenth century to the nineteenth, as the writings of Staël, Condorcet, and Mary Wollstonecraft (among others) make abundantly clear. However, one side effect of the French Revolution was a pervasive sense that society needed stabilization, and politically minded medical theorists like Cabanis were eager to provide that by evoking the notion of "indelible" femininity as a reason to relegate women to a highly restricted cultural role.[89]

A related factor was the new definition of genius that emerged in the final decades of the eighteenth century, when, as Christine Battersby has argued, the ancient Latin concept of genius (male procreativity, or the begetting spirit embodied in the males of a clan) merged with that of ingenium (innate or God-given mental capacity, wit, artistic talent) to form a single model in which creative energy and vigor of mind were seen as deriving from male strength—indeed, quite literally from male sperm.[90] Revolutionary-era biomedical researchers like Xavier Bichat also proposed a theory of limited vital energy, according to which an individual with highly developed intellectual faculties was necessarily underdeveloped in other areas.[91] Applying this theory, the medical vulgarizer Julien-Joseph Virey declared that women were destined by nature never to enjoy what he called "the ardent transports of genius."[92] The limited vital energy theory also had implications for intellectuals in general: Virey argued that there was an essential antagonism between the "cerebral" and "genital" poles in men (a topic to which I will return in the next chapter).[93]

Given Staël's literary fame and very public persona, we might expect her to have mounted a vigorous challenge to the Bonapartist era's narrow definition of women's social role and mental abilities. However, Staël's writings are full of contradictions: she fashioned herself as both a daughter of the Enlightenment and a social exile who identified deeply with Rousseau; and she championed the cause of the "exceptional" woman even while accepting the constraints that Rousseau and others perceived in women's capacities for study and creative achievement.[94] As a public figure, Staël was branded a virago by Napoleon, among others;[95] yet as a literary/social theorist, she did not make gender the major issue in her effort to uphold the principles of genius, refined sensibility, and individual self-improvement.[96] Her most famous fictional work, the novel *Corinne, ou l'Italie* (1807), is likewise rife with ambiguity: written against the backdrop of the French Enlightenment cult of the great creative genius, *Corinne* is designed to celebrate a great *woman* genius, but it spends as much time evoking Corinne's beauty, femininity, and amorous longings as it does describing what makes her so exceptional as a thinker and artist.

One way to understand those ambiguities is to consider the psychological condition that Staël attributed not just to Rousseau, but also to her fictional heroine: melancholy. Corinne does not start out as a melancholiac; that role initially falls to her admirer Lord Oswald Nelvil, who suffers from both a splenetic constitution and psychological anguish (he is racked with guilt over having not lived up to his late father's expectations). Nor does she contract melancholy from excessive mental work: although she periodically whips herself into a state of enthusiasm while doing a poetic improvisation, we do not see her absorbed in study or isolating herself from society in pursuit of learning. The novel doesn't, in fact, give us much information about Corinne's intellectual training. In "Corinne's Story" ("Histoire de Corinne"), the four-chapter epistle she writes to Oswald to explain the mysteries of her half-Italian, half-English heritage, Corinne passes quickly over the instruction she received as a youth, declaring simply that when she arrived in England to rejoin her father at the age of fifteen, "my talents, my tastes, my very character were already formed."[97] Initially, at least, Corinne's temperament is as sunny as the climate of Italy: she is "a miracle of nature" (166), an astonishing person who possesses "diverse charms that would seem mutually exclusive: sensibility, gaiety, depth, grace, abandonment, modesty" (93). Staël thus takes pains to avoid making Corinne constitutionally melancholic, just as she avoids giving her heroine even the slightest air of pedantry.

Corinne is unfailingly ladylike: amid the joyous fanfare that accompanies her opening appearance as "the most famous woman of Italy . . . poet, writer, *improvisatrice*, and one of the most beautiful people of Rome," she performs her every gesture—even that of receiving a crown on the steps of the Capitol—with such touching "nobility, modesty, sweetness and dignity" that her main observer, Oswald, is moved to tears (49, 54). This tableau of Corinne at her greatest moment of public triumph ends, moreover, with a highly conventional exchange of glances: Oswald looks in her eyes and sees a gaze that implores "the protection of a [male] friend, protection that no woman, however superior she may be, can do without; and he thought to himself that it would be sweet to be the defender of one who would need a defender solely because of her sensibility" (54). The narrator's delineation of sex roles in this passage—the male as strong, valiant protector; the woman as meek, sensitive, and in need of protection—is identical to that of separate-sphere advocates like Rousseau or Roussel; and Staël goes to great lengths to depict Corinne as a woman who could be a wonderful domestic companion to the sensitive, somber Oswald (212). Corinne is a hybrid, but she does not defy the gender stereotypes of the day: rather, she fuses typically feminine qualities with what her creator saw as the mythic, superhuman qualities of genius.

Nor, contrary to what some critics have contended, is Lord Nelvil a gender hybrid, if we keep in mind the historical context from which he arises.[98] Far from feminizing him, Oswald's melancholy and tendency to cry easily place him squarely in the tradition of the noble-hearted male as defined in the sentimental tradition. It is, precisely, Oswald's sensitive, suffering qualities (in addition to his handsome figure and heroic feats) that make him deeply appealing to Corinne: "There existed between Oswald and Corinne a singular and all-powerful sympathy: their tastes were not the same, their opinions rarely agreed, and yet, deep down in their soul, there were similar mysteries, emotions drawn from the same source, in short a sort of secret resemblance that supposed a same nature" (398–99). In other words, Staël simultaneously adheres to gender conventions in constructing the novel's lovers, and designs them to be "sister souls," morally superior beings whose heightened capacity for feeling and reflection draws them together even as it sets them apart—fatally, for Corinne—from contemporary society.

Although his melancholy originates in his natural temperament as an Englishman and is exacerbated by his remorse over memories of his dead father, Oswald also suffers from the "contrast between his soul and society, such as it is in general" (308). This, the narrator underscores, is the sign of a noble spirit: "Pain in our modern times, in the midst of our social state, so cold and oppressive, is the most noble thing there is in man; and, in our day, a person who has not suffered, has never felt or thought" (216). This "cold and oppressive" social state is represented by the rigidly proper English country life from which Corinne fled during her adolescence. However, we should not overlook the narrator's insistence on "modern times," nor on the era to which modernity is contrasted in the next sentence: antiquity, an age when "there was something nobler than pain: it was heroic calm, it was the sense of one's strength that could develop in the midst of free and open institutions" (216–17). A distinctly antique quality attaches to Corinne, evident in the admiration she expresses for ancient Roman statues and monuments throughout the long walking tours she and Oswald take in books 4 to 9, in the Sapphic undertones of her role as *improvisatrice*, and above all in the lengths to which she goes to develop her intellectual strengths in the relative freedom of Italy. This aspect of her persona is confirmed by Oswald's late father in the letter he writes to Corinne's father to explain why he has rejected her as a match for his son: "Your daughter is charming; but I seem to see in her one of those beautiful Greeks who enchanted and subjugated the world" (466). Corinne is, in short, larger than life, not of this world; and the all-consuming passion that kills her and her genius once Oswald abandons her for her younger half-sister Lucile has an explicitly mythic, Phaedra-like quality.

Clearly, the aspect of Corinne that Staël wants most ardently to defend and illustrate is her status as a "superior" being—one who, like Rousseau, should be admired for her immense creative powers, heeded like an oracle, and handled with the precautions befitting a profoundly sensitive heart. However, as Corinne underscores in her long epistolary self-portrait, that world is full of mediocre people who, slavishly devoted to what they call duty, are incapable of appreciating an intellectually distinguished person's enthusiasm, delicate moral sensibility, and need for respect and expansive expression—whether the person in question is a man or a woman (366). The novel flirts with the idea that Corinne's brilliance makes her not only inimitable but also above convention: as the admiring Oswald exclaims, "Who could resemble you? And can one make laws for a unique person?" (86). If we disregarded the ominous elements that shade the lovers' brief, intense scenes of bliss, we might think that Oswald and Corinne could marry happily if only the austere mores of his English homeland were softened to accommodate the gifts that Corinne possesses on top of her mainstream feminine charms. Indeed, Corinne raises the possibility that she would have found a more hospitable climate in the company of the superior beings drawn to more cosmopolitan places like London or Edinburgh (369). However, because the enemy camp of unfeeling or mediocre characters not only outnumbers but resents deep-feeling, deep-thinking souls, neither Corinne nor Oswald can find enduring happiness.

Corinne is too much of an anomaly to exist outside of the tolerant, art-loving, but—as the novel underscores—politically impotent, emasculating climate of contemporary Italy (156–65). Lady Edgermond, Corinne's hostile, rigidly English stepmother, is assigned the task of passing the most damning judgments on Corinne and her genius. In a heated debate with Oswald over Corinne's respectability, Lady Edgermond declares: "I set no store by talents that divert a woman from her true duties" and insists that, because Corinne has forsaken her family name for a public life, she is as good as dead in the eyes of proper society (458). She warns Oswald that Corinne will have a corrupting, denaturing influence on his character if he proceeds with his plan to marry her (461). Clearly, however, Corinne is not an agent but a victim of moral contagion: she becomes despondent as soon as Oswald reads her self-portrait, and she swiftly falls ill to the unspecified contagious malady that happens to be raging through Rome (401–6).

Although Corinne recovers from that illness, it nonetheless hastens her definitive decline into melancholy. Moved by Oswald's passionate devotion to her while she is ill (406), Corinne turns to loving him with "idolatry" and resolves to follow him without knowing what fate awaits her. As the narrator observes, "When passion takes over a superior mind, it entirely separates reason from action"—a way of foreshadowing the reckless acts Corinne is about to commit out of passion for Oswald. She creates a veritable cult for him: "I regard you as an angelic being, as the purest and noblest character who has appeared on the earth . . . all this genius, which in the past inflamed my thought, is now nothing more than love. Enthusiasm, reflection, intelligence, I no longer have anything except what I share with you" (440, 443). And she follows him, secretly, when he returns to Scotland, eventually learning that he has become attached to her half-sister Lucile but hesitates to marry her because he still loves Corinne. After a series of torturous scenes in which she spies, ghostlike, on Oswald and Lucile, Corinne resigns herself to what appears to be her fate: she writes a letter freeing Oswald of his promise to her, then returns to Italy in a state of unrelenting fever and utter dejection (510).

Corinne's melancholy carries unmistakable traits of the amorous and religious brands of melancholy. Yet it also has an intellectual dimension that brings to mind the "Aristotelian" class of melancholiacs featured in certain medical works of the period: "Lord Nelvil was wrong to believe . . . that the brilliant faculties of Corinne could give her means of happiness independent of her affections. When a person of genius is endowed with a true sensibility, her chagrins are multiplied by her very faculties: she makes discoveries in her own pain, as in the rest of nature, and the unhappiness of the heart being inexhaustible, the more one has ideas, the more one feels it" (419). Corinne's melancholy is thus another of her hybrid qualities, a malady rooted in futile love but driven to pathological extremes by her exquisite sensibility and highly developed mind: "If anyone can guess how a person reaches madness, it is surely when a single thought seizes hold of the mind and no longer allows the succession of objects to vary its ideas. Corinne was, moreover, a person with such a lively imagination that it would consume itself when her faculties no longer had any outside source" (470). When Oswald abandons her to marry Lucile, she blames the loss of her talents not on him but on her amorous passion—the force that makes her imagination turn solely around her idealizing cult for her lost lover (565). Corinne finally wastes away from moral anguish, but not before reproducing herself (after a fashion) by transforming Oswald's daughter Juliette into a Corinne-like artistic talent and instructing his wife, Lucile, on how to live harmoniously with him (575, 578).[99] She also manages to stage a somber public recital in which a young woman dressed in white sings Corinne's swan song: "my genius, if it still subsists, can be felt only through the force of my pain . . . of all the faculties of the soul I received from nature, that of suffering is the only one that I fully exercised" (583–84).

In the end, Staël's fictional woman genius is, indeed, an ambiguous being—but not in the terms that Cabanis had in mind when he applied the term to women intellectuals. She joins Rousseau by developing, via melancholy, an extraordinary "vigor and life in myself for suffering" (LC, 207).[100] Corinne exemplifies the fate of a sensitive, intellectually superior person living in an inhospitable world; and what she, like "Jean-Jacques," embraces as her mantle is the prerogative of self-definition—a prerogative that clearly existed in tension with contemporary definitions of the intellectual, including some that emanated from medical discourse.

Medicine was not, for all of that, inhospitable to Staël. Contemporary alienists frequently cited her works to support their theories on the passions or suicide.[101] Dr. Réveillé-Parise included Staël in his gallery of thinkers found, during autopsy, to have possessed extraordinarily large brains.[102] *Corinne* itself was turned into a medical document, of sorts, in *Études cliniques: Traité théorique et pratique des maladies mentales* (1852–53), where Bénédict Auguste Morel quoted two long excerpts from the novel to illustrate "primitive or simple lypemania." "Lypemania," as Morel defined it, was a "state of sadness and despondency with or without tears"—a condition of profound heartache that eventually led to "a prostration of all the intellectual forces . . . a cruel state that, depriving the individual of all her energy, seems to leave her with nothing but the sad faculty of suffering."[103] No one, in his eyes, had described this state more eloquently than Staël when she depicted Corinne's dejection after returning from Scotland to Florence: she tried "a thousand resources to calm that devouring faculty of thought that no longer presented her, as it once did, with the most varied reflections," but she failed, and realized with anguish that she had lost her creative talent.[104] Morel could not, as he put it, "resist the pleasure of citing this description."[105]

Chapter 6

Refashioning Intellectual Pathologies in the Wake of the Revolution

The medical profession underwent its own revolution in the wake of France's great political Revolution: it took on overtly anthropological dimensions and claimed authority in various areas of intellectual and social experience.[1] Significant changes also occurred in the way that medical theorists conceived of nervous disorders, which were central to the pathologies from which *gens de lettres* were held to suffer. Enlightenment-era physicians had spoken more or less interchangeably of "nervous," "hypochondriac," and "hysteric" disorders, a trio of adjectives featured together in a 1765 treatise by the English nerve doctor Robert Whytt; and they generally agreed with the rapprochement of hysteria and hypochondriasis that had been proposed by the seventeenth-century theorists Thomas Willis and Thomas Sydenham—an alignment that made the two disorders "sibling syndromes with similar symptomatologies that traced to the nervous system."[2] That mixed concept (which also included melancholy) was abandoned after 1790, around the same time that a new theory of sexual incommensurability set in across Europe.

A significant body of historical work has been done on the ways in which hysteria was separated out from its former "sibling syndromes" and redefined as a properly *female* disease at the end of the eighteenth century. One of the best-known contributions to this endeavor was Jean-Baptiste Louyer-Villermay's *Recherches historiques et médicales sur l'hypocondrie, isolée, par l'observation et l'analyse, de l'hystérie et de la mélancolie* (1802), which refeminized hysteria by reviving the age-old uterine theory of its origins.[3] Less attention has been paid to the efforts made by Villermay and other medical theorists to redefine hypochondria as a male disorder—and to associate it particularly with male intellectuals.

Mental medicine, the field in which those efforts were carried out, took over part of the discussion of "learned" ailments during the Revolutionary and Bonapartist eras. For the most part, the doctors who founded psychiatry in France endorsed the heroic vision of the laboring scholar that had been advanced in many pro-Enlightenment works—thereby positioning themselves against Jean-Jacques Rousseau, to some extent. Some took direct aim at Rousseau's provocative statement that "if she [Nature] destined us to be healthy, I almost dare to say that the state of reflection is unnatural [*un état contre nature*], and that the man who meditates is a depraved animal."[4] The alienist Maurice Roubaud-Luce set the phrase in direct contrast with a countercitation from Voltaire, which he considered more "correct" and philosophical: "The mind [*L'âme*] is a fire that one must feed / And that extinguishes itself if it does not expand."[5] The heroic, Voltairian perspective on intellectual endeavor was also fostered by the new measures that anthropologically minded physicians devised for classifying people and peoples, systems in which "cerebral men" were placed at the top of the chain of human existence.[6]

A classifying impulse also underpinned hygiene, a branch of medicine that "was institutionalized as a scholarly and pedagogical field only during the Revolution."[7] As this field expanded, theoreticians of hygiene focused increasingly on the laboring classes versus those higher up the chain of identified human types. However, hygienic discourse still produced some works targeted specifically at *gens de lettres*—including two with particularly grandiose titles, which I will examine in the last part of this chapter: Étienne Brunaud's *De l'hygiène des gens de lettres ou Essai médico-philosophique sur les moyens les plus propres à développer ses talens et son aptitude naturelles pour les sciences, sans nuire à sa santé et sans contracter des maladies* (1819), and Joseph-Henri Réveillé-Parise's *Physiologie et hygiène des hommes livrés aux travaux de l'esprit, ou Recherches sur le physique et le moral, les habitudes, les maladies et le régime des gens de lettres* (1834).

Gender Identity and Diseases of the Learned in Early French Psychiatry

The early French alienists were not staunchly mentalist in regard to the diseases that they perceived as stemming from intellectual exertion:

although clearly intent on identifying psychic disorders, many of these doctors insisted that such disorders had their seat in an organic lesion, usually in the stomach.[8] Nor did they maintain that civilization itself placed its inhabitants at dire risk of mental illness.[9] Rather, writing in the immediate wake of the Terror and anxious to contribute to the remaking of the nation, these doctors took a guardedly optimistic, meliorist view of civilization. Many belonged to the larger circle of thinkers—linguists and social and moral philosophers, as well as biomedical thinkers—known as the Idéologues, who believed they could build a new set of social institutions on the foundations of reason, and who styled themselves as architects of a healthier, calmer, and more reasonable society.[10]

When alienists discussed intellectuals as a patient group, they did so in works more generally concerned with the proper classification of nervous or mental disorders. Philippe Pinel was seminal in this regard: his *Nosographie philosophique, ou la méthode de l'analyse appliquée à la médecine* (1797) was reedited five times, up to 1813. The word *névrose* wasn't introduced into French until 1785, when Pinel coined it as an equivalent to the term "neurosis" in his translation of William Cullen's *First Lines of the Practice of Physics* (1777).[11] However, the general idea of nervous ailments was already well established, thanks both to theoretical developments in neurophysiology and medicine and to the general culture of nervousness that pervaded the eighteenth century.

Early psychiatric depictions of nervous illness carried few of the connotations of flightiness, lethargy, or decreased/fixated psychic vitality associated with neurosis in the modern, Freudian sense.[12] Pathological nervousness in the early nineteenth century had both psychological and physical components, particularly in the case of hypochondria. That approach was consistent with the perspective of predecessors like Samuel-Auguste Tissot, who, in *De la santé des gens de lettres*, divided hypochondria into two species: "the kind that is simply nervous and . . . is the effect of mental exertion," versus the kind "that depends on the engorgement of the viscera of the lower abdomen and digestive disturbance, which always results from inaction. It is easy to understand how these two sorts of illness are found in combination among Men of Letters. It is rare that they not be affected by them to some degree, and so difficult to cure them entirely" (*SGL*, 76). Tissot's suggested therapies to counter hypochondria also interwove the moral and the physical. At one point, after noting that hypochondriacs tend to be glum and silent, he offered a psychological remedy: "I have seen more than once hypochondriacs who began to read aloud, out of a forced courtesy, and who cheered up as they were reading; this aid should often be included in the curative plan proposed for them" (106). At another point, however, he singled out tea as a cause for the rise of hypochondria in his day: teapots, he declared, "spread sadness and despair," which could be alleviated by stopping or cutting back on tea consumption (192). This flexible perspective persisted in early nineteenth-century accounts of the illness, which often cited symptoms of visceral discomfort along with psychological conditions like taciturn moroseness. Villermay, for example, warned that hypochondria could be induced by undertaking mental work too soon after eating, or by eating and thinking at the same time.[13]

Well into the 1820s, French doctors maintained that the seat of hypochondria resided in the abdomen, not the brain. In the most radical expression of this view, the controversial medical theorist François-Joseph-Victor Broussais declared that it was all a matter of gastritis.[14] Locating hypochondria and its sibling syndromes in the viscera served both practical and theoretical purposes. First, it provided physicians with a justification for prescribing body-based treatment options like exercise and manual labor, purgatives and other digestive remedies, and hydrotherapy. Those therapies persisted despite the introduction of Pinel's famous moral treatment, which aimed to cure mental illness either by distracting the patient or by shaking up his or her imagination in order to break the "vicious chain of ideas" that had taken hold of it.[15] Second, the visceral location of these disorders adhered to the triadic conception of human physiology that had been advanced by the influential vitalist theorists of the Montpellier medical faculty, who regarded the abdomen as one of the body's three vital centers.[16] Finally, it provided a handy anatomical framework for drawing gender distinctions between male versus female sufferers. Following that logic, French doctors tended increasingly to reserve the terms "vaporous" or "hysterical" for women, on the theory that they were suffering from uterine spasms, and to call men "hypochondriacal." To a degree, therefore, hypochondria made it possible for turn-of-the-century *gens de lettres* to be nervous in a manly way—and somewhat more curable than the patient groups to which they were set in opposition.

Scholarly men were nonetheless seen as vulnerable to the full range of mental/nervous disorders explored by these physicians, from hypochondria (the mildest condition), to melancholy (more serious), all the way to stark raving mania. In *Nosographie philosophique*, Pinel grouped these diseases, along with hysteria, in the general class of nonfebrile "*vésanies*, or mental alienations" but insisted that men could contract only hypochondria, melancholy, and mania in their true forms. Women, he maintained, could develop those disorders, too, as a result of their extreme sensibility and the energy of their passions, but hysteria almost always complicated their symptoms.[17] Villermay systematized this sexually dimorphic view of nervous illness in his *Recherches historiques et médicales sur l'hypocondrie*, where he declared that "hypochondria almost always follows from the sedentary life and forced work of the library. . . . That is why Hoffmann called it the disease of men of letters; whereas hysteria arises more often from disturbances in the functions exclusive to sex, or in the imperious laws of reproduction."[18]

Arguing that earlier theorists had failed to note crucial differences between these different species of nervous disease, Villermay and others in the Pinel circle transformed hysteria into the principal pathological "other" to hypochondria. At the same time, they continued to view melancholy as lurking on the horizon of the hypochondriacal symptoms that seemed so prevalent among men of letters. Hypochondria, as they portrayed it, involved worrisome emotional states as well as abdominal symptoms like constipation, slow digestion, and flatulence. Pinel tied hypochondria to sadness and capriciousness of character (sometimes aggravated by changes in the atmosphere), whereas Villermay proposed a longer list of symptoms that included panic attacks and exaggerated anxieties like fretting about one's health.[19] Melancholy was held to involve more violent, somber, obsessive passions, including a stubborn, sometimes delirious fixation on a single idea. It was also more closely linked than hypochondria to a particular temperament, one that these doctors claimed was most common among dark-haired men with slow gaits and perpetually sad demeanors.[20] Yet hypochondria could, they warned, degenerate into melancholy, especially when the viscera remained in a chronic state of irritation due to overstudy, habitual overeating, or other causes.[21]

What made the nervous suffering of *gens de lettres* manly, in their estimation, was the relentless, exhausting mental exertion and deep reflection that underpinned it—qualities that were utterly incompatible with women's moral and physical nature, according to the dimorphic vision of the sexes to which these doctors subscribed. Specialists of mental medicine depicted great male thinkers who succumbed to nervous or mental ailments as driven by an extraordinary need for sensations, which derived directly from their exceptionally developed minds.

Dr. Jean-Etienne-Dominique Esquirol, the inventor of such neologisms as *lypémanie* and the more popular "monomania" (both proposed as replacement terms for melancholy), took that perspective at the outset of his treatise *Des maladies mentales* (1838), where he refuted Rousseau's misanthropic *boutade* about the "unnaturalness" of reflection along with the proximity that the English Restoration poet John Dryden had posited between genius and madness.[22] As Esquirol put it:

> The most extensive geniuses in the sciences and arts, the greatest poets, the most talented painters have retained their reasoning faculties up to old age. If we have seen some painters, poets, musicians and artists go mad, that is because, on top of having a very active imagination, those individuals had serious lapses in their regimen, to which their constitution made them more vulnerable than other men. It is not because they exercised their intelligence that they lost their minds; it is not the cultivation of sciences, arts and letters that is to blame: men endowed with great powers of thought and imagination have a great need for sensations.[23]

This view made nervous and mental disorders a consequence not of civilization, *tout court*, but of the needs and bad habits typical of those with a certain temperament. Pinel had made a similar argument earlier in his *Nosographie philosophique*, where he emphasized that it was the lack of moderation and method in conducting intellectual work that placed scholars at risk for nervous diseases. Evoking the "wise precepts established by Plutarque, Ramazzini, Tissot," he criticized the misguided notion to which many scholars subscribed that they had to sacrifice their health to succeed in the world of learning. Philosophical medicine could, he assured, guide intellectuals toward ways of developing their talents without contracting illnesses.[24]

Broadly speaking, early French psychiatrists echoed Xavier Bichat's insistence that it was impossible for any one person to perfect all of humankind's various sensory and intellectual capacities; this was one of the consequences he drew from his theory of "limited vital energy." As Bichat put it in his *Recherches physiologiques sur la vie et la mort* (1802), "The universality of knowledge in a single individual is a chimera; that notion goes against [physical] organization, and if history presents a few examples of extraordinary geniuses who were equally brilliant in several fields of knowledge, they were exceptions to those rules."²⁵ Arguing that the average person's aptitude for a given profession was determined by the organ that he or she exercised most frequently, Bichat divided human occupations into three general classes.²⁶ In the first class, he placed fields that mainly used the senses, like painting, music, sculpture, the arts of the perfumer, and haute cuisine. The second comprised professions that involved brain work, a grouping Bichat subdivided into imagination-based occupations like poetry, memory-driven fields like nomenclature, and judgment-dominated professions like the advanced sciences. In the third class, he placed professions that required muscular prowess, such as dance, equitation, and the mechanical arts. And to prove his thesis that no one could excel in more than one of these occupational classes, Bichat sketched a portrait of a hopelessly uncoordinated scholar: "Look at that scholar who, in his abstract meditations, constantly exercises his internal senses and, in the silence of his study, condemns to inaction his external senses and locomotive organs; if you see him trying out, by chance, a bodily exercise, you will laugh at his clumsiness and his awkward air. His sublime conceptions astonished you, but the slowness of his movements will amuse you."²⁷ He then offered a counterportrait of a dancer who, although gracious and captivating in motion, was quite dull in conversation. Bichat added that just as the locomotive organs, brain organs, and senses couldn't be perfected simultaneously, a man shouldn't be forced to undertake several different sorts of study all at once—a verity he considered to be not just a philosophical maxim, but also a physio-anatomic fact: "to increase the strength of one organ, you have to diminish it in others."²⁸

Aptitude or lack of aptitude for particular fields of study was a common theme among alienists who discussed *gens de lettres* in their writings. For example, Jean-Pierre Falret, a Restoration-era physician who specialized in hypochondria and suicide, warned that "when intellectual work is not in harmony with the particular disposition of the individual's mind, or when it goes violently against the grain of a natural penchant, it can predispose the person to suicide."²⁹ By the 1830s, it was a truism in French psychiatric discourse that the different thinking professions had varying degrees of susceptibility to nervous and mental illnesses.

While many alienists simply repeated some version of Pinel's declaration that musicians, poets, and artists were at the top of the "at-risk" list for madness because they tended to overwork their imaginations, Esquirol's protégé Étienne-Jean Georget offered a more fine-tuned ranking of intellectual professions in *De la physiologie du système nerveux, et spécialement du cerveau* (1821). Initially, Georget took a broad view, arguing that "almost all *gens de lettres*, scholars, philosophers, etc.," were susceptible to chronic hypochondriacal ailments because they tended to ignore the warning signs of imminent physical dysfunction: for example, irascibility and hypersensitivity to both cold and heat (this discussion is part of a long section entitled "Travaux intellectuels ou de l'esprit," full of dramatic anecdotes of overstudy—many drawn directly from Tissot's *De la santé des gens de lettres*).[30] The laws of nature eventually took their revenge on those who overtaxed their brains, leaving them with weakened faculties, chronically dysfunctional stomachs, and little hope of producing vigorous offspring (dangers that, as Georget noted, had been sounded earlier by Tissot).[31] Yet Georget then proceeded to exempt some intellectuals from this general rule: namely, those who engaged in mental operations involving memory, or the accumulation and combination of facts.[32] Professions that involved that sort of thinking seldom damaged mental health or health in general. By contrast, those that placed the mind in an exalted state wore out its organic *ressorts*, triggering a cerebral excitation that could become pathological. Thus, Georget concluded—citing for support the eighteenth-century naturalist Bonnet—"Scholars who are only observers, like chemists, naturalists, and botanists, are generally in better health than poets, philosophers, and artists."[33] Observational knowledge, in other words, was healthier and saner because it strained the brain less than did more complicated or abstract forms of thinking.

Georget's explanation of the varying incidence of nervous disorders among different varieties of intellectuals may have been inspired by the work of the phrenologists Franz-Joseph Gall and Johann Gaspar Spurzheim, who had recently undertaken to pinpoint loci or "organs" within the brain where specific sorts of ideation and feeling were seated. His admiration for their work was a departure from the reaction of some other alienists, including Pinel, who opposed the anatomical approach Gall and Spurzheim took to mental function.[34] In any case, Georget's typology did little more than confirm the emerging image of *gens de lettres* in alienist discourse, according to which scholars working in the exact sciences— except for those with a pronounced speculative bent, like mathematicians— were less inclined to fall ill than those specializing in imagination-bound or passion-stirring modes of cerebration.

Interestingly, doctors placed themselves in the high-risk category for hypochondria and melancholy, arguing that the training and practice involved in the medical profession endangered the mental health of those who took it up. First, studying medicine was dangerous because of the sort of reading it entailed, which could cause the reader to develop symptoms of whatever disease he or she read about (a similar effect of misplaced identification was, we should remember, commonly attributed to novel reading).[35] Alienists reported having observed this phenomenon not just among fretful nonprofessional readers—a group that they sometimes depicted in tones evocative of Molière's famous "imaginary invalid"—but also among medical students and established physicians.[36] Second, the sort of thinking done by physicians was itself mentally distressing: Villermay commented that practicing medicine produced an abundance of serious, severe, often sad ideas that made physicians vulnerable to nervous and mental disorders.[37] In his essay on hypochondria as a possible cause of suicide, Falret combined the two arguments to insist that hypochondria did not originate in the stomach, after all: the fact that doctors sometimes came down with it after seeing a number of patients and reading medical books proved that its true seat was not visceral but cerebral—by which he meant, rooted in the brain tissue.[38]

On balance, these doctors' attitudes toward study-induced nervous and mental ailments were ambivalent. Although they bemoaned the apparent prevalence of hypochondria and melancholy among *gens de lettres*, they also spoke of these diseases as an inevitable side effect of the glorious contributions scholars were making to the advancement of humankind's collective knowledge. In the words of Georget, "the progress of civilization and development of the human understanding" should be counted among the chief predisposing causes of hypochondria.[39] He included among those achievements the hard-earned advances that he and his fellow physicians were making, sometimes at the cost of their own health.

Georget—who, like Falret, regarded hypochondria as cerebrally located—provided an exceptionally detailed account of the five-month bout of hypochondria that he had himself endured as a result of excessive mental exertion. He fell ill in early March 1820, when, after approximately eighteen months of "continuous mental labors," he was suddenly struck with a "dull but continuous cephalagia" and "some difficulty in forming ideas, without any disorder in the other organs."[40] He persisted in his work but was soon overcome with fatigue and a great heaviness in his head; but when he lay down, the blood rushed to his head, which became hot and very painful.

Other symptoms included ringing in the ears, troubled sleep, bloodshot eyes, and difficulty in forming ideas, all of which made it impossible for him to work for more than a few hours each day. Although he exhibited no signs of muscular weakness or spasmodic contractions and had only a slight loss of appetite, he experienced some "sympathetic" symptoms in his heart and lungs: heart palpitations, pain in his lungs, and dry cough, all of which made him worry that he had tuberculosis.[41] He nonetheless pursued his research and writing as much as possible until April 17, when his symptoms became so bad that he had to give up his studies altogether. Because he appeared healthy, his attending physician regarded him as an "imaginary invalid" and prescribed fifteen days of rest and two bleedings, some cold applications on his head, tepid baths, and mustard-plaster footbaths. Thanks to these remedies, he was able to finish the writing project he was so reluctant to abandon, although he continued to suffer in his head, lungs, and heart (but never in the stomach). After twenty-five days of rest and recreation, he recovered completely, and by September he was able to resume his project without danger. During the next spring, he felt a slight tinge of hypochondria, which dissipated and then reappeared several times; however, he had no symptoms whatsoever the following summer. Georget concluded, "It appears that my brain has been toughened [*aguerri*] and gotten used to intellectual exercise."[42]

We can draw three general lessons from Georget's personal illness narrative. First, the "thinking as labor" paradigm was just as compelling for him and other alienists writing in the 1820s as it had been for eighteenth-century physicians. Second, far from exempting themselves from the nervous diseases incident to mental labor, these doctors saw themselves as acutely susceptible to them. Finally, Georget's concluding line suggests that scholars could overcome study-induced hypochondria and accustom themselves to the rigors of intellectual exercise. That was a common refrain in alienist discourse, although it coexisted with the observation that certain nerve-sick *gens de lettres* never recovered. The latter observation was often illustrated by the example of Nicolas Gilbert, a failed poet and *antiphilosophe* of the late eighteenth century who (by some accounts) succumbed to suicidal melancholy after being snubbed by the literary-philosophical establishment. Jean-Guillaume Fourcade-Prunet summed up that case as follows: "Gilbert, unhappy, persecuted, fell into the most pronounced melancholy and soon into complete dementia."[43]

Perfectibility, Temperament, and the Scholarly Constitution

Georget's emphasis on toughening up the brain echoed some of the arguments that were advanced by medical "invigorators" like Pierre-Éloi Fouquier de Maissemy. Author of the dissertation *Avantages d'une constitution faible* (1802), Fouquier argued that although the current generation of intellectuals was not as vigorous as their more solitary precursors from France's glory days (by which he meant the seventeenth century), their frailty was not necessarily unhealthy and could be remedied through fortifying methods. There were, he proclaimed, advantages to be found in the constitutions of "sickly poets" like Voltaire and Rousseau: although lacking in brawn, they possessed the heightened sensitivity and perfected intelligence toward which contemporary European society was evolving.[44] Although Fouquier was keen in his practice to increase the muscular strength of nervous sorts—for example, by administering *nux vomica*, also known as strychnine, with which he experimented extensively on his patients—he was also intent on refuting the notion that the human race was declining in Europe: "what people call degeneration is, in the human race, a true improvement."[45]

Some contemporaries regarded Fouquier's thesis as a clever paradox, like its reviewer in the *Dictionnaire des sciences médicales* of 1815.[46] However, others echoed his emphasis on the positive aspects of the nerve-dominated bodily constitution they deemed typical of scholars. Dr. Étienne Tourtelle of Strasbourg included a special appendix on *gens de lettres* in his *Éléments d'hygiène* (1796–97), where he argued that study, when pursued moderately, was as useful to the mind as exercise and labor were to the body. Both sorts of activities induced a sense of enjoyment that spread via the nerves throughout the organs, helping to maintain the balance of action among the different centers of sensibility and the harmony of functions that ensured good health; it was therefore not unusual, Tourtelle noted, to see men who were accustomed to regular study fall seriously ill when they interrupted their mental efforts.[47] Tourtelle's work was reprinted in 1838 under the title *Traité d'hygiène* in a volume that also included writings by Jean-Noël Hallé, a nephew of Anne-Charles Lorry, and the first holder of the Chair of Hygiene at the Paris Faculté de Médecine.[48] In 1798, Hallé had proposed a new hygienic category called "percepta," or the study of the sensations and intellectual and affective functions.[49] Both of these physicians contested the notion that the exercise of the mind necessarily shortens life; at the same time, however, they repeated the standard caution that excessive mental work could destroy even the strongest constitution.

These theoreticians worked within a conceptual framework still dominated by the psycho-physiology of sensation and stimuli. That perspective, as Philip Sarasin puts it, created "dangerous possibilities—excess, illness, and early death"; the task that hygienists assigned themselves was to reduce those dangers by showing that the body could be both knowable and controllable.[50] Health could be achieved by scrutinizing the body's signs and regulating the stimuli to which it was exposed, with the aim of keeping in check the tendency of individual parts to seek out more stimuli, more pleasure, than was good for the whole. Although it may not have had the poetic appeal of the Romantic ethos of intense living, the ethic of moderation underpinned much of the writing that hygienists directed at *gens de lettres* in the early decades of the nineteenth century. Intellectual pathologies were, in their minds, a true risk, but they were also reversible.

The medical Idéologue Pierre-Jean-George Cabanis also presented a normative image of the scholarly constitution in the *Rapports du physique et du moral de l'homme* (1802), an influential contribution to early nineteenth-century medical and social theory. Cabanis's book was controversial in some French intellectual circles because of the comparison he made between the stomach and the brain in his remark "the brain digests impressions, as it were, and produces organically the secretion of thought."[51] Viscera interested Cabanis for reasons that extended beyond that notorious analogy: he saw visceral weakness not just as a consequence of overstudy but also as a prerequisite for intellectual talent. As he argued, "The greatest aptitude for work that requires either a strong, active imagination, or persistent and profound meditations, often depends on a generally ill state introduced into the system by the disturbance of the functions of certain abdominal organs."[52]

To appreciate the implications of that claim, we should consider the context in which it was made: memoir 5 of the *Rapports du physique et du moral*, where Cabanis addressed the influence of sex differences on the character of ideas. As he described it there, dyspepsia was a specifically *masculine* trait, one analogous to—but not conflatable with—the generally weak, excitable, capricious state created in the female system by the functions of the uterus and ovaries. Chronic visceral disturbance, in other words, had different consequences for each sex. It was a constitutional factor that enabled men of a certain temperament to excel in the intellectual realm, even as it exposed them to hypochondriacal nervous affections.[53] For women, by contrast, this sort of disturbance was directed downward toward their reproductive organs, whose eminent sensibility was accompanied in the female body by a general softness that extended to the "cerebral pulp."[54] Women were simply not capable of deep thinking, in Cabanis's estimation: the healthy woman, although naturally intelligent, was "rightly put off by intellectual work that can't be carried out without long and profound meditations"; she preferred lighter subjects that required no more than a lively wit and imagination.[55] In response to reports that nervous ailments gave some women patients enhanced intellectual powers—as, for example, in bouts of vapors—he insisted that the effect was temporary: "nothing is less rare than to see them acquire during their vaporous attacks a penetration, a wit, an elevation of ideas and eloquence that they didn't have; those advantages, which are simply the result of the illness, disappear when health is restored."[56] He returned to this question in memoir 7, on the influence of illness on ideas, where he alluded to the claims made by magnetizers like the Lyon doctor Jacques-Henri-Désiré Petetin (author of the *Mémoire sur la découverte des phénomènes que présentent la catalepsie et le somnambulisme*, 1787) that female cataleptics exhibited symptoms like heightened intelligence and the ability to see and even smell through their internal organs. Cabanis dismissed such claims by declaring that "catalepsies, ecstasies, and all states of exaltation that are characterized by ideas and an eloquence that rise above the education and habits of the individual, are usually due to spasms in the organs of generation"—which is why those illnesses and the enhanced intelligence they sometimes produced were observed "mainly in women."[57]

By contrast, the enhancement effect was permanent in men who had an innately melancholic temperament or who had acquired a chronically dyspeptic state through force of habit. As he explained in memoir 7 of the *Rapports*, nervous affections in melancholic men "are conducive to attention and meditation; they accustom the senses and the organ of thought to exhaust, in a sense, the subjects of study to which they are attached. They expose the individual to all the errors of the imagination; but they can also enrich the genius with several precious qualities; they often lend talent a great deal of elevation, strength, and brilliance."[58] Cabanis thus gave an intriguing spin to the scholar's age-old "bad stomach" complaint: he interwove it with the sexually dimorphic model of human nature popularized by Rousseau and Roussel, while also linking it to the theory of limited perfectibility to which he, like his contemporary Bichat, subscribed. Seen from this perspective, visceral sickliness in men was not the result of but the enabling mechanism of sustained, intense mental labor.

This view of nervous affections provided a new way of finding value in the pathologies connected to thinking. The anecdotes reported (and sometimes dismissed) by Cabanis that patients suffering from a nervous or mental disorder sometimes exhibited extraordinary intelligence can be tied to a longer tradition, reaching back to Montaigne, of philosophical musing on the vagaries of the human mind and body. Denis Diderot made a brief but piquant contribution to that tradition: "A given person may be a fool while awake, and dream like a witty man [*un homme d'esprit*]. The variety of spasms which the intestines can create on their own corresponds to all the variety of dreams and all the variety of deliriums, to the full range of dreams of the healthy man who sleeps, and the full range of deliriums of the sick man who is awake but not in possession of his senses."[59] We can consider Diderot's clever-dreaming stupid man a cousin to the temporarily smart and eloquent cataleptic woman described by Cabanis: both personae morphed back into their true, dim-witted selves when they woke up or emerged from a trance. By contrast, the dyspeptic male cerebralist envisioned by Cabanis was likely to stay brilliant: his constitution, shaped both by habits and his melancholic temperament, tended to make him perpetually sickly—but also well disposed to intellectual exertion of the highest order.

This sort of reasoning was repeated in the section on education in *De la physiologie du système nerveux*, where Georget gallantly excluded women from the ranks of serious thinkers by arguing that Venus's forehead was too petite and pretty to support the same intensity of thought as Apollo's "handsome" profile—a comparison intended to illustrate the idea that women could not possess the power of reasoning, depth of mind, or power of meditation possible in men.[60] Although a woman might be sagacious, she would rarely have the "sublime faculty" necessary for abstract thinking, and the existence of a small number of exceptions to that rule did not refute the rule itself. As Georget put it, "We won't turn Woman into a metaphysician, a philosopher, a legislator; her powers cannot lift her to those heights, and her social duties do not agree with that sort of study."[61] Women could, however, fruitfully cultivate the sciences of observation, the fine arts, languages, and literature: even though they were ordinarily inferior to men in those fields, they could acquire enough to know and judge competently.

Around the same time, Julien-Joseph Virey advanced a more rigid and sweeping theoretical justification for the exclusion of women from scholarly pursuit, including the "softer" fields of literature and the arts. As he declared, the "ardent transports of genius" could be enjoyed only by males who had reached the so-called virile age, which was also the age at which study-induced hypochondria typically began.[62] Although he strongly disliked Cabanis's materialism, Virey shared his emphasis on the interdependence of body and mind, and a similar conviction that one of the primary tasks of contemporary medicine was to establish a system of human types—with sex difference leading his list of factors to be analyzed.[63] Virey first discussed women writers and intellectuals in *De l'influence des femmes sur le goût dans la littérature et les beaux-arts* (1810), later republished as the final section of his global analysis of female nature, *De la femme sous ses rapports physiologique, moral et littéraire* (1823). In a long note to *De la femme* entitled "The Influences of Love and of the Generative Functions on the Mind and Moral Character of the Feminine Sex," he rebutted the "zealous admirers of the fair sex" who claimed that women could produce literary works as brilliant as men's: "Does one find in them [women's writings] that sublimeness, that virile energy, that elevation or depth of thought that is the indelible mark of true genius, I would even say of the force of generation?" He explained the existence of great woman writers like the Greek poet Sappho by analyzing her personal history, from which he concluded that Sappho was a genius only because her "ardent, fiery temperament . . . made her almost a man," as evidenced by the "erotomania" she expressed in her poetry (442). All the women who had excelled in literature did so only because they had a "more masculine complexion," which gave them brief flashes of genius but also an unladylike lust. However "virile" they were, not a single one of these "impassioned Héloïses" escaped the mental and physical ravages of hysteria, a dire illness caused by the strange and overpowering impressions the uterus made upon the female mind, which usually led to madness (443–45).

In short, Virey maintained that the misplaced virility of exceptionally intelligent women did little more than make them oversexed: nature eventually avenged itself for their abnormal mental faculties through channels proper to the female body. True virility, as he conceived it, was "the greatest vital energy," a glorious creative force that only men could possess because they had sperm (427–28, 442). However, according to his peculiar application of the principle of limited vital energy, male scholars had to observe extreme caution while engaging in acts of physical virility—that is, sexual intercourse—lest they exhaust their mental powers through the "abuse of voluptuous pleasures" (442–43). Better yet, they should abstain from carnal relations altogether: "By abstaining from bodily generation, one becomes more capable of intellectual generation, one has more internal genius [*ingenium*], and for the same reason men of genius are less capable of engendering physically. . . . Newton died a virgin, as did W. Pitt, so they say. Kant hated women, and none of the great men of antiquity was very keen on women, according to Bacon of Verulam" (439–40). Although Virey took that theory to an extreme, most particularly in an 1840 speech, "Du contraste entre le pôle génital et le pôle cérébral dans l'homme et la série des animaux," the idea itself was not unique to him. The hygienists Tourtelle and Hallé also warned that "*gens de lettres* should rarely indulge in the pleasures of love, which are not only detrimental to their health, but also weaken the energy of the brain, necessary for the production of thought. Minerva rarely frequents the gardens of Idalie."[64]

Ardor, Glory, and Big Brains in Brunaud and Réveillé-Parise

Deterministic perspectives on the scholarly constitution also abounded in Brunaud's *De l'hygiène des gens de lettres* and Réveillé-Parise's *Physiologie et hygiène des hommes livrés aux travaux de l'esprit*. These armchair physicians lavished praise on intellectuals for perfecting the human spirit through their mental labors. They also proposed to guide them toward better, more healthful habits, ranging from how to eat to what sorts of women to frequent. If the mission of the early French alienists was to "console and classify" or "understand and treat," then one might say that Brunaud and Réveillé-Parise sought to preserve and glamorize the intellectual as a type.[65]

Brunaud, a Strasbourg physician and corresponding member of the Paris Société Médicale de l'Emulation, had published little before his medico-philosophical essay *De l'hygiène des gens de lettres*, other than a medical thesis and a short observation in the 1810 *Bulletin des sciences médicales* on the extraordinary expansion of the bladder that he had noticed in some cases of urinary retention. Although not an alienist, Brunaud dedicated his essay to Pinel and presented it as an answer to the question raised in Pinel's *Nosographie philosophique* regarding the health dangers of intellectual pursuit. Departing deliberately from Rousseau, Brunaud took a positive view of the moral and social effects of learning.[66] His goal in writing was to "direct wisely the zeal and ardor of those who, through extensive and diversified fields of knowledge, enlighten the human race and contribute so powerfully to the order and harmony of the social body"—and to avoid provoking in his scholarly readers "vain or exaggerated fears about the dangers they face" (18). Brunaud aligned his project with that of "the doctor of Lausanne"—that is, Tissot.

Like Tissot, Brunaud stressed how difficult it was to persuade *gens de lettres* to adopt healthful practices: they were inclined to find happiness only in "the continuous exercise of the operations of the intelligence," and their love of glory often seemed to stifle the natural desire for self-conservation (18). Doctors should therefore foster in these patients an "irresistible penchant" for other, more recreational sorts of pleasure, like music, gardening, hiking, and social commerce (22). Brunaud emphasized that the mind of the *homme de lettres* was utterly different from that of the *homme du monde* in its constitution and inclinations. The worldly man, while capable of keen focus, never drifted off into "that state of isolation of thought that detaches the attention from all surrounding objects; never does he experience the impetuous leaps of the imagination that transport the soul and engender genius" (41–42). The scholar, by contrast, lived in a perpetual state of distraction, and when gripped by an idea, he slipped into trances of ecstatic absorption: all the muscles of his face tensed, as if in a convulsion; his eyes became fixed, red, and bloodshot; and he didn't really see the objects in front of his eyes. Brunaud's portrait of the absorbed scholar then became downright erotic: when excited by the pleasures of study, the brain experienced a fever, or "erection," accompanied by a rapid influx of blood to it and to the face, followed by a climax in the form of a dramatic gushing forth of ideas (45).

Given the intensity of the pleasures derived from knowledge seeking, it was no easy task for doctors to convince scholars to balance them with more moderate, sociable enjoyments. Like Tissot, Brunaud believed that excessive absorption in intellectual matters could have worrisome side effects. Disregard for domestic affairs had, he warned, led to paternal negligence in the case of Corneille, and to death for Archimedes and the humanist Guillaume Budé (46–48). He also drew attention to the tendency of *gens de lettres* to neglect their bodies, which were typically scrawny and underdeveloped as a result of inaction. Rousseau, for example, had remarkably thin legs by the end of his life, perhaps because all the blood and vital action had been constantly carried to his head in order to fuel his literary genius (50). Similarly, the astronomer Lalande had a head much bigger than his other body parts, particularly his abdomen, which was extremely thin and frail (51). Whereas scholars could remedy the first problem by changing their bad habits, the second was more intractable because it arose from the peculiar bodily conformation that developed when one repeatedly exerted one's mind.

Brunaud used a curious sort of analogical reasoning to demonstrate this last theory. He compared the brain to three lower internal organs: the stomach, the bladder (the subject of his 1810 essay), and the uterus. Just as those organs acquired an exceptional degree of strength and volume when used habitually—as in men inclined to overeat, people with the "vicious" habit of retaining their urine for a long time, and women who were frequently pregnant—so, too, the scholarly brain expanded in size and power "through the effect of long and habitually sustained exercises and efforts" (37). As a consequence, they had larger, more developed brains than individuals whose intellectual faculties were rarely exercised. This was proven, Brunaud argued, by Pinel's observation in the *Traité de la manie* that people afflicted with idiotism had smaller cranial cavities than those of normal intelligence (39).

Although Brunaud's brain-bladder comparison was unconventional, his belief that great minds were housed in big skulls, with disproportionately smaller body parts elsewhere, echoed ideas in other strands of early nineteenth-century biomedical discourse. For example, the alienist Georget emphasized that the forehead was typically quite large on thinkers, judging from the busts that had been sculpted of Socrates, Bacon, Locke, Leibniz, Voltaire, and Rousseau.[67] As Michael Hagner explains, the brains and skulls of geniuses were a topic of keen interest to anatomists and anthropologists like Franz Joseph Gall, who by the end of his life "possessed a huge collection of skulls, casts of heads, and casts of brains," including anatomical exemplars of 103 illustrious men.[68] Brunaud did not entirely approve of Gall's organology: although he praised him as a skilled anatomist, he shied away from a system that seemed to threaten the unity of the thinking/feeling self (38–39). Yet he clearly agreed with Gall's idea that the brains of geniuses were bigger and heavier than others.

However, what concerned Brunaud more than big head size were the potentially life-shortening aspects of the muscular weakness, nervous ailments, and digestive disorders produced by unrelenting sedentary library work. For scholars, the key to long life was prudence in managing "the cerebral excitation produced by sustained intellectual activities"; the scholar should thus avoid overly prolonged study and regularly seek out moderating diversions (85–86). Nonetheless, a cloistered, studious existence had some healthful advantages over the constant agitation and noisy pleasures of worldly life, in that it protected the scholar against "intense and hotheaded passions" (82–85). Echoing the quantitative approach of Louis-René Villermé, Adolphe Quetelet, and other leaders of the early nineteenth-century public health movement, Brunaud gave some statistics.[69] He cited the theoretical estimate of seventy years as the maximum average human life span, which Buffon had made in the *Histoire naturelle de l'homme* (1749), applied it to a sample set of famous scholars, and found the results to be encouraging. He supported this with a statistical table showing the ages that had been attained by approximately three hundred men who had distinguished themselves through the sciences or letters; these examples ranged from Winkelmann, who died the youngest (of murder) at age 50, to Hippocrates, purported to have lived to 109 (490–96). Based on these findings, Brunaud calculated that cerebralists who led a sober, healthy life typically exceeded the average life span by six years, regardless of the climate in which they lived and the degree of "ardor" with which they pursued their studies (88).

Good scholarly hygiene, as Brunaud described it, entailed careful attention to all of the circumstances surrounding study. Those included the care that tutors should take to adapt their young charges' reading to their tastes and capacities (120–21); the small social circles that *gens de lettres* should form among themselves (179–96); the women of wit, refinement, and modesty whom they should seek out (207–17); and the attention they should pay to the nonnaturals—from air and diet to the secretion of seminal fluid, about which scholars should be extremely careful, given their tendency toward excessive excitation of the cerebral sort (360).

In short, Brunaud's *De l'hygiène des gens de lettres* was a compilation of received ideas regarding scholars intermingled with some curious new elements, like his orgasmic model of the brain in action, his brain-bladder analogy, and the correlation he drew between big brains and thin legs. It is worth noting that Brunaud took a somewhat more catholic view of genius vis-à-vis gender than did some contemporaries. Even while echoing the standard admonition that women should not seek to appear learned simply to burnish their social reputation, he praised women whose exceptional scientific talents "had elevated them to the highest conceptions," like

Hypatia, Caroline Herschel, and the Marquise Du Châtelet, and those who had excelled in literature, such as Marguerite de Navarre, Mlle de Gournay, and Mesdames Deshoulières, Graffigny, de Puisieux, La Fayette, and de Staël (212). Nonetheless, the real value Brunaud saw in learned women was the exceptionally rich conversation they could provide for male scholars, an idea he underscored by setting his illustrious examples side by side with women who had inspired or encouraged figures like Descartes, Condillac, Zimmermann, and Frederick of Prussia (208–9, 213).

* * *

Many of those ideas reappear in Joseph-Henri Réveillé-Parise's three-part treatise *Physiologie et hygiène des hommes livrés aux travaux de l'esprit*, which built upon his *Considérations médico-philosophiques sur ce mot d'Aristote, "Que la plupart des hommes célèbres sont atteints de mélancolie"* (1833).[70] According to one biography of Réveillé-Parise, he published a well-received treatise on ocular hygiene in 1816, became a member of the French Académie de Médecine in 1823, and served as a "major surgeon in the elite gendarmerie" until losing that position as a result of the 1830 Revolution, after which "he retreated into the practice of his art and his literary work, through which he has earned a distinguished rank among contemporary scholars."[71]

Thinkers clearly had a special physiology in Réveillé-Parise's estimation —and never more so than in the modern era, when the demands of social life were so pressing that few could lead the quiet, uniform life enjoyed by intellectuals in bygone days. Although contemporary scholars and *littérateurs* were no less driven than their predecessors by the "lively passion" for study, they were "devoured" by public life as well.[72] The increased social importance of *gens de lettres* had its benefits, in that it had made their profession more "dignified," respected, and influential, especially given their prominent role in journalism (vol. 2, 432). At the same time, however, it added to the sources of exhaustion with which they had to contend: by participating in the social whirlwind, intellectuals multiplied the passions to which they were susceptible, and their ardent internal constitutions drove them to be just as consumed by public affairs as they were by the quest to create something glorious and immortal.

What Réveillé-Parise saw when he perused the field of contemporary intellectual life was both the culmination of humankind's ongoing march toward greater complexity or "perfection" and the ravages created by a bodily organization in which sensibility was disproportionately concentrated in the brain and nerves. Those endowed with such a constitution embodied human perfectibility: "In truth, they are more men than other men, for good or for bad. . . . Physiological preeminence is the principle for supremacy in intelligence, and consequently for social preeminence. It has been said that great men are the aristocracy of our species, and that is true. . . . Their power is truly by divine right" (vol. 1, 102). However, such a physiology had its drawbacks by intensifying the passions: "The privileged men thus endowed have more joy, more chagrin, more love, more aversion, more transports, more ardor, more passions, more happiness and unhappiness than those with an inferior organization. . . . They are both the weak and the strong members of the human race, Heaven's chosen ones, the delight of their century and of posterity and yet, too often, the wretched of this world." There was, in other words, a price to pay for the privilege of residing at the top of the great chain of intelligent being: great thinkers felt everything too well and too much.

This argument was not, of course entirely new: it echoed the melancholic theories on perfectibility and superiority that had been proposed earlier in the century by Staël and Benjamin Constant.[73] However, Réveillé-Parise gave those theories a pronounced physiological aspect (one that those earlier theoreticians, who contested philosophical sensualism, would probably have rejected). He contended that the heightened vitality of the thinker's brain and nerves caused an imbalance in the distribution of the body's forces, creating (among other things) a deficit in the muscular realm: "The most poetically organized man is, in truth, lacking in material strength; that, perhaps, is the meaning of the saying of an ancient writer: 'heroic souls have no bodies'" (vol. 1, 104). To illustrate this thesis, he cited the irregular circulatory function observed in some superior minds, like the palpitations that Staël reported having experienced in her youth while reading *Clarissa*, especially the kidnapping scene (vol. 1, 108). He also evoked the frail, almost ethereal physique of other illustrious thinkers, attributing it to the intense mental activity taking place within their brains. Here, he cited the portrait of Voltaire sketched by Count Louis-Philippe Ségur: "His leanness bore witness to his long, incessant labors. . . . His piercing eye sparkled with genius and sarcasm . . . while his thin and bending form seemed nothing more than a slight envelope, almost transparent, through which beamed his genius and his soul."[74] As Réveillé-Parise described it, cerebral intensity exerted a physical effect more profound than upsetting the stomach or wearing out the eyes: it literally burned up the thinker's vital force.

Réveillé-Parise also ascribed disruptive moral consequences to the poetic constitution: the "great nervous mobility" it fostered sometimes produced abruptly changing moods and an "irascible" susceptibility to criticism and contradiction—traits shown by various famous thinkers, including Diderot, Voltaire, Rousseau, and Queen Christine of Sweden (vol. 1, 166–67, 190–94). High intelligence could, moreover, coexist with astonishing weakness of character, because the stable energy necessary for moral fortitude was difficult to sustain when one possessed a nervous system that reacted to the slightest impression. That was especially true of intellectuals who embraced an agitated, modern life (vol. 1, 176–77). When male thinkers did not learn how to master their emotions, their nervous constitution approached that of women: they became volatile, capricious, and histrionic, like the men of letters who had been observed crying over a lost parrot or moved to tears by the loveliest passages in Homer and Virgil (vol. 1, 168). All intellectuals, Réveillé-Parise warned, were susceptible to such weaknesses because of the fundamental laws of their physiology: artists, poets, and mathematicians alike exhibited the same "lively sensibility" that impassioned their ideas, and the same enthusiasm or "fanaticism" for their works, theories, or systems (vol. 1, 132). There was simply something in their nerves, veins, and fibers that moved them to exaggerate their feelings, ideas, or actions—that is, to experience life in "excess," in both moral and physical terms (vol. 1, 129–30).

However, although he worried about the volatility of "poetically" organized people, Réveillé-Parise plainly saw them as the embodiment of humanity at its best: "the poet, the artist, the scientist, the philosopher is the human being par excellence, the social and progressive being" (vol. 1, 172). He went to great lengths to glorify the toil and ardor involved in creative or scholarly production. This is particularly pronounced in chapter 15 of part I of *Physiologie et hygiène*, entitled "De l'enthousiasme, de la verve ou orgasme cérébral," where, citing Richerand, Réveillé-Parise waxed lyrical about the cerebral "oestrus" by which great thinkers worked themselves up into orgasmic-like explosions of ideas. That creative state could trigger a crisis in various body parts, evident in such examples as Grétry spitting up mouthfuls of blood, Mozart losing his senses, Montesquieu's hair turning white, Lagrange feeling his pulse become irregular, Rousseau suffering a fit of fever, Dryden experiencing a general trembling, and Alfieri's eyesight dimming (vol. 1, 306–11). Indeed, the effects of such cerebral "orgasms" could be so intense as to make the thinker lose all sense of self—a sort of madness through which the genius plummeted down from the summit of humanity into a bizarre, brutish state:

> Another no less remarkable effect of these impetuous movements, and without a doubt the saddest of all, is the loss of the sense of personality. . . . The concentration of repeated thinking force, pushed to its extreme, sometimes overwhelms and stupefies the nervous system. The man of genius suddenly descends to a state lower than the animal, who is at least guided by its instinct. Although in a minority, some poets, artists, and philosophers have lost their minds by wanting to fly too high or plunge too deeply into the obscure depths of metaphysics. (Vol. 1, 312)

Even in less extreme cases, long intellectual endeavors have scarred those who pursued them: "one could call them the marginal beings of our species, either because of the singularity of their opinions, which are at odds with those of their era, or because of the strangeness of their behavior and their states of almost somnambulic distraction."

Réveillé-Parise thus portrayed intellectuals as living in a state of mental intensity that was both devastating and sublime: although it overwhelmed their nerves and depleted their material bodies, it was also the motor of civilization and social progress. In keeping with the grand sweep of his vision—and his clear determination to make the most of the fifteen years that (according to his "Avant-Propos") he had devoted to consulting medical works, ancient and modern biographies, memoirs, and letters written by the most famous men in various fields (vol. 1, i–ii)—his pantheon of superior minds featured not just scholarly and literary celebrities but also political giants like Napoleon. In Réveillé-Parise's eyes, Napoleon deserved inclusion for multiple reasons: not only had he created ideas that changed the destiny of his era, but, like history's intellectual luminaries, he possessed a special physiology that concentrated his vital forces in his nerves and brain. This was proven by Napoleon's large, painfully sensitive head and the crushing melancholy he suffered in his final days (vol. 1, 59, 128; vol.

2, 358). In fact, Napoleon is surpassed only by Voltaire and Rousseau as the most frequently cited celebrity in *Physiologie et hygiène*, suggesting that Réveillé-Parise may have been eager to contribute to the myth-making particular to his era.

Despite his predilection for glamorizing the sufferings of civilization's giants, Réveillé-Parise adhered to the conventions of scholarly hygiene discourse by preaching the value of moderation in the name of health and self-preservation. Borrowing from Fouquier's *Avantages d'une constitution faible*, he maintained that those endowed with the nervous, intellectual temperament were generally better than muscular sorts at managing their health because their heightened sensitivity constantly alerted them to potential dangers (vol. 1, 318–19). Thus, although *gens de lettres* often experienced minor ailments, they succumbed less often to serious illness than did those with a more fleshy, "plethoric" body type; and, if they were wise, they regarded the temperance they were obliged to observe as a source of happiness and even glory (vol. 1, 320). Réveillé-Parise offered portraits of scholars who had successfully avoided the dangers to which their special physiology exposed them, either because they had "Herculean" muscles as well as energetic nerves, like Plato and Buffon, or because they had adopted a sober, balanced regimen to counterbalance their "extreme" intellectual work (vol. 1, 92; vol. 2, 43). He also included a chapter featuring "biographical proofs" of the power of judicious personal hygiene. Focusing particularly on octogenarian thinkers like Newton, Fontenelle, and Voltaire, he argued that many intellectuals who had enjoyed a long life had started out frail in constitution but mastered early "the art of living and sustaining their strength" (vol. 2, 175). Newton, for example, knew that he had been born weak and delicate and therefore took care to save his strength for his cerebrations: he adhered to an austere dietary regimen, did some physical exercise, stopped working when he was tired, and stayed detached from all passions, even that of glory (vol. 2, 176–78). Fontenelle, for his part, succeeded in juggling the roles of *homme de lettres* and *homme du monde* through a clocklike physical regimen and moderation in the moral realm (vol. 2, 179–80).

Réveillé-Parise insisted that preserving one's health was a mode of self-knowledge that each individual scholar should develop. Accomplishing this entailed scrutinizing three things: first, one's constitution, by which one could establish the "individual vital dynamometry" specific to one's body type; second, the specific "modifying agents" that exerted an influence on one's organic functions; and, third, the effects of those agents on the overall organism or animal economy (vol. 2, 159–61). When they had gathered all of that information, scholars could establish the rule for healthy living that best suited their temperament and circumstances, thus ensuring "full use and free expansion of the intellectual faculties" (vol. 2, 161).

Réveillé-Parise was less inclined to glean case histories directly from medical practice (to which he seems to have devoted less time than to his literary pursuits, after 1830) than to draw on historical and biographical literature about famous thinkers. He justified this choice by arguing that it was the best way for a physician to get behind-the-scenes glimpses of their habits and temperaments (vol. 2, 176). He also interwove into *Physiologie et hygiène* the voices of some possibly fictional *gens de lettres*. One was a skeptical magistrate to whom he addressed a long letter near the end of part III in order to present his views on the health effects of the passions and defend them against the charge of materialism (vol. 2, 298–347). Another was a "man of letters, long in my care," who appeared in a chapter on the patient-doctor relationship. In response to this character's arguments that the doctor's prescriptions were overly restrictive for a person who was addicted to the heady pleasures of scholarly life, Réveillé-Parise countered that health, not glory, was the first and most important of all riches for the intellectual, and that physical suffering should not be regarded as the inevitable companion to the cultivation of talent and genius (vol. 2, 116–32). However, he also addressed doctors, offering them practical tips on treating the illnesses of intellectuals. First, they should never forget that this patient group typically had an overactive nervous system, which made "sedative" measures the most effective remedies for most of their ailments (vol. 2, 79). Second, they should remember that scholars seldom gave up their intellectual work voluntarily, which meant that moral therapies were especially important for dealing with them. A wise doctor could, for example, cure a melancholic poet simply by giving him an audience for his work (vol. 2, 96–97). The lucky scholar was one who found a doctor who was not only skilled in the medical arts but also "a compassionate friend" who sympathized with his suffering, knew the traits and anomalies of intellectuals, and understood the sensitive, sometimes stormy nature of "all those whom genius, talents, and celebrity drag from the sleep of the mind and the habits of average life" (vol. 2, 109).

In sum, Réveillé-Parise combined two rather different sorts of discourse in his treatise: idealization of the "poetic" constitution, and the more pedestrian genre of the personal hygiene manual. This mixture was evident even when he responded to philosophical objections that he was "animalizing" genius: alluding to the reactionary spiritualism of Joseph de Maistre, Réveillé-Parise denied that he was a materialist but nonetheless insisted that there was no use denying that history's great thinkers had huge heads, nervous ailments, and all of the other bodily symptoms that he had described over the course of his treatise (vol. 2, 302). Biography and posthumous observation proved that there was, indeed, a correlation between intelligence and bodily organization. Despite objecting to some of Gall's theories on that topic, he agreed that there was a direct correlation between the perfection of the brain and its volume (vol. 2, 293). This hypothesis was supported by the postmortem appearance of the heads of several famous thinkers—Pascal, Voltaire, Rousseau, Mme de Staël, Napoleon Bonaparte, Byron, Cuvier, and Gall himself—some of which had been kept in jars, autopsied, or measured for circumference, and all of which contained a considerable quantity of cerebral matter (vol. 2, 296–301).

Physiologie et hygiène des hommes livrés aux travaux de l'esprit enjoyed considerable success: after winning a Prix Montyon in 1835, it was reedited three times, reprinted regularly until 1881, and translated into German and Italian. The Italian criminologist Cesar Lombroso referred to it at the outset of his influential work *L'uomo di genio: In rapporto alla psichiatria, alla storia ed all'estetica* (1888; English translation, *The Man of Genius* [1891]) while reviewing earlier books that had supplied "proofs" of the tendency of men of genius to experience hallucinations or monomania.[75] Dr. Édouard Toulouse also cited it, approvingly, in the introduction to his 1896 study *Émile Zola: Enquête médico-psychologique sur les rapports de la supériorité intellectuelle avec la névropathie*, where he singled out Réveillé-Parise's observation that "the faculty of feeling, of having emotions, grows with the intelligence, as much in the series of living beings as in the range going from savages to civilized men."[76] The work's reputation as a hygiene guide for scholars endured as late as 1921, when the Dominican priest and philosopher Antonin Gilbert Sertillanges praised its fundamental idea: namely, that "the thinker has a special physiology: he must look after it, and not hesitate to seek out expert advice on the matter."[77]

Epilogue: Not So Singular, After All?

In many ways, Joseph-Henri Réveillé-Parise's three-part opus on the special physiology and hygiene of scholars marked the apogee of the disease syndrome known as *maladies des gens de lettres*. Not only was it the last in the line of grand, synthetic treatises on the health of intellectuals, but it appeared at a time when biomedical experts were less inclined to pay particular attention to cerebralists as a medical type. The fading of that trend is confirmed by the listings under the heading "Hygiène des gens adonnés aux travaux de l'esprit (Tc^{33})" in the 1857 volume of the *Catalogue des sciences médicales* of the Bibliothèque Impériale (which would soon turn into the Bibliothèque Nationale de France): this category ended with an entry for an 1842 analytic review of Réveillé-Parise's treatise by M. L.-B. Caffe.[1] Other nineteenth-century librarians, like the indexers for the Library of the U.S. Surgeon General's Office, nonetheless continued to single out publications that dealt with this topic: in 1885, Dr. John S. Billings grouped them under the rubric "Hygiene (mental) and hygiene of literary men."[2] The exceptionalness of intellectuals' mental and physical constitution was also emphasized in the medical dictionaries that proliferated throughout this century, ranging from the articles "Contemplatif" and "Contemplation," which Dr. Antoine-François Jenin de Montègre contributed to the *Dictionnaire des sciences médicales* in 1813, to the 1869 *Dictionnaire encyclopédique des sciences médicales*, whose entry on "Lettres (Gens de), Hygiène" praised Samuel-Auguste Tissot as a useful source on the subject.[3]

Focus on cerebralists persisted in some new areas of biomedical investigation: for example, the theory that genius went hand in hand with susceptibility to hallucinations and other forms of mental alienation, which was promoted in works like Louis-Francisque Lélut's *Le Démon de Socrates* (1836) and *De l'Amulette de Pascal, étude sur les rapports de santé de ce grand homme à son génie* (1846). The psychiatrist Jacques-Joseph Moreau de Tours contributed to this sort of theorizing in *La Psychologie morbide dans ses rapports avec la philosophie de l'histoire, ou De l'influence des névropathies sur le dynamisme intellectuel* (1859), where, building on Lélut's ideas and those that Bénédict Auguste Morel had advanced in his *Traité des dégénérescences physiques, intellectuelles, et morales de l'espèce humaine* (1857), he proposed an overarching theory of nervous illnesses that placed great painters, musicians, and scientists on a branch of the tree of "idiosyncratic hereditary nervous states"—with criminals, prostitutes, and idiots occupying other, closely connected branches.[4] However, even alienists seeking to categorize genius as a form of neurosis or degeneracy (hereditary or acquired) were often less interested in cerebralists than in other human types, like alcoholics, opium eaters, criminals, the chronically malnourished, the sexually deviant, and so-called primitive peoples. By the 1840s, the era in which doctors fretted particularly about the health or physiology of thinkers was over.

This decline in interest in the supposed physio-moral exceptionalness of intellectuals was tied to larger developments in French culture. One was the post-Revolutionary reshaping of France's educational system around the ideal of meritocracy, a process in which the anti-materialist philosopher Victor Cousin played a central role. Cousin's philosophical psychology, which was widely disseminated in French lycées from 1830 to 1848, assiduously avoided the biologically based explanations of mental phenomena favored by many of the physicians whom I examined earlier (particularly those who accepted, in part or whole, the theories of phrenology and organology). As John Carson puts it, "Cousin gave little attention to the varieties of actual individual minds," taking an approach to human nature that "evinced little concern with explaining why talents varied and what those differences might mean."[5] Because of Cousin's enormous influence in the philosophical world of early to mid-nineteenth-century France, the physiology of difference that was so important to many in the medical world was not as culturally prominent during the Bourbon restoration. (Also pertinent was the diminished prominence or power of the holistic view of sensibility, which had underpinned a good deal of French medical theory up to this time: biomedical investigations into the brain and nerves shifted firmly away from the "high" end of the chain of being toward the low end—as, for example, in François Magendie's vivisectionist experiments on animals.[6]) Biologically grounded theories of intelligence did find traction in other realms: this period saw the rise of anthropology and the so-called science of race, in which physicalist conceptions of mental capacity were frequently applied both to various animal species and to various human groups, often in hierarchical terms that were predicated on assumptions of Western superiority vis-à-vis less "civilized" peoples.[7] That branch of naturalist inquiry was, however, more intent on investigating ethnic groups (particularly those outside of Europe) than on individuals such as the suffering cerebralist.

Another factor in the waning of medical concern over intellectuals was the public hygiene movement, whose proponents were more preoccupied with illnesses arising from poverty or dangerous working conditions than with those that might be tied or imputed to overstudy.[8] The health reformers who became prominent in the 1820s and 1830s were just as meliorist and moralizing as Enlightenment-era physicians, but they worked in a very different social and ideological context. What distinguished these "new sanitarians" from their predecessors (aside from their statistically grounded methodology) was, first, their emphasis on public versus personal hygiene, and, second, the new perspective they took to occupational medicine—the field that, as we'll recall, had been a major impetus in the rise of scholar-specific hygiene writing, starting with Ramazzini. As Ann La Berge explains, "The prevailing opinion of leading hygienists—Villermé, Chevallier, and Parent-Duchâtelet—was that it was not occupations per se that caused workers' health problems, but living conditions resulting from poverty. . . . Hygienists debunked what they regarded as myths about the dangers of various occupations."[9] Among the myths debunked was the notion that *gens de lettres* suffered from a distinct set of occupation-specific health risks and thereby formed a distinct, privileged patient group.

Take, for example, the updated version of Ramazzini's theories that Philibert Patissier proposed in his *Traité des maladies des artisans et de celles qui résultent de diverses professions d'après Ramazzini* (1822). Although he devoted a nine-page section to the illnesses of *gens de lettres* and cited his contemporary Étienne Brunaud on their "ardent" labors, Patissier emphasized only the most pedestrian aspects of intellectual work, like the fact that scholars sat for too long in a hunched position, forgot to go to the bathroom, and breathed in too much bad, stale air.[10] In other words, rather than waxing lyrical (like Brunaud) about the poetic magic happening to the mind during cerebral exertion, Patissier focused on the prosaic conditions in which that activity was performed. He thus proposed purely body-based remedies for the ailments tied to it: *gens de lettres*, he recommended, should exercise to offset the dangers of sedentariness, take *tisanes apéritives* to clear out their bowels and tobacco to diminish headaches, protect their eyes by rubbing them with a mixture of water and *eau de vie* and wearing a "gardevue" in the light, and, if they wrote a lot, use a table "à la Tronchin" (a standing table invented by the eighteenth-century physician Théodore Tronchin).[11] Moreover, Patissier broadened the medical classification of *gens de lettres* to include more humble workers like secretaries who wrote letters dictated by the "grands seigneurs" who employed them. This classification anticipated the tendency of later nineteenth-century French hygienists and sociopolitical commentators to place scholars in the general category of "office men" or bourgeois urban "mental workers," a group sometimes belittled as debilitated functionaries.[12] By the 1890s, when the physical culture movement got into swing in France, the status of cerebral work as a desirable vocation for young men had declined: far from being lionized, intellectuals were now grouped with functionaries and dandies in "a single category of decadent and weak men."[13]

That is not to say that myths related to the specialness of the scholarly psycho-physiology disappeared altogether. Balzac, an avid reader of contemporary medicine and science, incorporated many components of the suffering-scholar persona into his novels.[14] Medical notions of the effects of intense cerebration inspired some of his most striking characters, like Louis Lambert, an intellectual prodigy whose existence is dubbed an "anomaly" on the third page of the story, and the big-foreheaded scientist Balthazar Claës of *La Recherche de l'Absolu* (1834).[15] Balzac also created a female version of the suffering genius: Félicité des Touches of *Béatrix* (1845), a George Sand–like woman of letters whose pen name is Camille Maupin and who is labeled a "monstrosity" by both her neighbors and a former lover.[16] Balzac's works are full of tales that dramatize the tension between deep thinking and the rest of life—not just love, family life, and social engagement, but life in the vital sense as well. The only long-lived intellectuals in his fictional universe, the only ones not burnt out by the devouring flame of their superior minds, are those who live in obscurity, like the distracted professor Saint-Vandrille of *Entre savants* (1845).[17]

Poetic melancholy and other forms of intellectual pathology were popular among other nineteenth-century French authors as well. Gustave Flaubert and Charles Baudelaire cultivated their own personal myths of being "hysterical," while others embraced the contemporary equation of genius with madness—or, at least, of superior intelligence with some form of neuropathy.[18] Moreover, a heroic quality was still attached to the diagnoses that some physicians proposed of celebrated intellectual figures, as in Édouard Toulouse's meticulously detailed case history of Émile Zola's health, *Enquête médico-psychologique sur les rapports de la supériorité intellectuelle avec la névropathie* (1896). Although he concluded that the novelist was "truly a neuropath" with traits like "nervous disequilibrium" and "morbid exaggerated emotivity," Dr. Toulouse also interpreted Zola's struggle against obesity as testimony to the novelist's extraordinary willpower.[19] The diagnosis pleased Zola himself, who wrote Toulouse a letter expressing thanks and relief to know that he would no longer be disparaged as a "beast of burden" but, rather, recognized as a "poor flagellant [*écorché*] . . . trembling and suffering with the slightest breeze, and sitting down every morning to his daily task only in anguish."[20] In his preface, Toulouse aligned his effort to observe "high intellectual personalities" currently alive with his examination of asylum patients, "subjects who are less illustrious but no less interesting"; his general hope was to open up a fertile new path for "cerebral physiology."[21]

Clearly, *gens de lettres* were still inclined to see themselves as suffering for their artistic or intellectual efforts. However, they were less inclined to regard heightened sensitivity as something that could or should be kept in check. Enlightenment-style meliorism gave way in the self-construction of prominent intellectuals to the embrace of degeneration, if not out-and-out decadence. To cite Angus McLaren, "Reacting against what they took to be the crassness of contemporary mass democratic society, a number of late nineteenth-century French writers were drawn to the themes of ineptitude, decadence, and failure. Their novels were studded with references to the pathological, the psycho-somatic, and the sterile. . . . The old notion that the life of the mind countered the demands of body was given new life."[22] Nathalie Heinich likewise emphasizes that differentiation from a "stigmatized bourgeoisie" was crucial to the construction of the new, elite social category known as the Artist—which, "for the first time in western culture, brought together the various domains of creation and sometimes, too, the interpreters and performance of music, theater, and dance."[23]

In fact, it may have been writers and artists—that is, those most likely to be placed in Réveillé-Parise's category of "poetically" organized beings—who contributed the most decisively to the decline of *les maladies des gens de lettres* as a jointly medical and literary enterprise. (Another reason, however, may have been that physicians had less tolerance for the literary in styles of clinical observation.[24]) Although literary authors were often keenly aware of established and emerging medical theories on the pathologies tied to mental exertion, they were more skeptical than their predecessors about the claims doctors made regarding the relationship between health and cerebral intensity. As Juan Rigoli emphasizes, writers like Nodier, Balzac, and Nerval vigorously contested the policing function that some contemporary alienists tried to assume over literary production, like the denunciation of "fantastic" literature as conducive to nervous illness, which appeared in the pages of the *Gazette médicale de Paris* in 1832; and they also tended increasingly to question the competence of doctors to interpret the altered states to which geniuses were susceptible—most particularly when those altered states appeared to border on madness.[25] Only those who possessed the poetic temperament, these writers seemed to suggest, could understand its often perplexing effects on the mind and body, or convey those effects in creative form. A new, more dissonant tone thus entered into the ongoing medical-cultural dialogue over exceptional minds and the qualities that made them singular.[26]

Notes

Introduction

1. Balzac, *Louis Lambert*, in *La Comédie humaine*, vol. 11 (Paris: Gallimard, Éditions de la Pléiade, 1980), 612. All translations from the French are my own unless otherwise noted.

2. "Introduction par Félix Davin," in *La Comédie humaine*, vol. 10 (1979), 1215. Balzac developed this idea in the "Avant-Propos" to *La Comédie humaine*, where he explained that the general goal of the *Études philosophiques* was to show the "ravages of thought . . . sentiment by sentiment" (*La Comédie humaine*, vol. 1 [1976], 19).

3. See these three chapters, Aristotle (or a follower of Aristotle), "Brilliance and Melancholy"; Ficino, "Learned People and Melancholy"; and Burton, "Melancholic States"—especially the section "Love of Learning, or Overmuch Study"—in Janet Radden, ed., *The Nature of Melancholy, from Aristotle to Kristeva* (Oxford: Oxford University Press, 2000), 55–60, 87–94, and 129–56. On ancient conceptions of melancholy and mental illness, see Jackie Pigeaud, *La Maladie de l'âme: Étude sur la relation entre l'âme et le corps dans la tradition médico philosophique antique* (Paris: Les Belles Lettres, 1981). On Burton, see Angus Gowland, *The Worlds of Renaissance Melancholy: Robert Burton in Context* (Cambridge: Cambridge University Press, 2006). On Bartholi, see John J. Renaldo, *Daniello Bartoli—a letterato of the seicento* (Naples: Nella sede 'dell'Istituto, 1979).

4. An epidemiological transition occurred in eighteenth-century Western Europe "from a society whose disease pattern was dominated by infectious diseases to a more modern situation where chronic diseases are prevalent"; Laurence Brockliss and Colin Jones, *The Medical World of Early Modern France* (Oxford: Clarendon, 1997), 356–70.

5. Michael Stolberg, *Experiencing Illness and the Sick Body in Early Modern Europe*, trans. Leonhard Unglaub and Logan Kennedy (New York: Palgrave Macmillan, 2011), 89–156. See also E. C. Spary, "Health and Medicine in the Enlightenment," in *The Oxford Handbook of the History of Medicine*, ed. Mark Jackson (Oxford: Oxford University Press, 2011), 81–99.

6. Cited in Rudy Le Menthéour, *La Manufacture de maladies: La dissidence hygiénique de Jean-Jacques Rousseau* (Paris: Classiques Garnier, 2011), 38. The vapors were a nebulous genre of ailments that included both nervous convulsions and intestinal

windiness. Tronchin maintained that their supposed prevalence was caused by bad remedies, ignorance, and mischief on the part of those who "manufactured" such illnesses.

7. Recent studies of this period's ideas on genius include Darrin M. McMahon, *Divine Fury: A History of Genius* (New York: Basic Books, 2013); Ann Jefferson, *Genius in France: An Idea and Its Uses* (Princeton, N.J.: Princeton University Press, 2015); and Kathleen Kete, *Making Way for Genius: The Aspiring Self in France from the Old Regime to the New* (New Haven, Conn.: Yale University Press, 2012). See also Ann Jefferson and Jean-Alexandre Perras, eds., *Thinking Genius, Using Genius / Penser le génie à travers ses usages, L'Esprit créateur* 55:2 (Summer 2015); and Joyce E. Chaplin and Darrin M. McMahon, eds., *Genealogies of Genius* (New York: Palgrave Macmillan, 2016).

8. See http://artflsrv02.uchicago.edu/cgi-bin/dicos/pubdico1look.pl?strippedhw =singulier (DAF [1694]).

9. Lilti, *Figures publiques. L'invention de la célébrité (1750–1850)* (Paris: Fayard, 2014).

10. Montesquieu, "Mes pensées," in *Œuvres complètes*, ed. Roger Caillois, 2 vols. (Paris: Gallimard, Éditions de la Pléiade, 1949), vol. 1, 1298.

11. Ibid.

12. Books that explore those connections in different centuries or national traditions include Juan Rigoli, *Lire le délire: Aliénisme, rhétorique et littérature en France au XIXe siècle* (Paris: Fayard, 2001); Irina Sirotkina, *Diagnosing Literary Genius: A Cultural History of Psychiatry in Russia, 1880–1930* (Baltimore: Johns Hopkins University Press, 2002); Dino Franco Felluga, *The Perversity of Poetry: Romantic Ideology and the Popular Male Poet of Genius* (Albany: State University of New York Press, 2005); Françoise Grauby, *Le corps de l'artiste: Discours médical et représentations littéraires de l'artiste au XIXe siècle* (Lyon: Presses Universitaires de Lyon, 2001); and Helen Deutsch, *Resemblance and Disgrace: Alexander Pope and the Deformation of Culture* (Cambridge, Mass.: Harvard University Press, 1996) and *Loving Dr. Johnson* (Chicago: University of Chicago Press, 2005).

13. Roland Barthes used the term "marvelous singularity" when reflecting upon the mythic function of the modern French intellectual, embodied by a photograph of André Gide reading Bossuet while sailing down the Congo. "L'Écrivain en vacances," in *Mythologies* (Paris: Seuil, 1957), 31–32.

14. On the Enlightenment "cult" of intellectuals and other great men, see Jean-Claude Bonnet, *Naissance du Panthéon: Essai sur le culte des grands hommes* (Paris: Fayard, 1998); and David A. Bell, *The Cult of the Nation: Inventing Nationalism, 1680–1800* (Cambridge, Mass.: Harvard University Press, 2001), 107–39.

15. Darrin M. McMahon, *Enemies of the Enlightenment: The French Counter-Enlightenment and the Making of Modernity* (Oxford: Oxford University Press, 2001), 32.

16. I am adapting a question raised by Ian Hacking in *Mad Travelers: Reflections on the Reality of Transient Mental Illnesses* (Charlottesville: University Press of Virginia, 1998), 55.

17. I explored this question at length in *Enlightenment and Pathology: Sensibility in the Literature and Medicine of Eighteenth-Century France* (Baltimore: Johns Hopkins University Press, 1998). There are many fine studies on sensibility in the eighteenth-century British and early American contexts. See in particular Graham J. Barker-Benfield, *The Culture of Sensibility: Sex and Society in Eighteenth-Century Britain* (Chicago: University of Chicago Press, 1992); Lynn M. Festa, *Sentimental Figures of Empire in Eighteenth-Century Britain and France* (Baltimore: Johns Hopkins University Press, 2006); and Sarah Knott, *Sensibility and the American Revolution* (Chapel Hill: University of North Carolina Press, 2009). For an incisive overview, see Alexander Cook, "Feeling Better: Moral Sense and Sensibility in Enlightenment Thought," in *The Discourse of Sensibility: The Knowing Body in the Enlightenment*, ed. H. M. Lloyd, *Studies in History and Philosophy of Science* 35 (2013), 85–103.

18. On eighteenth-century French medical vitalism, see Elizabeth A. Williams, *The Physical and the Moral: Anthropology, Physiology, and Philosophical Medicine in France, 1750–1850* (Cambridge: Cambridge University Press, 1994), *A Cultural History of Medical Vitalism in Enlightenment Montpellier* (Burlington, Vt.: Ashgate, 2003), and "Of Two Lives One? Jean-Charles-Marguerite-Guillaume Grimaud and the Question of Holism in Vitalist Medicine," *Science in Context* 21:4 (2008), 593–613. See also the overviews provided in Roselyne Rey, *Naissance et développement du vitalisme en France de la deuxième moitié du 18e siècle à la fin du Premier Empire*, SVEC 381 (2000); and Charles T. Wolfe, ed., *Vitalism Without Metaphysics? Medical Vitalism in the Enlightenment*, *Science in Context* 21:4 (2008).

19. On the German context, see Albrecht Koschorke, "Physiological Self-Regulation: The Eighteenth-Century Modernization of the Human Body," *MLN* 123 (2008), 469–84. On sensibility in Scottish medical and social theory, see Christopher Lawrence, "The Nervous System and Society in the Scottish Enlightenment," in *Natural Order: Historical Studies of Scientific Culture*, ed. Barry Barnes and Steven Shapin (Beverly Hills, Calif.: Sage, 1979), 19–40; and Megan J. Coyer and David E. Shuttleton, eds., *Scottish Medicine and Literary Culture, 1726–1832* (Amsterdam: Rodopi, 2014). On the history of the theory of "diffused" sensibility and contractility, see Michael Gross, "The Lessened Locus of Feelings: A Transformation in French Physiology in the Early Nineteenth Century," *Journal of the History of Biology* 12:2 (1979), 231–71. For overviews of sensibility in relation to mechanism in European natural philosophy, see Stephen Gaukroger, *The Collapse of Mechanism and the Rise of Sensibility: Science and the Shaping of Modernity, 1680–1760* (Oxford: Oxford University Press, 2010), and *The Natural and the Human: Science and the Shaping of Modernity, 1739–1841* (Oxford: Oxford University Press, 2016); and Peter Reill, *Vitalizing Nature in the Enlightenment* (Berkeley: University of California Press, 2005).

20. Lisa Wynne Smith notes this about consultation letters written by English and French women patients during this era: "humoralism fundamentally shaped sufferers' experiences of their bodies, as revealed by descriptions of internal sensations and body/mind overlap"; "'An Account of an Unaccountable Distemper': The Experience of Pain in Early Eighteenth-Century England and France," *Eighteenth-Century Studies* 41:4 (2008), 459–80, citation at 463.

21. Williams, *Physical and the Moral*, 8.

22. Jean-Jacques Rousseau, *Les Confessions*, *Œuvres complètes*, vol. 1, ed. Bernard Gagnebin, Marcel Raymond et al. (Paris: Gallimard, 1959), 409.

23. Denis Diderot, *Le Rêve de d'Alembert*, *Œuvres complètes*, ed. Herbert Dieckmann, Jacques Proust, and Jean Varloot (Paris: Hermann, 1987), vol. 17, 127–29 (henceforth abbreviated DPV).

24. Janković, "Exposed and Vulnerable," in *Confronting the Climate: British Airs and the Making of Environmental Medicine* (New York: Palgrave Macmillan, 2010), 15–40.

25. Michel Foucault, *Histoire de la folie à l'âge classique* (Paris: Gallimard, 1972), 314.

26. See Alexander Cook, "The Politics of Pleasure Talk in Eighteenth-Century Europe," *Sexualities* 12 (August 2009), 451–66.

27. This is drawn from Gary Hatfield's historical account of psychology in "Remaking the Science of Mind: Psychology as Natural Science," in *Inventing Human Science: Eighteenth-Century Domains*, ed. Christopher Fox, Roy Porter, and Robert Wokler (Berkeley: University of California Press, 1995), 184–231, see esp. 189–96.

28. See Stéphane Van Damme's overview in "Philosophe, Philosopher," in *Cambridge Companion to the French Enlightenment*, ed. Daniel Brewer (Cambridge: Cambridge University Press, 2014), 153–66, and his more developed remarks in *A toutes voiles vers la vérité. Une autre histoire de la philosophie au temps des Lumières* (Paris: Éditions du Seuil, 2014). See also Dinah Ribard, "Philosophe ou écrivain? Problèmes de délimitation entre histoire littéraire et histoire de la philosophie en France, 1650–1850," *Annales. Histoire, Sciences Sociales* 55:2 (2000), 355–88.

29. Fernando Vidal, *Les sciences de l'âme, XVI–XVIIIe siècle* (Paris: Honoré Champion, 2006), 23; Hatfield, "Remaking the Science of Mind," 196.

30. Karl M. Figlio, "Theories of Perception and the Physiology of Mind in the Late Eighteenth Century," *History of Science* 13 (1975), 177–212, at 197. Figlio is paraphrasing Haller's discussion of the mental faculties in *First Lines of Physiology*, ed. William Cullen (Edinburgh: Charles Elliot, 1786).

31. Tobias Cheung, "Omnis Fibra Ex Fibra: Fibre Economies in Bonnet's and Diderot's Models of Organic Order," in *Transitions and Borders Between Animals, Humans and Machines 1600–1800*, ed. Tobias Cheung, Charles T. Wolfe, and Ann Thomson (Leiden: Brill, 2010), 66–104, at 67–68. On the centrality of the "fiber body" in the British context, see Hisao Ishizuka, *Fiber, Medicine, and Culture in the British Enlightenment* (New York: Palgrave Macmillan, 2016).

32. Charles Bonnet, *Essai analytique sur les facultés de l'âme* (Geneva: Slatkine Reprints, 1970), xiii.

33. *Essai de psychologie ou considérations sur les opérations de l'âme, sur l'habitude et sur l'éducation* (London: s.n., 1755), 13–14, analyzed in Cheung, "Omnis Fibra Ex Fibra," 88–89.

34. "Another model of the soul-body-interface is the puppeteer-marionette-relation," which Julien Offray de la Mettrie mentioned in *L'homme machine* (1748); Cheung, "Omnis Fibra Ex Fibra," 89, n61.

35. Caroline Jacot Grapa, *Dans le vif du sujet: Diderot corps et âme* (Paris: Classiques Garnier, 2009), 267–90.

36. Guillaume Barrera notes that the analogy between the mind/soul and a spider in its web can be found in works by Stoics like Chrysippe and in Pierre Bayle; Montesquieu, "Essai sur les causes qui peuvent affecter les esprits et les caractères," in *Œuvres complètes de Montesquieu*, ed. Jean Ehrard and Catherine Volpilhac-Auger, 22 vols. (Oxford: Voltaire Foundation, 2006), vol. 9, 241n78.

37. Cheung, "Omnis Fibra Ex Fibra," 69.

38. Montesquieu, "Essai sur les causes," 241. For discussions of Montesquieu's use of the "spider in its web" analogy, see Vidal, *Les Sciences de l'âme*, 118, and Josué Harari, *Scenarios of the Imaginary: Theorizing the French Enlightenment* (Ithaca, N.Y.: Cornell University Press, 1987), 94–95.

39. Montesquieu, "Essai sur les causes," 241. The "unsuspected" body parts to which Montesquieu was alluding were the reproductive organs: in the next paragraph, he shifted to the topic of eunuchs (241–42).

40. Montesquieu, "Essai sur les causes," 253.

41. See Julien-Joseph Virey's treatment of racial types in *Histoire naturelle du genre humain*, 2nd expanded ed. (1824), discussed in Claude Blanckaert, "J.-J. Virey, observateur de l'homme (1800–1825)," in *Julien-Joseph Virey, naturaliste et anthropologue*, ed. Claude Bénichou and Claude Blanckaert (Paris: Vrin, 1988), 97–182.

42. Roger Chartier, for example, refers briefly to Tissot in "The Man of Letters," in *Enlightenment Portraits*, ed. Michel Vovelle, trans. Lydia G. Cochrane (Chicago: University of Chicago Press, 1997), at 176–78.

43. Caricatures did, of course, persist. See, for instance, Alexandre Wenger, "Sangrado and Eighteenth-Century Caricatures of the Physician," in *Portrayals of Medicine, Physicians, Patients, and Illnesses in French Literature from the Middle Ages to the Present: A Collection of Essays*, ed. Philippa Kim and Lison Baselis-Bitoun (New York: Mellen Press, 2011), 207–36.

44. See Catriona Seth, *Les rois aussi en mourraient: Les Lumières en lutte contre la petite vérole* (Paris: Editions Desjonquères, 2008), and "Textually Transmitted Diseases: Smallpox Inoculation in French Literary and Medical Works," SVEC 2013:04, 125–38.

45. Daniel Roche, *Les Républicains des lettres: Gens de culture et Lumières au XVIIIe siècle* (Paris: Fayard, 1998), 308–30.

46. On the role of the *Encyclopédie* and Paris medical journalism in circulating medical information, see Williams, *Cultural History of Medical Vitalism*, 120–29.

47. See, for example, Le Camus, *Abdeker, ou l'art de conserver la beauté* (1754), and Paumerelle, *La Philosophie des vapeurs* (1774).

48. Janković, *Confronting the Climate*, 36.

49. Séverine Pilloud and Micheline Louis-Courvoisier, "The Intimate Experience of the Body in the Eighteenth Century: Between Interiority and Exteriority," *Medical History* 47:4 (2003), 451–72, at 455.

50. Alain Corbin points out the value of diaries for historians interested in hearing the "murmuring of the viscera to which the elite . . . were so attentive before the emergence of psychoanalysis"; *Time, Desire and Horror: Toward a History of the Senses*, trans. Jean Birrell (Cambridge, U.K.: Polity Press, 1995), 185.

51. See Colin Jones, "The Great Chain of Buying: Medical Advertisement, the Bourgeois Public Sphere, and the Origins of the French Revolution," *American Historical Review* 101:1 (February 1996), 13–40.

52. See Philip Rieder, "Médecins et patients à Genève: Offre et consommations thérapeutiques à l'époque moderne," *Revue d'histoire moderne et contemporaine* 52:1 (2005), 39–63; Micheline Louis-Courvoisier and Séverine Pilloud, "Le malade et son entourage au XVIIIe siècle: Les médiations dans les consultations épistolaires adressées au Dr Tissot," *Revue médicale de la Suisse romande* 120 (2000), 939–44; and Pilloud, *Les mots du corps: Expérience de la maladie dans les lettres de patients à un médecin du 18e siècle: Samuel Auguste Tissot* (Lausanne: Éditions BHMS, 2013), 111–69.

53. E. C. Spary, *Eating the Enlightenment: Food and the Sciences in Paris, 1670–1760* (Chicago: University of Chicago Press, 2012), 1, 6.

54. Brockliss and Jones, *Medical World of Early Modern France*, 441–73.

55. Baldine Saint Girons emphasizes that eighteenth-century notions of genius carried traces of two distinct ancient notions: on the one hand, "the conception of genius as furor, delirium, divine or demoniacal inspiration, enthusiasm . . . , and on the other hand, the conception of genius as *ingenium*, natural dispositions or talent"; "Génie," in *Le Dictionnaire européen des Lumières*, ed. Michel Delon (Paris: Presses Universitaires de France, 1997), 496–99, at 496.

56. See Sarah Knott and Barbara Taylor, "General Introduction," in *Women, Gender and Enlightenment*, ed. S. Knott and B. Taylor (Basingstoke, U.K.: Palgrave Macmillan, 2005), xv–xxi, at xvii. Adeline Gargam does a comprehensive survey of such efforts in the "long" eighteenth-century French context, in *Les Femmes savantes, lettrées et cultivées dans la littérature française des Lumières, ou, La conquête d'une légitimité (1690–1804)*, 2 vols. (Paris: Champion, 2013).

57. See Huguette Krief, "Retraite féminine et femmes moralistes au siècle des Lumières," *Dix-huitième siècle* 48 (2016), 89–101.

58. Châtelet, *Discours sur le bonheur* (Paris: Payot et Rivages, 1997), 53. Barbara Whitehead points out the highly personal tone of this short essay—a trait that set it apart from the universalizing tendencies of contemporary male moralists who wrote

on happiness: "The Singularity of Mme Du Châtelet: An Analysis of the *Discours sur le bonheur*," SVEC 2006:01, 255–76.

59. See Judith P. Zinsser, *La Dame d'esprit: A Biography of the Marquise Du Châtelet* (New York: Viking, 2006).

60. Renaud Redien-Collot, "Émilie Du Châtelet et les femmes: Entre l'attitude prométhéenne et la pleine assomption du statut de minoritaire," SVEC 2006:01, 277–91.

61. See Julie Chandler Hayes, "Sex and Gender, Feeling and Thinking: Imagining Women as Intellectuals," in *Cambridge Companion to the French Enlightenment*, 91–104, at 93; and Joan de Jean, *Ancients Against Moderns: Culture Wars and the Making of a Fin de Siècle* (Chicago: University of Chicago Press, 1997), 75–77.

62. See Lorraine Daston, "The Naturalized Female Intellect," *Science in Context* 5:2 (1992), 209–35.

63. "The most poetically organized man is, in truth, lacking in material strength; that, perhaps, is the meaning of the saying of an ancient writer: 'heroic souls have no bodies' ": Réveillé-Parise, *Physiologie et hygiène des hommes livrés aux travaux de l'esprit ou Recherches sur le physique et le moral, les habitudes, les maladies et le régime des gens de lettres* [1834], 4th ed., 2 vols. (Paris: Chez G.-A. Dentu, 1843), vol. 1, 104.

64. See Philip Rieder's analysis of Charrière in *La Figure du patient au XVIIIe siècle* (Geneva: Droz, 2010), 90–111.

65. Hayes, "Sex and Gender," 97.

66. Gary Kelly, "Bluestocking Work: Learning, Literature, and Lore in the Onset of Modernity," in *Bluestockings Now! The Evolution of a Social Role*, ed. Deborah Heller (Burlington, Vt.: Ashgate, 2015), 175–208, at 186.

67. Anne Thérèse de Lambert, *Réflexions nouvelles sur les femmes* (Paris: Côté-Femmes Éditions, 1989), 39. After circulating in manuscript form among Mme de Lambert's friends, this work was published without her permission in 1727.

68. On the "avalanche" of antifeminist comedies produced during the eighteenth century (particularly by *anti-philosophe* playwrights), see Florence Lotterie, *Le Genre des Lumières: Femme et philosophe au XVIIIe siècle* (Paris: Classiques Garnier, 2013), 38–48; and Gargam, *Les Femmes savantes, lettrées*, vol. 2, 537–618. Gargam's inventory includes avatars of the *femme savante* persona who appeared in narrative fiction as well as theater. On the longer tradition of *femme savante* parodies—and efforts to refute them—see Linda Timmermans, *L'Accès des femmes à la culture (1598–1715)* (Paris: Champion, 1993), esp. 320–35.

69. Jean-Noël Pascal notes that, despite the eighteenth century's valorization of sociability, many sorts of writing stressed the coexistence of community and solitude, of "participation in society and distance from the world": "Du cabinet du sage à la chaumière des amants: Variations poétiques sur la retraite (1760–1810)," *Dix-huitième siècle* 48 (2016), 103–19, at 104.

70. I am adapting an expression from Van Damme, "Philosophe, Philosopher," 155.

71. The term "pathography," as McMahon notes, was coined by the nineteenth-century German neurologist Paul Julius Möbius "to describe what was by then a flourishing genre" (*Divine Fury*, 162).

72. See Heinich, *L'Élite artiste: Excellence et singularité en régime démocratique* (Paris: Gallimard, 2005), and "Genius Versus Democracy: Excellence and Singularity in Postrevolutionary France," in Chaplin and McMahon, *Genealogies of Genius*, 29–42.

73. Christopher Forth, *The Dreyfus Affair and the Crisis of French Manhood* (Baltimore: Johns Hopkins University Press, 2004), 13.

74. See Anne Deneys-Tunney, *Écritures du corps: De Descartes à Laclos* (Paris: Presses Universitaires de France, 1992); Natania Meeker, *Voluptuous Philosophy: Literary Materialism in the French Enlightenment* (New York: Fordham University Press, 2006); and Mary Helen McMurran and Alison Conway, eds., *Mind, Body, Motion, Matter: Eighteenth-Century British and French Literary Perspectives* (Toronto: University of Toronto Press, 2016). See also Caroline Bynum's remarks on constructivist theoretical approaches to the body in "Why All the Fuss About the Body? A Medievalist's Perspective," *Critical Inquiry* 22:1 (Autumn 1995), 1–33, esp. 1–6.

75. Studies examining intellectual identity from the angle of sexuality include Raymond Stephanson, *The Yard of Wit: Male Creativity and Sexuality, 1650–1750* (Philadelphia: University of Pennsylvania Press, 2004); and A. D. Nuttall, *Dead from the Waist Down: Scholars and Scholarship in Literature and the Popular Imagination* (New Haven, Conn.: Yale University Press, 2003).

76. Bertrand Taithe and Mark Jenner describe the "sexual fix" as the collapsing of the history of the body into the history of sexuality and sexual difference; "The Historiographical Body," in *Medicine in the Twentieth Century*, ed. John Pickstone and Roger Cooter (New York: Harwood, 2000), 187–200, at 198–99.

77. See Jean Starobinski, "Brève histoire de la conscience du corps," *Revue française de psychanalyse* 45:2 (1981), 261–80; and François Azouvi, "Quelques jalons dans la préhistoire des sensations internes," *Revue de synthèse*, 3rd ser., T. CXV, no. 113–14 (1984), 113–33. For a general overview of this period's widespread insistence on the organic underpinnings of human nature, see Xavier Martin, *Régénérer l'espèce humaine: Utopie médicale et Lumières, 1750–1850* (Bouère: Dominique Martin Morin, 2008), 9–59.

78. Clark Lawlor makes a similar point about "the mediation between the biomedical and cultural perspectives on disease" in eighteenth-century Britain: *Consumption and Literature: The Making of the Romantic Disease* (Basingstoke, U.K.: Palgrave, 2006), 4.

79. I am borrowing loosely from the lecture of January 10, 1979, in Foucault, *The Birth of Biopolitics: Lectures at the Collège de France, 1978–1979*, ed. Michel Senellart, trans. Graham Burchel (New York: Palgrave Macmillan, 2010), 19.

80. On epistolary medical consultation, see (among other studies) Patrick Singy, "Medicine and the Senses: The Perception of Essences," in *The Cultural History of the Senses in the Enlightenment*, ed. Anne C. Vila (London: Bloomsbury, 2014), 133–53;

and Micheline Louis-Courvoisier, "Rendre sensible une souffrance physique: Lettres de mélancoliques au 18e siècle," *Dix-huitième siècle* 47:1 (2015), 87–101.

81. See J. Taschereau et al, *Catalogue des sciences médicales. Bibliothèque impériale, Département des imprimés*, 3 vols. (Paris: Firmin Didot Frères, Fils et Cie, 1857–89). In his preface, Taschereau singled out the alienist Dubois d'Amiens, then Perpetual Secretary of the French Academy of Sciences, as the main architect of the classifications used in this catalog: "A son Excellence Monsieur le Ministre de l'Instruction publique et des Cultes," *Catalogue des sciences médicales*, vol. I, i–iii, at ii. See Foucault, *Naissance de la clinique. Une archéologie du regard médical* (Paris: Presses Universitaires de France, 1963); and *Histoire de la folie à l'âge classique*.

82. See Pilloud, *Les mots du corps*, 279–81. On the broader topic of medical storytelling during the eighteenth century and its connections to literature, see Sophie Vasset, ed., *Medicine and Narration in the Eighteenth Century*, SVEC 2013:04. On the role of textual practices in the invention of hysteria, see Sabine Arnaud, *L'invention de l'hystérie au temps des Lumières (1670–1820)* (Paris: École des Hautes Études en Sciences Sociales, 2014), translated into English as *On Hysteria: The Invention of a Medical Category Between 1670 and 1820* (Chicago: University of Chicago Press, 2016).

83. On Lamy, Caraccioli, and the larger tradition of introspection, see Jacot Grapa, *Dans le vif du sujet*, 54–66. As she emphasizes, the vocabulary of interiority also led toward the insides of the body, particularly among thinkers intent on articulating psyche and soma (184–85).

84. Fernando Vidal, "Brains, Bodies, Selves, and Science: Anthropologies of Identity and the Resurrection of the Body," *Critical Inquiry* 28 (2002), 930–74, at 936.

85. See, for example, Christopher Lawrence and Steven Shapin, eds., *Science Incarnate: Historical Embodiments of Natural Knowledge* (Chicago: University of Chicago Press, 1998); Sirotkina, *Diagnosing Literary Genius*; Rieder, *La Figure du patient*; and Miriam Nicoli, *Les savants et les livres. Autour d'Albrecht von Haller (1708–1777) et Samuel-Auguste Tissot (1728–1797)* (Geneva: Slatkine, 2013).

86. See Marcel Proust, "Contre Sainte-Beuve" [1908], in *Marcel Proust on Art and Literature, 1896–1919*, trans. Sylvia Townsend Warner, 2nd ed. (New York: Carroll and Graf, 1997), 17–276; and Michel Foucault, "What Is an Author?" [1969], in *Textual Strategies: Perspectives in Post-Structuralist Criticism*, ed. Josué V. Harari (Ithaca, N.Y.: Cornell University Press, 1979), 141–60.

87. On *physiologie* as a literary genre, see Juan Rigoli, "Le Roman de la médecine," in *Littérature et médecine: Approches et perspectives*, ed. Andreas Carlino and Alexandre Wenger (Geneva: Droz, 2007), 199–226; and Valérie Stiénon, *La Littérature des physiologies: Sociopoétique d'un genre panoramique (1830–1845)* (Paris: Classiques Garnier, 2012). On "physiological" or "semiological" literary criticism and reactions against it, see Rigoli, *Lire le délire*, 552–89.

Chapter 1

1. *Pensées choisies de Blaise Pascal: Publiées sur les manuscrits originaux et mises en ordre à l'usage des lycées et des collèges* (Paris: J. Delalain et Fils, 1882), 256. While he

valorized the Christian paradigm of suffering, Pascal did not advocate the Christian condemnation of knowledge.

2. On the rise of the intellectual in eighteenth-century Europe, see (among many studies) Didier Masseau, *L'invention de l'intellectuel dans l'Europe du XVIIIe siècle* (Paris: Presses Universitaires de France, 1994).

3. On monomania and obsession, see Jan Goldstein, *Console and Classify: The French Psychiatric Profession in the Nineteenth Century* (Chicago: University of Chicago Press, 1987), 152–96; Lennard J. Davis, *Obsession: A History* (Chicago: University of Chicago Press, 2008); and Marina Van Zuylen, *Monomania: The Flight from Everyday Life in Literature and Art* (Ithaca, N.Y.: Cornell University Press, 2005). Studies of the nineteenth-century writer or artist as a "sick" hero include Alan Pasco, *Sick Heroes: French Society and Literature in the Romantic Age, 1750–1850* (Exeter, U.K.: University of Exeter Press, 1997); Pascal Brissette, *La Malédiction littéraire: Du poète crotté au génie malheureux* (Montreal: Presses de l'Universite' de Montréal, 2005); Felluga, *Perversity of Poetry*; Grauby, *Le corps de l'artiste*; and Myriam Roman, "Avatars romanesques du penseur chez Mme de Staël, Balzac et Hugo," *Romantisme* 34:124 (2004), 89–102.

4. Letual, *Essai sur la mélancolie* (Strasbourg: Levrault, 1810), 1.

5. Rousseau, "Préface à *Narcisse, ou l'Amant de lui-même*" (1752), in *Œuvres complètes*, ed. Bernard Gagnebin, Marcel Raymond et al., 5 vols. (Paris: Gallimard, 1964), vol. 2, 966; Preface to Narcisse, in *Collected Writings of Rousseau*, ed. Roger D. Masters and Christopher Kelly; trans. Judith R. Bush, Roger D. Masters, and Christopher Kelly, 13 vols. (Hanover, N.H.: University Press of New England, 1992), vol. 2, 192, translation slightly modified.

6. Rousseau, *Discours sur l'origine et les fondements de l'inégalité parmi les hommes* (1755), in *Œuvres complètes*, vol. 3 (1964), 138; *Discourse on the Origins of Inequality (Second Discourse)*, in *Collected Writings of Rousseau*, vol. 3, 23, translation slightly modified.

7. See Ronan Chalmin, *Lumières et corruption* (Paris: Honoré Champion, 2010); and Sean M. Quinlan, *The Great Nation in Decline: Sex, Modernity and Health Crises in Revolutionary France c. 1750–1850* (Aldershot, U.K.: Ashgate, 2007).

8. See, for example, François Azouvi's preface to the 1981 re-edition of Tissot, *La santé des gens de lettres* (Geneva: Slatkine Reprints, 1981), v.

9. On the rise of hygiene as a medical branch, see Brockliss and Jones, *Medical World of Early Modern France*, 441–79; Matthew Ramsey, "Medicine in France, 1650–1900," in *The Popularization of Medicine, 1650–1850*, ed. Roy Porter (London: Routledge, 1992), 97–133; and William Coleman, "Health and Hygiene in the *Encyclopédie*: A Medical Doctrine for the Bourgeoisie," *Journal of the History of Medicine* (October 1974), 399–421.

10. See Dinah Ribard, "Pathologies intellectuelles et littérarisation de la médecine: Une voie pour l'histoire du travail intellectuel," in *Littérature et médecine: Approches*

et perspectives (XVIe–XIXe siècle), ed. Andrea Carlino and Alexandre Wenger (Geneva: Droz, 2007), 113–34.

11. Pomme, *Essai sur les affections vaporeuses des deux sexes* (Paris: Desaint et Saillant, 1760), 28–29.

12. Pressavin, *Nouveau traité des vapeurs, ou Traité des maladies des nerfs, dans lequel on développe les vrais principes des vapeurs* (Paris: Chez la Veuve Reguilliat, 1770), 222–24.

13. Ramazzini, *De Morbis Artificium diatriba* (Modena: Typis Antonii Capponi impressoris episcopalis, Capponi, Antonio 1700); translated as *Treatise of the Diseases of Tradesmen, Shewing the Various Influence of Particular Trades Upon the State of Health* (London: Andrew Bell, Ralph Smith, Daniel Midwinter et al., 1705), 246. Other citations to this work appear parenthetically in the text. On the historical significance of this work, see Arlette Farge, "Les artisans malades de leur travail," *Annales. Histoire, Sciences Sociales* 32:5 (1977), 993–1006; and J. S. Felton, "The Heritage of Bernardino Ramazzini," *History of Occupational Medicine* 47:3 (1997), 167–79.

14. On those groups, see Lindsay Wilson, *Women and Medicine in the French Enlightenment* (Baltimore: Johns Hopkins University Press, 1993), 141–48.

15. See Roche, *Les Républicains des lettres*, 308–30.

16. See George S. Rousseau's introduction to John Hill, *Hypochondriasis: A Practical Treatise, 1766* (Los Angeles: William Andrews Clark Memorial Library, 1969), i–xii; German E. Berrios, "Hypochondriasis: A History of the Concept," in *Hypochondriasis: Modern Perspectives on an Ancient Malady*, ed. Vladan Starcevic and Don R. Lipsitt (New York: Oxford University Press, 2001), 3–20; and Guenter B. Risse, "In the Name of Hygieia and Hippocrates: A Quest for the Preservation of Health and Virtue," in *New Medical Challenges During the Scottish Enlightenment*, Clio Medica, vol. 76 (Amsterdam: Editions Rodopi, 2005), 135–69.

17. Nicholas Robinson, *A New System of the Spleen, Vapours, and Hypochondriack Melancholy, Wherein All the Decay of the Nerves, and Lowness of the Spirit, Are Mechanically Accounted For* (London: Bettesworth, Innys, and Rivington, 1729), 22, cited in Carolyn Houlihan Flynn, "Running Out of Matter: The Body Exercised in Eighteenth-Century Fiction," in *The Languages of Psyche: Mind and Body in Enlightenment Thought*, ed. G. S. Rousseau (Berkeley: University of California Press, 1991), 147–85, at 156.

18. Anita Guerrini, *Obesity and Depression in the Enlightenment: The Life and Times of George Cheyne* (Norman: University of Oklahoma Press, 2000), 150. Guerrini borrows the last term from Thomas W. Laqueur, "Bodies, Details, and the Humanitarian Narrative," in *The New Cultural History*, ed. Lynn Hunt (Berkeley: University of California Press, 1989), 176–204. See also Sylvie Kleiman-Lafon, "The Healing Power of Words: Medicine as Literature in Bernard Mandeville's Treatise of the Hypochondriack and Hysterick Diseases," *SVEC* 2013:04, 161–81.

19. On Le Camus, see Alexandre Wenger, *La fibre littéraire: Le discours médical sur la lecture au XVIIIe siècle* (Geneva: Droz, 2007), 90–95, passim; Mary Terrall, "Material

Impressions: Conception, Sensibility and Inheritance," in *Vital Matters: Eighteenth-Century Views of Conception, Life, and Death*, ed. Helen Deutsch and Mary Terrall (Toronto: University of Toronto Press, 2012), 109–29; and Gaukroger, *Natural and the Human*, 144–45.

20. "Hypochondriacal (passion or affection): This is the term ordinarily used by physicians to designate a species of malady related to melancholy, since atrabile is also its morbific humor, which infects the entire mass of fluids . . . but settles particularly on the organs or viscera of the lower abdomen"; "Hypochondriaque," in *Encyclopédie, ou dictionnaire raisonné des sciences, des arts et des métiers, etc.*, ed. Denis Diderot and Jean le Rond d'Alembert, University of Chicago, ARTFL Encyclopédie Project (Spring 2016), ed. Robert Morrissey and Glenn Roe, http://encyclopedie.uchicago.edu, vol. 8, 408–9 (hereafter abbreviated as ENCYC plus volume and page numbers).

21. On Fabre, see my article "The *Médecin philosophe* as Drama Critic: Pierre Fabre's Natural History of French Theater," *SVEC* 314 (1993–94), 231–48.

22. Pinel, *Traité médico-philosophique sur l'aliénation mentale, ou la manie* (Paris: Richard, Caille et Ravier, an IX [1800]; reprint, Paris: l'Harmattan, 2006), 111; cited in Rigoli, *Lire le délire*, 434.

23. The "pauvre diable" figure is exemplified by the case of Nicolas Gilbert, a failed poet and *anti-philosophe* of the late eighteenth century, whom I discuss in Chapter 6. More generally, see Henri Duranton, ed., *Le Pauvre diable: Destins de l'homme de lettres au XVIIIe siècle* (Saint-Etienne: Publications de l'Université de Saint-Etienne, 2006).

24. Ribard, "Pathologies intellectuelles," 125–32.

25. Tissot, *De la santé des gens de lettres*, 3rd rev. ed. (Lausanne: Grasset, 1775), 128. Henceforth abbreviated as *SGL* and cited in parentheses in the text. This edition is the source of all citations I make to this book.

26. On the Renaissance topos of idleness, see Virginia Krause, *Idle Pursuits: Literature and Oisiveté in the French Renaissance* (Newark: University of Delaware Press, 2003). Anson Rabinbach locates the disappearance of idleness and an accompanying shift to an association of work with fatigue in the nineteenth century; *The Human Motor: Energy, Fatigue, and the Origins of Modernity* (New York: Basic Books, 1990), 1–44.

27. Garnier, *L'homme de lettres* (Paris: Panckoucke, 1764). On Garnier, see Rémy G. Saisselin, *The Literary Enterprise in Eighteenth-Century France* (Detroit, Mich.: Wayne State University Press, 1979), 135–40; and Chartier, "Man of Letters."

28. Pierre Saint-Amand, *The Pursuit of Laziness: An Idle Interpretation of the Enlightenment*, trans. Jennifer Curtiss Gage (Princeton, N.J.: Princeton University Press, 2011).

29. Roche, *Les Républicains des lettres*, 233.

30. Montesquieu, "Discours prononcé à la rentrée de l'Académie de Bordeaux" [1717], in *Œuvres complètes*, vol. 1, 6–7.

31. "Both *gens de bras* and *gens de métier* engaged in manual labor, but only the labor of the *gens de métier* was raised by the application of intelligence to the level of art"; William Hamilton Sewell, *Work and Revolution in France: The Language of Labor from the Old Regime to 1848* (Cambridge: Cambridge University Press, 1980), 21–22.

32. "The glorious professions that produce, to varying degrees, esteem and distinction, and that all tend to foster the public good, are religion, arms, justice, politics, the administration of state revenues, commerce, letters, and the fine arts. Honest professions are farming and useful trades"; Jaucourt, "Profession," in ENCYC, vol. 13: 426; cited in Roche, *Les Républicains des lettres*, 235.

33. Tissot, for instance, depicted the simple life of the peasant as healthful but devoid of interesting sensations or sentiments; *Essai sur les maladies des gens du monde* [1770] (Paris: Chez Didot, 1771), 26–36.

34. The 1762 *Dictionnaire de l'Académie française* describes "contention" as referring primarily to a debate or dispute involving two parties, but it also mentions the intellectual meaning that was ascribed to the term: "People say *mental exertion* to refer to great, extreme application of the mind. *He is working on that, he is applying himself with great mental exertion. Mental exertion is altering his health*" (382; italics in the original) (accessed via the ARTFL Project, https://artfl-project.uchicago.edu/content/dictionnaires-dautrefois).

35. Diderot, "Contention," in ENCYC, vol. 4: 111–12.

36. "It is the effect of a considerable effort. It is said about the body and the mind, and it is sometimes used to refer to the work itself: people say both the work and the fatigue of war; yet one is the cause, and the other the effect. We must also point out that in the example we just gave, the word 'work' can have two meanings, one relative to the person, and the other to the piece of work"; Diderot, "Fatigue," in ENCYC, vol. 6: 429. By 1776, the exhaustion created by mental exertion was deemed specific enough to warrant a separate dictionary entry: see Frédéric Grunwald, "Exercice immodéré de l'esprit (Physiologie)," in *Supplément à l'Encyclopédie ou dictionnaire des sciences, des arts et des métiers*, ed. Jean Baptiste Robinet, 4 vols. (Amsterdam: Chez M.M. Rey, 1776–77), vol. 2, 915.

37. See the definition of *surmener* in the 1762 *Dictionnaire de l'Académie française*. The *Trésor de la langue française* traces the first occurrence of the noun *surmenage* to a discussion of veterinary medicine in an 1845 re-edition of Boyer's *Traité des maladies chirurgicales*. Cadart's *Le surmenage au collège* (1888) illustrates the later, pedagogical use of the term—whose use increased greatly after 1880, according to the *Dictionnaire vivant de la langue française* (http://dvlf.uchicago.edu/mot/surmenage).

38. Cited in Roche, *Les Républicains des lettres*, 226.

39. "I do not think that anyone can deny the existence of a general spasm during major mental exertions: this is indicated by the very word 'exertion,' because it supposes an extraordinary effort. These sorts of labors entail a rallying of all the [body's] activated forces, which are directed toward the organs whose functioning is necessary for the operations being meditated. . . . Whoever speaks of mental exertion implies a

excessive tension in the nervous system; I'd go so far as to say that the exhaustion which follows intense meditations is a clear sign that a considerable action has taken place"; Robert, *Traité des principaux objets de la médecine* (Paris: Lacombe, 1766), 51.

40. Vandermonde, *Dictionnaire portatif de santé*, 2nd ed., 2 vols. (Paris: Chez Vincent, 1760), vol. 2, 80–81.

41. Sèze, *Recherches physiologiques et philosophiques sur la sensibilité* (Paris: Chez Prault, 1786), 226–27. This is a close paraphrase of a scenario presented in Roussel's *Système physique et moral de la femme* (1775), which Sèze praised in a note at the outset of his chapter (Sèze, *Recherches physiologiques*, 216); Roussel, *Système physique et moral de la femme, suivi du système physique et moral de l'homme, et d'un fragment sur la sensibilité* (Paris: Crapart, Caille et Ravier, 1805), 57.

42. Sèze, *Recherches physiologiques et philosophiques sur la sensibilité*, 228.

43. See, for example, the anonymous medical article "Oisiveté" in the *Encyclopédie*: "Work is the remedy to all the ailments that idleness brings with it. That is why the celebrated Locke ordains making young people exercise a lot, and getting them accustomed from an early age to work. This method would be more useful, and *gens de lettres* could take up the different exercise of the body, which would make them healthier and more robust" (ENCYC, vol. 11: 446).

44. On the therapeutic powers that eighteenth-century British novelists and physicians attributed to exercise, see Flynn, "Running Out of Matter," esp. 156.

45. Montesquieu, letter 87 of *Les Lettres persanes*, in *Œuvres complètes*, vol. 1, 261.

46. Vandermonde, *Dictionnaire portatif*, vol. 2, 80–81.

47. Lorry, *Essai sur l'usage des alimens, pour servir de commentaire aux livres diététiques d'Hippocrate* [1754], 2nd ed., 2 vols. (Paris: Vincent, 1757), vol. 2, 234.

48. Zimmermann, *Von der Erfahrung in der Arzneikunst* [1763]; French trans., *Traité de l'expérience en général, et en particulier dans l'art de guérir, traduit de l'allemand par Le Febvre de Villebrune (réimprimé sur l'édition de 1797)*, bound with P. J. Barthez, *Traité des maladies goutteuses* (Paris: A. Delahays, 1855), 477.

49. Ibid., 478.

50. Ménuret, "Manie (Médecine)," in ENCYC, vol. 10: 32.

51. The epigraph beginning this section is taken from a letter from Bonnet to Tissot, cited in Charles Eynard, *Essai sur la Vie de Tissot: Contenant des lettres inédites de Tronchin, Voltaire, Haller, Zimmermann, Rousseau, Bonnet, Stanislas Auguste II, Napoléon Bonaparte, etc.* (Lausanne: Ducloux, 1839), 153–54.

52. "The beauty of our country, our academy, and M. Tissot attract foreigners from every country, of all ages and all characters," writes Cécile's mother regarding Lausanne; *Lettres écrites de Lausanne*, in Isabelle de Charrière / Belle de Zuylen, *Oeuvres complètes*, ed. Jean-Daniel Candaux, et al., 10 vols. (Amsterdam: G. A. van Oorschot / Geneva: Editions Slatkine, 1980), vol. 8, 145.

53. Tissot is also regarded as a pioneer in neurology, particularly in the fields of migraine research and epileptology; see K. Karbowski, "Samuel Auguste Tissot (1728–1797): His Research on Migraine," *Journal of Neurology* 233:2 (April 1986), 123–25.

54. Vincent Barras and Micheline Louis-Courvoisier, eds., *Tout autour de Tissot* (Geneva: Georg Editeur, 2001), 1.

55. Three exceptions are F.-G. Boisseau's 1826 re-edition (which reproduced the Paris 1769 edition) and the 1859 re-edition by Bertrand de Saint-Germain and 1991 re-edition by Christophe Calame, which are both based on the 1775 edition.

56. One notable omission to Tissot's list of predecessors is the Dutch physician Nicolaas Heerkens, who had published a didactic poem *De valetudine literatorum* in 1749 and expanded it in 1790, in what Yasmin Haskell calls a "rather testy engagement" with Tissot; Haskell, "Physician, Heal Thyself! Emotions and the Health of the Learned in Samuel Auguste André Tissot (1728–1797) and Gerhard Nicolaas Heerkens (1726–1801)," in Lloyd, *Discourse of Sensibility*, 105–24, at 105.

57. M. de Brenles was Jacques Abram Daniel Clavel de Brenles (1717–71), a renowned lawyer and juris consult, and the friend of Voltaire as well as Tissot. See the notice about him in Albert de Montet, *Dictionnaire biographique des Genevois et des Vaudois qui se sont distingués dans leur pays ou à l'étranger par leurs talents, leurs actions, leurs œuvres littéraires ou artistiques* (Lausanne: G. Bridel, 1878), 173–74. For an analysis of the Brenles eulogy, see Ronan Y. Chalmin and Anne C. Vila, "Malade de son génie: Raconter les pathologies des gens de lettres, de Tissot à Balzac," *Dix-huitième siècle* 47:1 (2015), 55–71, at 64–68.

58. On Tissot's use of the stringed-instrument metaphor for nervous operations, see Alain Cernuschi, "Des 'cordes qui vibrent' aux 'cordes cachées.' Acoustique et musique dans le *Traité des nerfs* de Tissot," in *Tout autour de Tissot*, 295–311.

59. "I have known a gentlewoman of a most active mind, who, when intensely thinking, had all the nervous filaments of her forehead, and part of her visage, as visibly twitched and agitated, as the wires of a harpsichord are, when vibrating some sprightly air in music"; Kirkpatrick, "Annotator's Preface," in Tissot, *An Essay on Diseases Incident to Literary and Sedentary Persons, with Proper Rules for Preventing Their Fatal Consequences, and Instructions for Their Cure, with a Preface and Notes by J. Kirkpatrick, M.D.*, trans. James Kirkpatrick (London: Norse and Dilly, 1769), xx–xxi.

60. François Rosset, "Samuel-Auguste Tissot: Le Docteur écrivain," in *Tout autour de Tissot*, 245–59, at 251.

61. This case came directly from Tissot's correspondence with Zimmermann, not from the *Traité de l'expérience* (even though Tissot attributed it to that work). Zimmermann first referred to it in a letter dated May 22, 1766, where he spoke of "a very intelligent young man who is incapable of any sustained attention and is suffering numerous pains as a result of extreme mental exertion"; Tissot and Zimmermann, *Correspondance 1754–1797*, ed. Antoinette Emch-Dériaz (Geneva: Slatkine, 2007), 332. In his letter of September 10, 1766, Zimmermann explained that "the observation concerning the Swiss gentleman . . . is not in the original" treatise (360).

62. On Rousseau's paradoxical aspects, see Jean Starobinski's classic study *Jean-Jacques Rousseau: La Transparence et l'obstacle* (Paris: Gallimard, 1971).

63. Tissot describes his hour-and-a-half meeting with Rousseau in a letter to Zimmermann dated July 13, 1762: "this short period of time will be a milestone in my life. I left liking the man as much as I admired the author; kind, polite, humble, frank, speaking with both ease and precision; and forcibly, neither talkative nor taciturn. Because he deeply loves his fellow human beings and does not question the notion that retreat is necessary to his health, he seeks only ways to make them [other people] happy; but . . . he has taken the firm resolution no longer to write because he no longer feels up to it"; *Correspondance 1754–1797*, 202.

64. Zimmermann, *Traité de l'expérience*, 286.

65. See Le Menthéour, *La Manufacture de maladies*, 82, 178, 249–51.

66. Singy, historiographical essay, in *L'usage du sexe: Lettres au Dr Tissot, auteur de L'Onanisme (1760)* (Lausanne: Éditions BHMS, 2014), 1–42.

67. Ibid., 29–30.

68. In his *Traité des nerfs et de leurs maladies,* Tissot asserted that "people are right in saying that it is up to medicine to treat the passions"; he also devoted a long chapter to the effects of various passions on nervous maladies. *Traité des nerfs et de leurs maladies*, 5 vols. (Paris: P. F. Didot le jeune, 1778–80), vol. 1, xxviii, and vol. 3 (Tome II, Part I), 280–444.

69. Singy, *L'usage du sexe*, 51.

70. Cited in ibid., 34.

71. "If a few men must be allowed to devote themselves to the study of the Sciences and Arts, it must be only those who feel the strength to walk alone in their footsteps and go beyond them. It is for these few to raise monuments to the glory of the human mind"; *Discours sur les sciences et les arts* [1750], in *Œuvres complètes*, vol. 3, 29; *First Discourse*, in *Collected Writings of Rousseau*, vol. 2, 21. Rousseau made that exception only for those of "vast" genius, "the Verulams [Bacon], the Descartes, the Newtons, those Preceptors of the human race."

72. Antoinette Emch-Dériaz, "The Non-Naturals Made Easy," in *The Popularization of Medicine, 1650–1850*, ed. Roy Porter (London: Routledge, 1992), 134–59. See also her discussion of *De la santé* in *Tissot, Physician of the Enlightenment* (New York: Peter Lang, 1992), 72–77.

73. Tissot's English translator, James Kirkpatrick, politely objected to his condemnation of tea drinking, calling it a product of Tissot's Swiss patriotism rather than his medical judgment; the Swiss, he commented, didn't import tea "at the lowest price" or consume it as much as the English (Tissot, *Essay on Diseases Incident*, 149).

74. Spary, *Eating the Enlightenment*, 250.

75. Williams conjectures that Tissot's views on overly intense educational programs were influenced by his "miserable days" as a medical student in Montpellier; *Cultural History of Medical Vitalism*, 60, 64.

76. Sauri, *Cours de philosophie : Élémens de métaphysique, ou Préservatif contre le matérialisme, l'athéisme et le déisme* (Paris: Chez Saillant et al., 1773), 177–215.

77. Buchan, *La Médecine domestique, ou traité complet des moyens de se conserver en santé, de traiter et de guérir les maladies par le régime et les remèdes simples*, trans. J. D. Duplanil, 3rd ed., 2 vols. (Paris: Chez Frouillé, 1783), vol. 1, 149. See Tissot, *SGL*, 134–35. Buchan acknowledged Duplanil's textual augmentations and thanked him for them in the preface to the 1790 edition; Buchan, *Domestic Medicine. Or, A Treatise on the Prevention and Cure of Diseases by Regimen and Simple Medicines*, 11th ed. (London: A. Strahan, 1790), v.

78. See Charles E. Rosenberg, "Medical Text and Social Context: Explaining William Buchan's *Domestic Medicine*," *Bulletin of the History of Medicine* 57 (1983), 22–42. Sharon Ruston contrasts Buchan's meliorist perspective on the bad health of learned men with the later Romantic notion of genius, in "The Medical Dangers of Literary Genius," *Literature and Medicine* 34: 2 (2016), 299–319.

79. Tissot, *De la santé des gens de lettres, suivi de l'Essai sur les maladies des gens du monde, nouvelle édition, revue sur les derniers manuscrits de l'auteur, et publiée par le Docteur Bertrand de Saint-Germain* (Paris: Techener, 1859), iii–v. Emch-Dériaz offers a chronology of the book's re-editions and translations in Tissot, *Physician of the Enlightenment*, 331–32.

80. Lloyd, "The Diseases of Occupation," in *Twentieth Century Practice: An International Encyclopedia of Modern Medical Science by Leading Authorities of Europe and America*, ed. Thomas L. Stedman, 20 vols. (London: Sampson Low, Marston, 1895), vol. 3, 312.

81. See Marijke Gijswijt-Hofstra and Roy Porter, eds., *Cultures of Neurasthenia: From Beard to the First World War* (Amsterdam: Rodopi, 2001).

82. Cited in Nicoli, *Les savants et les livres*, 145. See also the chapter on Bonnet in Rieder, *La Figure du patient*, 66–90.

83. Cited in Pilloud, *Les mots du corps*, 279.

84. Ibid., 279–81. For another analysis of the consultation letters that patients sent to Tissot, see Sonja Boon, *Telling the Flesh: Life Writing, Citizenship, and the Body in the Letters to Samuel Auguste Tissot* (Montreal: McGill-Queen's University Press, 2015).

85. Diderot, *Éléments de physiologie* [1778], in DPV, vol. 17, 334. A recent special issue of the journal *Literature and Medicine* explores the medical tradition of "pathological" reading since the Enlightenment. See particularly these articles: James Kennaway and Anita O'Connell, "Introduction: Pathological Reading"; and James Kennaway, "Two Kinds of 'Literary Poison': Diseases of the Learned and Overstimulating Novels in Georgian Britain," *Literature and Medicine* 34:2 (2016), 242–51, 252–77.

86. Boisseau, preface to Tissot, *De la santé des gens de lettres. Nouvelle édition augmentée d'une notice sur l'auteur et des notes*, ed. F.-G. Boisseau (Paris: J.-B. Baillière, 1826), xv–xvi.

87. Émile Beaugrand, "Lettres (Gens de), Hygiène," in A. Dechambre, et al., *Dictionnaire encyclopédique des sciences médicales*, 100 vols. (Paris: Masson et Asselin, 1868–89), sér. 2, vol. 2 (1869), 215–20, at 220.

88. On Rousseau's distrust of medicine, see Le Menthéour, *La Manufacture de maladies*. On his relationship with Tissot in the 1760s, see George Makari, *Soul Machine: The Invention of the Modern Mind* (New York: W. W. Norton, 2015), 289–90.

89. Rousseau, letter 121, in *Lettres (1728–1778)*, ed. Marcel Raymond (Lausanne: La Guilde du Livre, 1959), 243.

90. See Zimmermann, *Traité de l'expérience*, 480. Tissot described this illness in a letter of April 2, 1763; *Correspondance 1754–1797*, 218–19.

91. Voltaire was not, however, kind toward Tissot: he called him a "fabricator of little medical books" in a 1772 letter to the Marquise du Deffand; *Œuvres complètes de Voltaire. Correspondance générale*, 66 vols. (Paris: Chez Antoine-Augustin Renouard, 1819–25), vol. 56, 71.

92. *Correspondance 1754–1797*, 489. On the jointly physical and moral meaning of nostalgia in this period, see Helmut Illbruck, *Nostalgia: Origins and Ends of an Unenlightened Disease* (Evanston, Ill.: Northwestern University Press, 2012); and Kevis Goodman, "Uncertain Disease: Nostalgia, Pathologies of Motion, Practices of Reading," *Studies in Romanticism* 49:2 (2010), 197–227.

93. September 13, 1768, in *Correspondance 1754–1797*, 505.

94. February 18, 1769, in ibid., 531.

95. Tissot, *Vie de Zimmermann, conseiller d'Etat & premier médecin du roi d'Angleterre à Hanovre, chevalier de l'ordre de Wladomir, membre de plusieurs académies* (Lausanne: A. Fischer et Luc Vincent, 1797).

Chapter 2

1. Lilti, *Figures publiques*.

2. On the related broadness of the term "Republic of Letters," see Dan Edelstein, *The Enlightenment: A Genealogy* (Chicago: University of Chicago Press, 2010), 83–84.

3. See Bell, *Cult of the Nation*. As Elena Russo notes, barristers and *philosophes* alike were labeled *gens de lettres* because "both invoked similar concepts of genius and sentiment, and followed similar publication strategies"; *Styles of Enlightenment: Taste, Politics, and Authorship in Eighteenth-Century France* (Baltimore: Johns Hopkins University Press, 2007), 25.

4. On the persona of the philosopher, see Jochen Schlobach, "Philosophe," in *Le Dictionnaire européen des Lumières*, ed. Michel Delon (Paris: Presses Universitaires de France, 1997), 851–54; Conel Condren, Stephen Gaukroger, and Ian Hunter, eds., *The Philosopher in Early Modern Europe: The Nature of a Contested Identity* (Cambridge: Cambridge University Press, 2006); Catherine Wilson, "The Enlightenment Philosopher as Social Critic," *Intellectual History Review* 18:3 (November 2008), 413–25; Daniel Brewer, *The Enlightenment Past: Reconstructing Eighteenth-Century French Thought* (Cambridge: Cambridge University Press, 2008); and Van Damme, "Philosophe, philosopher." On the image and self-image of authors, see Christian Jouhaud and Alain Viala, eds., *De la publication: Entre Renaissance et Lumières* (Paris: Fayard, 2002); Gregory S. Brown, *A Field of Honor: Writers, Court Culture and Public Theater in French*

Literary Life from Racine to the Revolution (New York: Columbia University Press/ EPIC, 2002; electronic resource available from www.gutenberg-e.org); and Geoffrey Turnovsky, *The Literary Market: Authorship and Modernity in the Old Regime* (Philadelphia: University of Pennsylvania Press, 2010).

5. Voltaire, "Gens de lettres," in ENCYC vol. 7: 599–60, at 599.

6. Yvon, "Amour des sciences et des lettres," in ENCYC vol. 1: 368–69, at 368.

7. Descartes, *La Recherche de la vérité par la lumière naturelle* [1641], in *Oeuvres et lettres* (Paris: Gallimard, Bibliothèque de la Pléaide, 1953), 882.

8. Malebranche, *The Search After Truth: With Elucidations of the Search After Truth*, trans. Thomas M. Lennon and Paul J. Olscamp (Cambridge: Cambridge University Press, 1997), 138.

9. See Deborah Brown, *Descartes and the Passionate Mind* (Cambridge: Cambridge University Press, 2006), 42–46.

10. James, *Passion and Action: The Emotions in Seventeenth-Century Philosophy* (Oxford: Clarendon, 1997), 225. For a summary of seventeenth-century theories of the passions, see Stephen Gaukroger, ed., *The Soft Underbelly of Reason: The Passions in the Seventeenth Century* (New York: Routledge, 1998), 1–16.

11. Lorraine Daston and Katharine Park, *Wonders and the Order of Nature, 1150–1750* (New York: Zone Books, 1998), 327–28. See also the discussion of wonder in Philip Fisher, *Vehement Passions* (Princeton, N.J.: Princeton University Press, 2003).

12. Harold J. Cook emphasizes that the views that Descartes held of the relationship between body and soul were more complex than is often acknowledged by those who focus on the tenets of dogmatic Cartesianism; "Body and Passions: Materialism and the Early Modern State," *Osiris*, 2nd ser., 17 (2002), 25–48, at 40.

13. See Matthew L. Jones, *The Good Life in the Scientific Revolution: Descartes, Pascal, Leibniz, and the Cultivation of Virtue* (Chicago: University of Chicago Press, 2006).

14. For a summary of the influence of Locke's philosophy on emerging concepts of the self, see chap. 6 of Jerrold E. Seigel, *The Idea of the Self: Thought and Experience in Western Europe Since the Seventeenth Century* (Cambridge: Cambridge University Press, 2005). On the introduction of Locke's philosophy into France, see John Yolton, *Locke and French Materialism* (Oxford: Clarendon, 1991). On Boyers d'Argens, see Thomas M. Kavanagh, *Enlightened Pleasures: Eighteenth-Century France and the New Epicureanism* (New Haven, Conn.: Yale University Press, 2010), 52–70.

15. See Sophia Rosenfeld, "Thinking About Feeling, 1789–99," *French Historical Studies* 32:4 (2009), 697–706; and Rebecca L. Spang, "Paradigms and Paranoia: How Modern Is the French Revolution?" *American Historical Review* 108:1 (2003), 119–47.

16. Reddy, *The Navigation of Feeling: A Framework for the History of the Emotions* (Cambridge: Cambridge University Press, 2001), 162–63. Barbara H. Rosenwein stresses that Reddy's account of sentimentalism is based deliberately on "stereotypical sources"; "Worrying About Emotions in History," *American Historical Review* 107:3 (2002), 821–45, at 839.

17. Denby, *Sentimental Narrative and the Social Order in France, 1760–1820* (Cambridge: Cambridge University Press, 1994); Maza, "Luxury, Morality and Social Change in Pre-Revolutionary France," *Journal of Modern History* 69:2 (1997), 199–227, at 224.

18. Hunt, *Inventing Human Rights: A History* (New York: W. W. Norton, 2007): see esp. chap. 1, "'Torrents of Emotion.'"

19. On the last idea, see Jessica Riskin, *Science in the Age of Sensibility: The Sentimental Empiricists of the French Enlightenment* (Chicago: University of Chicago Press, 2002).

20. The unsentimental eighteenth century is explored in Simon Dickie, *Cruelty and Laughter: Forgotten Comic Literature and the Unsentimental Eighteenth Century* (Chicago: University of Chicago Press, 2011); and Anne Coudreuse, *Le refus du pathos au XVIIIe siècle* (Paris: Champion, 2001).

21. On the use of literally shocking techniques for the purposes of medical therapy and social reform, see Carolyn Purnell, "Instruments Endowed with Sensibility: Remaking Society Through the Body in Eighteenth-Century France," Ph.D. dissertation, University of Chicago, 2013.

22. See Lawrence E. Klein and Anthony J. La Vopa, eds., *Enthusiasm and Enlightenment in Europe: 1650–1850* (San Marino, Calif.: Huntington Library, 1998).

23. See Dena Goodman, *The Republic of Letters: A Cultural History of the French Enlightenment* (Ithaca, N.Y.: Cornell University Press, 1994); and Daniel Gordon, *Citizens Without Sovereignty: Equality and Sociability in French Thought, 1670–1789* (Princeton, N.J.: Princeton University Press, 1994).

24. Not all scholars, Duclos granted, were sociable; however, those who possessed varied and wide-ranging talents were sought out by polite company for their wit and learning, and in return gained knowledge they would not have derived from study alone; see "Gens de lettres," chap. 10 in *Considérations sur les moeurs de ce siècle* (Paris, 1751), 243–69.

25. Turnovsky, *Literary Market*, 19.

26. Antoine Lilti, "The Kingdom of Politesse: Salons and the Republic of Letters in Eighteenth-Century Paris," *Republic of Letters: A Journal for the Study of Knowledge, Politics, and the Arts* 1:1 (2008), 1, http://arcade.stanford.edu/rofl/kingdom-politesse-salons-and-republic-letters-eighteenth-century-paris. See also Lilti, *Le monde des salons: Sociabilité et mondanité à Paris au XVIIIe siècle* (Paris: Fayard, 2005).

27. "Discours en vers sur l'homme" (#5); cited in Emmanuel Bury, *Littérature et politesse: L'invention de l'honnête homme, 1580–1750* (Paris: Presses Universitaires de France, 1996), 215.

28. Russo, "Editor's Preface," in *Exploring the Conversible World, Yale French Studies* 92 (1997), 1–7.

29. Jaucourt, "Étude," in ENCYC, vol. 6: 86–87, at 86.

30. On negative seventeenth-century images of scholars, see Alain Viala, *Naissance de l'écrivain: Sociologie de la littérature à l'âge classique* (Paris: Editions de Minuit,

1982), esp. 271–72. As Elena Russo notes, "*Goût, finesse,* and *délicatesse* denoted in the seventeenth and eighteenth centuries a kind of empirical judgment that could be applied not only to the appreciation of aesthetic objects but also to discernment in worldly interactions" (*Styles of Enlightenment*, 143).

31. See, for example, Rollin's *Traité des études* (1730), discussed in Bury, *Littérature et politesse*, 227.

32. See Jean Dagen, *L'Histoire de l'esprit humain dans la pensée française de Fontenelle à Condorcet* (Paris: Klincksieck, 1977); and Jean Starobinski, "Le mot 'civilisation,'" in *Le Remède dans le mal: Critique et légitimation de l'artifice à l'âge des Lumières* (Paris: Gallimard, 1989), 11–59.

33. Jaucourt, "Sensibilité (morale)," in ENCYC, vol. 15: 52. See Lambert, *Réflexions nouvelles sur les femmes*, 49.

34. The Montpellier-trained physician Gabriel Venel implied that those who fretted over petty ailments like "digestion fougueuse" suffered mainly from self-absorption: he called them "the people who constantly *observe* or *listen* to themselves"; "Digestion," in ENCYC, vol. 4: 999–1003, at 1002, Venel's emphasis.

35. Fouquet made this dismissive remark on his earlier work in his *Discours sur la clinique* (Montpellier: Izar et Ricard, an XI [1802–3]), 79. I thank Elizabeth Williams for sharing her notes on this hard-to-find work.

36. Fouquet, "Sensibilité, Sentiment (*Médecine*)," in ENCYC, vol. 15: 38–52, at 40. Further citations to this work appear parenthetically in this paragraph.

37. See Williams, *Physical and the Moral*, 50–62.

38. Taking their cue from sentimentalist models of male heroism, some academic eulogists described their subjects as admirable not just for their brilliance but also for their caring and devotion to other human beings; see Bell, *Cult of the Nation*, 107–39.

39. See Anne Goldgar, *Impolite Learning: Conduct and Community in the Republic of Letters, 1680–1750* (New Haven, Conn.: Yale University Press, 1985); and Peter N. Miller, *Peiresc's Europe: Learning and Virtue in the Seventeenth Century* (New Haven, Conn.: Yale University Press, 2000).

40. Tencin's remark on Fontenelle is cited in Pierre Moreau, "Fontenelle," in *Dictionnaire des lettres françaises au XVIIIe siècle* (Paris: Librairie Arthème Fayard, 1960), vol. 1, 462–66, at 465. Madame de Lambert said this of Fontenelle: "He has a healthy mind, nothing astonishes or alters it; free of ambition, full of moderation, favored by Reason, [he is] a philosopher made by the hands of nature"; cited in Dinah Ribard, *Raconter, vivre, penser: Histoires de philosophes, 1650–1766* (Paris: Vrin, 2003), 150.

41. On Fontenelle's account of Malebranche's passionate reading of Descartes, see Ribard, *Raconter, vivre, penser*, 117–19. According to his biographer, Pierre Desmaisieux, Pierre Bayle often sequestered himself in his room during adolescence to "give himself over to the pleasures that arise from application and study," experiencing a love of philosophy so acute that it repeatedly made him ill; cited in Luc Weibel, *Le Savoir et le corps: Essai sur le Dictionnaire de Pierre Bayle* (Paris: Éditions L'Age d'Homme, 1975), 119–20.

42. Ribard, *Raconter, vivre, penser*, 205–6; Le Menthéour, *La Manufacture de maladies*, 137–41.

43. Cited in Ribard, *Raconter, vivre, penser*, 132.

44. Ibid., 132–34.

45. Algazi, "Scholars in Households: Refiguring the Learned Habitus, 1480–1550," *Science in Context* 16:1/2 (2003), 9–42, at 26.

46. Mercier, *Le Bonheur des gens de lettres*, in *Éloges et discours philosophiques* (Amsterdam: E. van Harrevelt, 1776), 9–10.

47. Mercier, *Discours sur la lecture*, in *Éloges et discours*, 257–58.

48. Letter of March 15, 1747, in Graffigny, *Vie privée de Voltaire et de Mme du Châtelet pendant un séjour à Cirey; par l'auteur des Lettres péruviennes, suivies de cinquantes lettres inédites, en vers et en prose, de Voltaire* (Paris: Treuttel et Wurtz, 1820), 283, 286. Although attributed only to Graffigny, this volume includes letters by various other authors, including Mme de Staal (Mme de Staal-Delaunay). The court of Sceaux, the scene of the episode related by Staal, was the "oppositional" court established by the Duc du Maine (the illegitimate son of Louis XIV and Mme de Montespan) and his culture-loving wife, the Duchesse du Maine. On the visit that Voltaire and Du Châtelet made there, see André Maurois, "Voltaire," in *Dictionnaire des lettres françaises XVIIIe siècle*, vol. 2, 648. On Graffigny's particular hostility toward Du Châtelet, see Marie-Thérèse Inguenaud, "La Grosse et le monstre: Histoire d'une haine," *SVEC* 2006:01, 65–90.

49. For other images, see René Pomeau, "Voltaire et Mme Du Châtelet à Cirey: Amour et travail," in *Cirey dans la vie intellectuelle / La Réception de Newton en France*, ed. François de Gandt, *SVEC* 2001:11, 9–15.

50. Voltaire, "Éloge historique de Madame du Châtelet," in *Oeuvres complètes de Voltaire / The Complete Works of Voltaire* (Geneva: Institut et Musée Voltaire / Toronto: University of Toronto Press / Oxford: Voltaire Foundation, 1968–), vol. 32A, 387–88. Henceforth abbreviated OCV. See Lotterie's discussion of Voltaire's various tributes to Du Châtelet and other women intellectuals, in *Le Genre des Lumières*, 100–111.

51. See Zinsser, *La dame d'esprit*, 237.

52. Doigny du Ponceau, *Épître à un homme de lettres célibataire* (Paris: Brunet et Demonville, 1773); Ducis, "Épitre contre le célibat," in *Oeuvres de J. F. Ducis* (Paris: Chez Nepveu, 1826), vol. 3, 34–45. These texts are discussed in Éric Walter, "Le complexe d'Abélard ou le célibat des gens de lettres," *Dix-huitième siècle* 12 (1980), 127–52.

53. Letter to Maupertuis, December 10, 1735; cited in Krief, "Retraite féminine," 97.

54. D'Alembert, "Essai sur la société des gens de lettres et des grands, sur la réputation, sur les mécènes, et sur les récompenses littéraires," in *Œuvres complètes de d'Alembert* (Geneva: Slatkine, 1967), vol. 4, 335–73, at 339.

55. Plutarch, "Marcellus," in *Plutarch's Lives*, trans. John Dryden, reviewed by Arthur Hugh Clough (New York: Modern Library, 1932), 378, 380. Kathleen Kete notes that Plutarch's descriptions of Archimedes are cited by modern-day theorists

who insist on the adversarial relationship between creative genius and society (*Making Way for Genius*, 27–28).

56. Montesquieu, "Discours sur l'Usage des glandes rénales" (1718), in *Œuvres complètes*, vol. 1, 20.

57. Condillac, *Traité des sensations* [1754] (Paris: Fayard, 1984), 30.

58. La Mettrie, *L'Homme machine* [1747] (Paris: Editions Brossard, 1921), 49.

59. Yvon, "Attention," in ENCYC, vol. 1: 842–43.

60. Levesque de Pouilly, *Théorie des sentiments agréables, où après avoir indiqué les règles que la nature suit dans la distribution du plaisir, on établit les principes de la théologie naturelle et ceux de la philosophie morale* (Paris: Chez David, 1748), 24. See Robert Mauzi's discussion in *L'idée du bonheur dans la littérature et la pensée françaises au XVIIIe siècle* [1960] (Geneva: Slatkine Reprints, 1979), 240–42.

61. Fouquet, "Sensibilité," in ENCYC, vol. 15: 38–52, at 46.

62. Zimmermann, *Traité de l'expérience*, 487.

63. Tissot, *Traité des nerfs*, vol. 3 (Tome II, Part I), 313–14. The *convulsionnaires* were a lightning rod throughout the century because of their troubling manifestations of alienated mental and sensory states; see Charly Coleman's recent discussion in *The Virtues of Abandon: An Anti-Individualist History of the French Enlightenment* (Stanford, Calif.: Stanford University Press, 2014), esp. 107–118.

64. Daston, "Attention and the Values of Nature," in *The Moral Authority of Nature*, ed. Lorraine Daston and Fernando Vidal (Chicago: University of Chicago Press, 2004), 100–126; Nicoli, *Les savants et les livres*, 143–55.

65. On related concerns in the British context, see John Sutton, "Carelessness and Inattention: Mind-Wandering and the Physiology of Fantasy from Locke to Hume," in *The Body as Object and Instrument of Knowledge: Embodied Empiricism in Early Modern Science*, ed. Charles T. Wolfe and Ofer Gal (New York: Springer, 2010), 243–63.

66. Hecquet, *Le Naturalisme des convulsions dans les maladies de l'épidémie convulsionnaire* (Soleure: Chez Andreas Gymnicus, 1733).

67. Garnier, *L'homme de lettres*, 112.

68. Ibid., 117–18.

69. *Les Confessions de Fréron (1719–1776). Sa Vie, souvenirs intimes et anecdotiques, ses pensées*, ed. Charles Barthélemy (Paris: Charpentier, 1876), 272.

70. Voltaire, "Gens de lettres," in ENCYC, vol. 7: 599–600, at 599.

71. Voltaire, "Lettres, gens de lettres, ou lettrés" (1764), *Dictionnaire philosophique*, in OCV, vol. 36, 285.

72. Denis Diderot, letters to Sophie Volland, October 20 and November 21, 1765, in *Correspondance (1742–1784)*, in *Oeuvres de Diderot* (Paris: Éd. Robert Laffont, 1997), vol. 5, 541–42, 556.

73. "This was an ideology of distance, both metaphorical and literal, from all human ties": Daston, "Enlightenment Fears, Fears of Enlightenment," in *What's Left*

of Enlightenment? A Post-Modern Question, ed. Keith M. Baker and Peter H. Reill (Stanford, Calif.: Stanford University Press, 2001), 115–28, at 121.

74. Russo, *Styles of Enlightenment*, 215. See also her essay "Slander and Glory in the Republic of Letters: Diderot and Seneca Confront Rousseau," *Republic of Letters: A Journal for the Study of Knowledge, Politics, and the Arts* 1:1 (2008), http://arcade.stanford.edu/rofl/slander-and-glory-republic-letters-diderot-and-seneca-confront-rousseau.

75. Diderot, letter of November 7, 1762, in *Correspondance*, 470. He gave a less eroticized version of the contrast in his letter to Sophie Volland of October 20, 1765, where he emphasized the compensatory satisfactions he enjoyed in society when he left behind the pleasures of studious retreat: see *Correspondance*, 541–42.

76. Ribard points out that the image put forth by Fontenelle omits mention of Leibniz's life as a courtly diplomat: *Raconter, vivre, penser*, 130.

77. Diderot, *Réfutation suivie de l'ouvrage d'Helvétius intitulé "de l'Homme"* (1775), in DPV, vol. 24, 538–39. Further citations to this work appear parenthetically within the paragraph.

78. Brewer, *The Discourse of Enlightenment: Diderot and the Art of Philosophizing* (Cambridge: Cambridge University Press, 1993), 33.

79. Diderot, "Bas (*Bonneterie, Peausserie*)," in ENCYC, vol. 2: 98–113, at 98. See Joanna Stalnaker's analysis in *The Unfinished Enlightenment: Description in the Age of the Encyclopedia* (Ithaca, N.Y.: Cornell University Press, 2010), 122.

80. This is a central theme in discours III, chapter 7 of Helvétius's earlier work, *De l'Esprit*, 246–53; cited in Albert O. Hirschman, *The Passions and the Interests: Political Arguments for Capitalism Before Its Triumph* (Princeton, N.J.: Princeton University Press, 1977), 27.

81. "One must not make poetry in life. Heros, lovers in novels, great patriots, inflexible magistrates, apostles of religion, outrageous philosophers, all of those rare and divine insane people make poetry in life, which is the source of their unhappiness. They are the people who, after death, provide inspiration for great paintings: they are excellent to paint. Experience tells us that nature condemns to unhappiness the person to whom she has given genius, and to the woman she had endowed with beauty; and it is because they are poetic beings": *Salon de 1767*, in DPV, vol. 16, 207.

82. "Distraction (*Morale*)," in ENCYC, vol. 4: 1061. On the positive cast given to mind-wandering elsewhere in the *Encyclopédie*, see David W. Bates, *Enlightenment Aberrations: Error and Revolution in France* (Ithaca, N.Y.: Cornell University Press, 2002), 19–40.

83. The term "enthusiasm" had different implications in the eighteenth century depending on the context in which it was invoked: it was generally condemned in discussions of religious fanaticism, but praised by aesthetic theoreticians and proponents of genius. See, among other studies, Coleman, *Virtues of Abandon*, 159–201; and Caroline Jacot-Grapa, "Le camisard et le philosophe: Sur l'enthousiasme," in *Les*

Extrémités des émotions: Du spectaculaire à l'inexprimable, Actes du colloque international de mars 2007, Littérales 42, ed. B. Boudou et L. Picciola (Paris: Université Paris Ouest Nanterre La Défense, 2009), 313–29.

84. Jaffe, "The Concept of Genius: Its Changing Role in Eighteenth-Century French Aesthetics," *Journal of the History of Ideas* 41:4 (1980), 579–99, at 596 (Jaffe's emphasis).

85. "Essai sur les causes," 253. See Thomas L. Pangle's comments on this passage in *Montesquieu's Philosophy of Liberalism: A Commentary on the Spirit of the Laws* (Chicago: University of Chicago Press, 1973), 155–57.

86. *Lettres persanes*, 356. Further citations to this work will appear parenthetically in the text.

87. See, for example, Starobinski, "Exil, satire, tyrannie: *Les Lettres persanes*," in *Le Remède dans le mal*, 91–121.

88. According to Robert Shackelton, Chabdan corresponds to October in the version of the hybrid French/Persian calendar adapted by Montesquieu for the dating of the novel's letters: see "The Moslem Chronology of the *Lettres persanes*," *French Studies* 8 (1954), 17–27; reprinted in *Essays on Montesquieu and the Enlightenment* (Oxford: Voltaire Foundation, 1988), 73–83. Starobinski cites Shackelton's essay in the appendix "Chronologie des *Lettres persanes*" in his edition of *Les Lettres persanes* (Paris: Folio, 2003), 401.

89. Harari, *Scenarios of the Imaginary*, 90.

90. For another nontragic reading of Usbek's fate, see Philip Stewart, "Toujours Usbek," *Eighteenth-Century Fiction* 11:2 (1999), 141–50.

Chapter 3

1. On the significance of this text, see Herbert Dieckmann's classic study *Le Philosophe: Text and Interpretation*, Washington University Studies 18 (St. Louis, 1948).

2. Cited in ibid., 46.

3. Bonneval, *Progrès de l'éducation, suite des Élémens de l'éducation* (Paris: Prault Père, 1743), 159–60.

4. Shank, *The Newton Wars and the Beginning of the French Enlightenment* (Chicago: University of Chicago Press, 2008), 33. See also Van Damme, "Philosophe, Philosopher."

5. Van Damme, "Philosophe, Philosopher," 510 (cited in the rest of the paragraph parenthetically). See Bury, *Littérature et Politesse*, 201–3; and Hans Ulrich Gumbrecht, *Making Sense in Life and Literature* (Minneapolis: University of Minnesota Press, 1992), 139. The version of "Philosophe" that appeared in the *Encyclopédie* expunged many of the 1743 text's openly materialist and combatively antireligious remarks (Dieckmann, *Le Philosophe*, 23).

6. Brewer, *Enlightenment Past*, 64–68.

7. See Jean-Claude Bonnet, "De la famille à la patrie," in *Histoire des pères et de la paternité*, ed. Jean Delumeau and Daniel Roche (Paris: Larousse-HER, 1990 [reprint,

2000]), 245–67. See also Meghan Roberts, "Philosophes Mariés and Épouses Philosophiques: Men of Letters and Marriage in Eighteenth-Century France," *French Historical Studies* 35:3 (2012), 509–39; and *Sentimental Savants: Philosophical Families in Enlightenment France* (Chicago: University of Chicago Press, 2016).

8. See Pierre Hartmann, ed., *Le Philosophe sur les planches: L'image du philosophe dans le théâtre des Lumières: 1680–1815* (Strasbourg: Presses Universitaires de Strasbourg, 2003); and Logan J. Connors, *Dramatic Battles in Eighteenth-Century France: Philosophes, Anti-philosophes and Polemical Theatre*, SVEC 2012:07.

9. Dieckmann, *Le Philosophe*, 71.

10. Ira Wade gives his estimate in *The Structure and Form of the French Enlightenment* (Princeton, N.J.: Princeton University Press, 1977), vol. 1, 14; see also Wade, *The "Philosophe" in the French Drama of the Eighteenth Century* (Princeton, N.J.: Princeton University Press, 1926). The CESAR website can be found at www.cesar.org.uk/cesar2.

11. Piis, *Aristote amoureux, ou le philosophe bridé* (Paris: Vente, 1780), 24.

12. See d'Andeli, *Le Lai d'Aristote*, intro. A. Héron (Rouen: Imprimérie Léon Gy, 1901). Coulet and Gilot cite this fabliau as a possible source of Marivaux's *Le Triomphe de l'amour*; in Marivaux, *Le Prince travesti / Le Triomphe de l'amour*, ed. Henri Coulet and Michel Gilot (Paris: Honoré Champion, 1983), 124.

13. "Le Philosophe soi-disant" in Marmontel, *Contes moraux*, 3 vols. (Paris: Chez J. Merlin libraire, 1765), vol 2, 1–42; discussed in Wade, *"Philosophe" in French Drama*, 83–87.

14. See Isabelle Martin, *Le Théâtre de la Foire: Des tréteaux aux boulevards*, SVEC 2002:10, 252–307.

15. See Nancy D. Klein, "Inscribing the Feminine in Seventeenth-Century Narratives: The Case of Madame de Villedieu," in *A Labor of Love: Critical Reflections on the Writings of Marie-Catherine Desjardins (Mme de Villedieu)*, ed. Roxane Decker Lalande (Madison, N.J.: Fairleigh Dickinson University Press, 2000), 87–100.

16. Villedieu, "Socrates," in *Amours des grands hommes*, translated as "Socrates" in *The Loves of Sundry Philosophers and Other Great Men* (London: Herringman and Starkey, 1673), 29–62.

17. See, for example, Saint-Foix, *Le Philosophe dupe de l'amour* (1726); Philippe Poisson, *Alcibiade* (1731); Charles-Simon Favart, *La Fille mal gardée, ou le pédant amoureux* (1758); and Jacques Tesseirenc, *La femme philosophe* (1759).

18. Jean d'Alembert used this expression to describe the fundamental theme of all of Marivaux's plays: "Éloge de Marivaux," in *Œuvres complètes de d'Alembert* (Geneva: Slatkine, 1967), vol. 3, 577–621, at 582.

19. Marivaux, *Le Triomphe*, act I, scene 1, 136. Skeptical interpretations of Hermocrate include Robert Tomlinson, "Marivaux dans les jardins de Socrate ou l'Anti-Banquet," *Études littéraires* 24:1 (1991): 39–49, and Raymond Joly, "La Haine du philosophe: Notes pour une lecture psychanalytique du *Triomphe de l'amour*," *Études littéraires* 24:1 (1991), 51–62.

20. Marivaux, *Le Triomphe*, I, 1, 135. Further citations to this work are in the text within parentheses.

21. On Marivaux's moral philosophy, see Jean Sgard, "Trois 'philosophes' de 1734: Marivaux, Prévost, et Voltaire," *Études littéraires* 24:1 (1991), 31–38. See also Pierre Hartman's sympathetic reading of Hermocrate in "Figures du philosophe dans le théâtre de Marivaux," in *Le Philosophe sur les planches*, 45–54.

22. Origny, entry for March 12, 1738, in *Annales du théâtre* [1788] (Geneva: Slatkine Reprints, 1970), vol. 1, 124.

23. According to Aleksandra Hoffmann-Lipońska, *Le Philosophe marié* attracted 80,000 spectators to the Comédie Française and was performed approximately 163 times from 1727 to 1754; "Destouches et Voltaire, relations et correspondance," *Cahiers de Varsovie* 10 (1982), 251–58, at 252. Both Michelle Bokobza Kahan and Gabriele Vickermann-Ribémont stress the novelty of Destouches's depiction of the *philosophe* character; Bokobza Kahan, "Mutations culturelles et construction du personnage du philosophe chez Destouches," in *Le Philosophe sur les planches*, 81–91; and Vickermann-Ribémont, "Introduction" to Philippe Néricault Destouches, *Le philosophe marié, ou Le Mari honteux de l'être*, ed. G. Vickermann-Ribémont (Geneva: Librairie Droz, 2010). See also Paul Pelckmans, "Du désert d'Alceste aux délices de la retraite partagée. À propos de quelques dénouements de Philippe Néricault Destouches," *Dix-huitième siècle* 1:48 (2016), 307–21. On Destouches's very successful dramatic career, see John Dunkley's introduction to Philippe Néricault Destouches, *L'Irrésolu: Comédie* (Paris: Klincksieck, 1995), v–xcvi; and A. Burner, "Philippe Néricault Destouches (1680–1754): Essai de biographie," *Revue d'histoire littéraire de la France* 38 (1931), 64–70.

24. Destouches, *Le philosophe marié*, in *Oeuvres dramatiques de N. Destouches* (Paris: Lefèvre, 1811), 6–11. Further references to this work appear parenthetically in the text.

25. Virey, *De la femme sous ses rapports physiologique, moral et littéraire* [1823], 2nd ed. (Brussels: Wahlen, 1826), 437.

26. Fagan's sympathetic depiction of the *philosophe* is, however, tempered by a passing evocation of the theme of scholarly impotence: see *La Pupille* in Jacques Truchet, ed., *Théâtre du XVIIIe siècle* (Paris: Gallimard, Bibliothèque de la Pléiade, 1972), vol. 1, 990.

27. On plays that showcased great historical thinkers and writers in domestic settings, see Russo, *Styles of Enlightenment*, 194–213.

28. Rousseau, *Discours sur les sciences et les arts*, 14; *First Discourse*, 10.

29. See Starobinski, "Le mot 'civilisation,'" in *Remède dans le mal*.

30. See Derek F. Connon, "Alexis Piron's Ha-Ha: Shifting Identities in 'La Métromanie,'" *Modern Language Review* 101:1 (2006), 62–74.

31. Cited in Anne Goldgar, *Impolite Learning*, 247. Another satirical example is *scribomanie*, used by Chassaignon in *Cataractes de l'imagination: Déluge de la scribomanie, vomissement littéraire, hémorrhagie encyclopédique, monstre des monstres, par*

Épiménide l'inspiré ([s.n.] Dans l'antre de Trophonius: au pays des visions, 1779), 4 vols. Arnaud discusses this work in *On Hysteria*, 156–59.

32. Desfontaines, *La Voltairomanie* [1738], ed. M. H. Waddicor (Exeter: University of Exeter, 1983), 6 and 25. On the dispute between Desfontaines and Voltaire, see Saisselin, *Literary Enterprise*, 104; and Shank, *Newton Wars*, 395–401.

33. The larger context was the "critical jousting that all men of letters engaged in within the Parisian wing of the Republic of Letters" (Shank, *Newton Wars*, 285). See also Olivier Ferret, *La fureur de nuire: Échanges pamphlétaires entre philosophes et antiphilosophes, 1750–1770, SVEC* 2007:03.

34. Cited by Desfontaines in his favorable review, in *Jugements sur quelques ouvrages nouveaux: 1744–1745* (Geneva: Slatkine Reprints, 1967), vol. 2, 128.

35. Fréron, *Lettres sur quelques écrits de ce temps* [1753] (Geneva: Slatkine Reprints, 1966), vol. 2, 203.

36. *Les Confessions de Fréron*, 256–57.

37. Linguet, *Le Fanatisme des philosophes* (London: De Vérité, 1764), 8–9.

38. "Les Honnêtetés littéraires" [1767], in Voltaire, *Mélanges* (Paris: Gallimard, Éditions de la Pléiade, 1961), 985.

39. Voltaire, *Le Pauvre diable* (Geneva: Cramer, 1758), 10. For a discussion of this work's publication history, see Ferret, *La fureur de nuire*, 143–80 and passim. Didier Masseau emphasizes the contrast Voltaire drew between the minor author working for a living and the *philosophe*, who worked exclusively for glory and the disinterested quest for truth: "La Promotion de l'homme de lettres chez Duclos et d'Alembert: Rapports de force et stratégies littéraires," in Voltaire, *Le Pauvre diable*, 311–20. See also Turnovsky, *Literary Market*, 116–18.

40. Daniel Desormeaux, *La figure du bibliomane: Histoire du livre et stratégie littéraire au XIX siècle* (Paris: Nizet, 2001), 38.

41. "Bibliomanie," in ENCYC, vol. 2: 228. D'Alembert had already denounced "the mania for *bel esprit*" in the "Discours préliminaire" to the *Encyclopédie*, blaming it for the decline in taste and good scholarly habits; see "Discours préliminaire des Éditeurs" (June 1751), ENCYC, vol. 1: i–xlv, at xxxiv.

42. Desormeaux, *La figure du bibliomane*, 57.

43. Bollioud-Mermet, *De la bibliomanie* [1761], ed. P. Chéron (Paris: Chez D. Jouaust, 1865), 66. For discussion of this book, see Yann Sordet, *L'amour des livres au siècle des Lumières: Pierre Adamoli et ses collections* (Paris: École Nationale des Chartes, 2001), 29–33 and passim; and Jennifer Tsien, *The Bad Taste of Others: Judging Literary Value in Eighteenth-Century France* (Philadelphia: University of Pennsylvania Press, 2012), 15–24 and passim.

44. Bollioud-Mermet, *De la bibliomanie*, 69–70. Amédée Paul Chéron, Bollioud-Mermet's nineteenth-century editor, slyly subverted the author's utilitarian aims by explaining that he had reprinted *De la bibliomanie* on luxurious paper in a limited edition to excite the passion of his fellow bibliomaniacs; see the preface to *De la bibliomanie*.

45. Tissot, *Traité des nerfs*, vol. 3 (Tome II, Part I), 442–43.
46. Descuret, *La Médecine des passions, considérées dans leurs rapports avec les maladies, les lois, et la religion* (Paris : Périsse, 1841), 719–30. On Flaubert, see Desormeaux, *La figure du bibliomane*, 99–126; and Jan Goldstein, "The Uses of Male Hysteria: Medical and Literary Discourse in Nineteenth-Century France," *Representations* 34 (Spring 1991), 134–65.
47. "Essai sur la société des gens de lettres," 350.
48. Thomas, "Discours de réception à l'Académie française, le jeudi 22 janvier 1767," in *Oeuvres de M. Thomas, de L'Académie Françoise, nouvelle édition* (Paris: Moutard, 1773), vol. 4, 325–63. On the polemics surrounding this speech, and Thomas's role as apologist for the "parti philosophique" within the Académie, see Bonnet, *Naissance du Panthéon*, 80–82. On the glorification of theater, see Brown, *Field of Honor*.
49. Jacques Neefs, "La 'haine des grands hommes' au XIXe siècle," *MLN* 116.4 (2001), 750–69.
50. Montesquieu, *Discours de réception à l'Académie des Sciences de Bordeaux : Prononcé le premier mai 1716*, in *Œuvres complètes*, vol. 1, 3–4.
51. *Les Lettres persanes*, 263–65.
52. See Brewer, *Enlightenment Past*, 79.
53. D'Alembert, "Éloge de M. Le Président de Montesquieu," in "Avertissement des Éditeurs," in ENCYC, vol. 5: ii–xviii, at xiv. D'Alembert used the same insect rhetoric as Montesquieu later in this eulogy, to contrast the response to Montesquieu's work in France versus England: "While Insects tormented him in his own country, England raised a monument to his glory" (xv).
54. Cited in McMahon, *Enemies of the Enlightenment*, 24.
55. The text of d'Alembert's "Réflexions" is reproduced in an appendix to Lucien Brunel, *Les philosophes et l'Académie française au dix-huitième siècle* (Paris: Hachette, 1884), 361–66. Further citations to "Réflexions" appear parenthetically in the text.
56. D'Alembert, "Essai sur la société des gens de lettres et des grands," 340–41. See, on this point, Antoine Lilti, "Sociabilité mondaine et réseaux intellectuels: Les salons parisiens au XVIIIe siècle," in *Réseaux de l'esprit en Europe—des lumières au XIXe siècle: Actes du Colloque international de Coppet (décembre 2003)*, ed. Vladimir Berelovič and Michel Porret (Geneva: Librairie Droz, 2009), 88–104.
57. On the evolution of d'Alembert's views regarding the condition of *gens de lettres*, see Olivier Ferret, "De la considération à la réputation: La mutation de la condition intellectuelle de l'homme de lettres dans les écrits théoriques de D'Alembert," in Voltaire, *Le Pauvre diable*, 299–310.
58. Bonnet traces this tendency to Fénelon; see *Naissance du Panthéon*, 41–49. This rhetoric was particularly evident in the writings of Voltaire; see John R. Iverson, "La Gloire humanisée? Voltaire et son siècle," *Histoire, Économie et Société* 20:2 (April–June 2001), 211–18.

59. Leroy, *Réflexions sur la jalousie, pour servir de commentaire aux derniers ouvrages de M. de Voltaire* (Amsterdam, 1772).

60. Peter Gay, *The Enlightenment: The Science of Freedom* (New York: W. W. Norton, 1969), 16.

61. See Anthony Levi's detailed analysis of Descartes' *Traité des passions* in *French Moralists: The Theory of the Passions, 1585 to 1649* (Oxford: Clarendon, 1964), 257–89.

62. Descartes, *Traité des passions de l'âme* [1649], in *Oeuvres et lettres*, 781. Further citations appear parenthetically in the text.

63. La Rochefoucauld, *Maximes* [fifth ed., 1678], ed. F. C. Green (1945; Cambridge: Cambridge University Press, 2015), maxim #28, 60.

64. Ibid., maxims #280 and 281, 96.

65. D'Alembert, "Envieux, Jaloux, (synon.)," in ENCYC, vol. 5: 738; Anon., "Envie, méd," in ENCYC, vol. 5: 735.

66. Anon., "Envie, méd," in ENCYC, vol. 5: 735.

67. According to János (Jean) Hankiss, this play was performed only three times, and it was soon followed by another unsuccessful play, *Les Philosophes amoureux*; Hankiss, *Philippe Néricault Destouches: L'homme et l'œuvre* [1918] (Geneva: Slatkine Reprints, 1981), 41–42.

68. D'Alembert, "Éloge de Destouches" [1776], in *Œuvres de d'Alembert*, vol. 3, 403–36; see esp. 410–11.

69. Hirschman, *Passions and the Interests*, 26.

70. "Émulation," in ENCYC, vol. 5: 601–2. Jaucourt's article was, as John R. Iverson points out, taken largely from La Bruyère's reflection on emulation and its negative opposite in *Les Caractères*; "Introduction" to "Forum: Emulation in France, 1750–1800," *Eighteenth-Century Studies* 36:2 (2003), 217–23, at 218.

71. Voltaire, "Discours en vers sur l'homme" (1738), in *Mélanges*, 221–23. In 1738, he also wrote his own play entitled *L'Envieux*, a minor work targeting Desfontaines, which was never performed.

72. Staël, *Lettres sur les ouvrages et le caractère de Jean-Jacques Rousseau* [1788], in *Oeuvres de jeunesse*, ed. John Isbell (Paris: Éditions Desjonquères, 1997), 98.

73. *De l'Interprétation de la nature* [1754], in DPV, vol. 9, 86.

74. *Éloge de Richardson* [1762], in DPV, vol. 13, 208; *Essai sur les règnes de Claude et de Néron, et sur les mœurs et les écrits de Sénèque* (*Essai sur Sénèque*) [1778], in DPV, vol. 25, 239.

75. *Le Neveu de Rameau ou Satire seconde* [1761–82/1805], in DPV, vol. 12, 72; *Denis Diderot's Rameau's Nephew: A Multimedia Edition*, trans. Kate Tunstall and Caroline Warman, ed. Marian Hobson, music dir. Pascal Duc (Cambridge: Open Book, 2014), 8–9. Further citations of these works appear parenthetically in the text.

76. Marc Buffat underscores how systematic LUI is in applying his reverse morality of grandeur in evil: "La Loi de l'appétit," in *Autour du "Neveu de Rameau,"* ed. Anne-Marie Chouillet (Paris: Champion, 1991), 37–57, at 54.

77. LUI uses the term "sublime" here in an anthropological sense to describe those who are superior, but without any moralizing connotation. See Baldine Saint Girons, *Le sublime de l'antiquité à nos jours* (Paris: Les Éditions Desjonquères, 2005), 56–57. See also Brian Elkner, "Diderot and the Sublime: The Artist as Hero," in *Studies in the Eighteenth Century: Papers Presented at the Second David Nichol Smith Memorial Seminar, Canberra 1970*, ed. R. F. Brissenden (Toronto: University of Toronto Press, 1970), 143–62; and McMahon, "Genius and Evil," in *Genealogies of Genius*, 171–82, esp. 176–78.

78. *Salon de 1767*, in DPV, vol. 16, 206.

79. On the complex interplay between masking and unmasking in *Le Neveu de Rameau* and in Diderot's dramatic theory, see Jean Starobinski, "L'accent de la vérité," in *Diderot et le théâtre* (Paris: Comédie-Française, 1984), 9–26.

Chapter 4

1. Diderot, *Éléments de physiologie*, in DPV, vol. 17, 334.

2. Diderot, *Lettre sur les sourds et muets*, in DPV, vol. 4, 140. Other sensationist anatomies include Condillac's statue-man fable in *Traité des sensations* (1754); the chapter "De l'homme" in Buffon's *Histoire naturelle* (1749–89); and Bonnet, *Essai analytique sur les facultés de l'âme* (1760).

3. The London remark is cited in Jacques van den Heuvel, *Voltaire dans ses contes: De "Micromégas" à "L'ingénu"* (Paris: A. Colin, 1967), 27. For the reference to Condillac, see Voltaire, "Sensation," *Dictionnaire philosophique*, in OCV, vol. 36, 530.

4. Voltaire, "Passions," *Questions sur l'Encyclopédie*, in OCV, vol. 42B, 377.

5. Ibid., 374.

6. Voltaire, *Lettres philosophiques* [1734], in *Mélanges*, 40.

7. Daniel Cottom, *Cannibals and Philosophers: Bodies of Enlightenment* (Baltimore: Johns Hopkins University Press, 2001), xii, 7.

8. *Réfutation suivie de l'ouvrage d'Helvétius intitulé 'de l'Homme'* [1775], in DPV, vol. 24, 605.

9. *La Lettre sur les aveugles* [1749], in DPV, vol. 4, 431–32; translation adapted from *Letter on the Deaf* in *Diderot's Early Philosophical Works*, trans. and ed. Margaret Jourdain (London: Open Court, 1916), 87.

10. Physiology and medicine were not, however, the only subjects Diderot discussed in the *Éléments*: he also drew on contemporary psychology, moral theory, and metaphysics. See Mayer, "Introduction," *Éléments de physiologie*, 273–86.

11. See Timo Kaitaro, *Diderot's Holism: Philosophical Anti-Reductionism and Its Medical Background* (Frankfurt: Peter Lang, 1997), 137–38.

12. Diderot, *Éléments de physiologie*, 511–12.

13. On Huber's paintings of Voltaire, see Christiane Mervaud, *Voltaire à table: Plaisir du corps, plaisir de l'esprit* (Paris: Editions Desjonquères, 1998), 9–13.

14. On Diderot's prodigious consumption of fine wine and food, see the chapter "Diderot gastronome," in Georges May, *Quatre visages de Denis Diderot* (Paris: Boivin,

1951), 13–33. On Voltaire's love of refined dining (despite his digestive woes), see Mervaud, *Voltaire à table*, esp. 17–94; and Jean Starobinski, "Le philosophe à table," in *Être riche au siècle de Voltaire, actes du colloque de Genève (18–19 juin 1994)*, ed. Jacques Berchtold and Michel Porret (Geneva: Librairie Droz, 1996), 279–93. Steven Shapin underscores the contrast between the traditional, abstemious image of the scholar, and the "sociable, merry, and moderately gormandizing philosopher of the eighteenth century"; "The Philosopher and the Chicken: On the Dietetics of Disembodied Knowledge," in *Science Incarnate*, 21–50, at 43.

15. See Jean-Claude Bonnet, "Le Système de repas et de la cuisine chez Rousseau," *Poétique* 6:22 (1975), 248–67, and "Le réseau culinaire dans l'*Encyclopédie*," *Annales. Économies, Sociétés, Civilisations* 31:5 (1976), 891–914.

16. Lorry, *Essai sur les alimens*, vol. 2, 237–38.

17. "Santé," in ENCYC, vol. 14: 628–30, at 630.

18. See Michel Jeanneret, *Les mets et les mots: Banquets et propos de table à la Renaissance* (Paris: José Corti, 1987); Fredrik Albritton Jonsson, "The Physiology of Hypochondria in Eighteenth-Century Britain," in *Cultures of the Abdomen: Dietetics, Digestion, and Fat in the Modern World*, ed. Christopher E. Forth and Ana Cardin-Coyne (New York: Palgrave, 2005), 15–30; and George Rousseau, "Coleridge's Dreaming Gut: Digestion, Genius, Hypochondria," in *Cultures of the Abdomen*, 105–26.

19. On restaurants and food science, see Rebecca L. Spang, *The Invention of the Restaurant: Paris and Modern Gastronomic Culture* (Cambridge, Mass.: Harvard University Press, 2000); and Spary, *Eating the Enlightenment*.

20. See Williams, *Physical and the Moral*, 38–39, 43–44, 51, 59; Williams, *Cultural History of Medical Vitalism*, 152–60; and Rey, *Naissance et développement du vitalisme*, 164–69.

21. Lacaze, *Idée de l'homme physique et moral* (Paris: Guérin et Delatour, 1755), 327, 343. The rest of the paragraph contains further parenthetical citations to this work.

22. Bordeu, *Recherches sur les maladies chroniques* (1775), in *Oeuvres complètes*, 2 vols. (Paris: Caille et Ravier, 1818), vol. 2, 831, 839.

23. Ibid., vol. 2, 806.

24. See Esquirol, *Des Passions considérées comme causes, symptômes et moyens curatifs de l'aliénation mentale* [1805] (Paris: Librairie des Deux Mondes, 1980), 17. Goldstein notes that, like Pinel, Esquirol favored visceral lesions over cerebral lesions as a theory for the localization of insanity; *Console and Classify*, 251. On the tensions between visceralism and cerebralism in nineteenth-century mental medicine, see Elizabeth A. Williams, "Neuroses of the Stomach: Eating, Gender, and Psychopathology in French Medicine, 1800–1870," *Isis* 98:1 (March 2007), 54–79; and Jackie Pigeaud, *Aux portes de la psychiatrie: Pinel, l'ancien et le moderne* (Paris: Aubier, 2001), 185–222.

25. Broussais, *De l'irritation et de la folie* [1828/1839], reprint of 2nd ed. (Paris: Fayard, 1986). See Jean-François Braunstein, *Broussais et le matérialisme. Médecine et philosophie au XIXe siècle* (Paris: Klincksieck, 1986).

26. As he wrote to Jean Robert Tronchin (Dr. Théodore Tronchin's brother), "The affairs of Saxony can go as they please, but I can't live without cassia. . . . Cassia absorbs all of my ideas"; letter 6720, October 12, 1757, in *Voltaire's Correspondence*, ed. Theodore Besterman (Geneva: Institut et Musée Voltaire, 1953–65), vol. 32, 110.

27. Épitre 76 (1748), in Voltaire, *Oeuvres complètes*, ed. Louis Moland, 107 vols. (Paris: Garnier frères, 1877–85), vol. 10, 346–47.

28. Ibid., 347.

29. Épitre 65 (1744), in ibid., 327–28.

30. October 25, 1724, in ibid., vol. 1, 291.

31. Voltaire wrote two extensive letters on indigestion and cassia to Mme du Deffand in 1775; see ibid., vol. 90, 34–35 and 174–75. On Mme du Deffand, see Marianne Charrier-Vozel, "Sociabilités de la maladie: Des manuels épistolaires aux lettres de Mme Riccoboni, de Mme du Deffand, de Mme d'Épinay, et de Mlle de Lespinasse," *Dix-huitième siècle* 47:1 (2015), 231–43.

32. Voltaire's poem about the colic of Frederick of Prussia is reprinted in Starobinski, "Le philosophe à table," 280–81, and in *Oeuvres complètes de Voltaire*, ed. Pierre Augustin Caron de Beaumarchais, Jean-Antoine-Nicolas de Caritat Condorcet (marquis de), and Jacques Joseph Marie Decroix, 60 vols. (Paris: Carez, Thomine et Fortic, 1820–26), vol. 11, 216–17.

33. See René Pomeau and Christiane Mervaud, *De la Cour au jardin*, in *Voltaire en son temps*, ed. René Pomeau, 5 vols. (Oxford: Voltaire Foundation, Taylor Institution, 1988), vol. 3, 168–77.

34. Letter 1443, May 20, 1738, in *Voltaire's Correspondence*, vol. 7, 182.

35. Vaillot, *Avec Madame Du Châtelet: 1734–1749*, in *Voltaire en son temps*, vol. 2, 367–68.

36. Deidre Dawson, *Voltaire's Correspondence: An Epistolary Novel* (New York: Peter Lang, 1994), 73.

37. Murray, *Voltaire's Candide: The Protean Gardener, 1755–1762*, SVEC 69 (1970), 54–55.

38. Ibid., 55–56.

39. Nicholas Cronk, "Le pet de Voltaire," in *La Figure du philosophe dans les lettres anglaises et françaises*, ed. Alexis Tadié (Paris: Presses Universitaires de Paris Ouest, 2010), 123–36. Regarding flatulent literature, Charrier-Vozel cites a letter in which Mme d'Epinay described the therapeutic farting she used to relieve her colic; "Sociabilités de la maladie," 237.

40. See, for example, letter 6731, written October 21, 1757 to Elie Bertrand, a Swiss pastor and theologian, in *Voltaire's Correspondence*, vol. 32, 129.

41. Letter 3451, written August 29, 1749, in ibid., vol. 17, 149.

42. Letter 11148, in ibid., vol. 53, 163.

43. On Tronchin's attitude toward Voltaire as a patient—and efforts to put an end to Voltaire's "frightening" consumption of remedies—see Henri Tronchin, *Théodore Tronchin: Un médecin du XVIIIe siècle* (Paris: Plon-Nourrit, 1906), 149–50, 160–65.

44. Cited in ibid., 160.
45. Letters D8056 and 8057, in *Voltaire's Correspondence*, vol. 41, 136–37.
46. Cited in Mervaud, *Voltaire à table*, 130.
47. Anita Guerrini, "The Hungry Soul: George Cheyne and the Construction of Femininity," *Eighteenth-Century Studies* 32:3 (Spring 1999), 279–91, at 280.
48. Cited by Roland Barthes in "Michelet mangeur d'histoire," in Barthes, *Oeuvres complètes*, 3 vols. (Paris: Seuil, 1993–95), vol. 1, 253–66, at 253.
49. "Vampires," *Questions sur l'Encyclopédie*, in OCV, vol. 43, 416–23.
50. "Ventres paresseux," in ibid., 432–43.
51. "Déjection. Excréments, leur rapport avec le corps de l'homme, avec ses idées et ses passions," in ibid., vol. 40, 357–58.
52. Pearson, *The Fables of Reason: A Study of Voltaire's Contes philosophiques* (Oxford: Clarendon, 1993), 225.
53. Undated letter from Voltaire to Tronchin, cited in H. Tronchin, *Théodore Tronchin*, 368.
54. *Les Oreilles du comte de Chesterfield* [1775], in OCV, vol. 76, 161. Further citations to this work appear parenthetically in the text.
55. On the redemption of illness through fiction, see Evelyne Ender, "'Speculating Carnally,' or, Some Reflections on the Modernist Body," *Yale Journal of Criticism* 12:1 (1999), 113–30.
56. Voltaire wrote this to Cideville on May 10, 1764: "I am extremely weak . . . and my soul [*âme*], which I call *Lisette*, is very uncomfortable in its doddering body"; *Correspondence and Related Documents*, in OCV, vol. 111, 368.
57. Cited in H. Tronchin, *Théodore Tronchin*, 161–62, 228.
58. Cited in Christiane Mervaud, *Le Dictionnaire philosophique de Voltaire* (Oxford: Voltaire Foundation, 1994), 39.
59. Cited in John N. Pappas, *Berthier's Journal de Trévoux and the Philosophes*, SVEC 3 (1957), 110.
60. On the construction of Robespierre and Danton as cultural units, see Ann Rigney, "Icon and Symbol: The Historical Figure Called Maximilien Robespierre," in *Representing the French Revolution: Literature, Historiography, and Art*, ed. James A. W. Heffernan (Hanover, N.H.: University Press of New England, 1992), 106–34; and Marie-Hélène Huet, *Mourning Glory: The Will of the French Revolution* (Philadelphia: University of Pennsylvania Press, 1997), 149–79.
61. Réveillé-Parise, *Physiologie et hygiène*, vol. 1, 104. He gave a detailed analysis of Voltaire's illnesses in vol. 2, 182–88.
62. Cited in Vaillot, *Avec Madame Du Châtelet*, 368.
63. Franck Nouchi, *Le Cerveau de Voltaire* (Paris: Flammarion, 2012).
64. Quoted in Brewer, *Discourse of Enlightenment*, 288n10.
65. Georges Daniel, *Le style de Diderot: Légende et structure* (Geneva: Droz, 1986), 2.
66. Diderot, *Éléments de physiologie*, 328–29.

67. See Jean Starobinski, "Diderot et la parole des autres," *Critique* 296 (1972), 3–22.

68. Fried, *Absorption and Theatricality: Painting and Beholder in the Age of Diderot* (Chicago: University of Chicago Press, 1980), 31.

69. *La Religieuse* [1770/1780–82], in DPV, vol. 11, 123–24.

70. Georges-Louis Leclerc, comte de Buffon and Louis-Jean-Marie Daubenton, *Histoire naturelle générale et particulière: Avec la description du Cabinet du Roy*, 21 vols. (Paris: Imprimerie royale, 1749–89), vol. 2, 429–36.

71. Denis Diderot and Louis Jean-Marie Daubenton, "Animal," in ENCYC, vol. 1: 468–74, at 470.

72. Ibid., 471. The comparison is designed to undermine Buffon's contention in his *Histoire naturelle* that the human mind always acts voluntarily. See Caroline Jacot Grapa, "Des huîtres aux grands animaux: Diderot, animal matérialiste," *Dix-huitième siècle* 42:1 (2010), 99–118; and Ann Thomson, "Diderot, le matérialisme et la division de l'espèce humaine," *Recherches sur Diderot et sur l'Encyclopédie* 26 (April 1999), 197–211.

73. See Jacot Grapa, *Dans le vif du sujet*, 394–95 and passim. On Diderot's interest in the dream state—and, more broadly, altered mental states—see also Aram Vartanian, "Diderot and the Phenomenology of the Dream," *Diderot Studies* 8 (1966), 217–53; and Coleman, *Virtues of Abandon*, 181–201.

74. Jean-Luc Martine, "L'article ART de Diderot: Machine et pensée pratique," *Recherches sur Diderot et sur l'Encyclopédie* 39 (2005), 2–29, at 5.

75. John Lough summarizes Chaumeix's critique of "Animal" and related *Encyclopédie* articles in *The Encyclopédie* (London: D. McKay, 1971), 171–75.

76. See the chapter "Heart Strings" in Downing Thomas, *Aesthetics of Opera in the Ancien Régime, 1647–1785* (Cambridge: Cambridge University Press, 2002), esp. 189–200.

77. For analyses of those metaphors, see Jacot Grapa, *Dans le vif du sujet*, 267–321; Wilda Anderson, *Diderot's Dream* (Baltimore: Johns Hopkins University Press, 1990), 42–76; Michael Moriarty, "Figures of the Unthinkable: Diderot's Materialist Metaphors," in *The Figural and the Literal: Problems of Language in the History of Science and Philosophy, 1630–1800*, ed. Andrew E. Benjamin, Geoffrey N. Cantor, and John R. R. Christie (Manchester, U.K.: Manchester University Press, 1987), 147–75; Annie Ibrahim, "Matière des métaphores, métaphores de la matière," *Recherches sur Diderot et sur l'Encyclopédie* 26 (April 1999), 125–33, and "Diderot et les métaphores de l'animal: Pour un antispécisme?" *Dix-huitième siècle* 42:1 (2010), 83–98; and Kate E. Tunstall, "The Early Modern Embodied Mind and the Entomological Imaginary," in *Mind, Body, Motion, Matter*, 202–29.

78. Diderot, *Le Rêve de d'Alembert* [1769], in DPV, vol. 17, 157. Other citations to this work appear parenthetically in the text.

79. See *D'Alembert Dream*, in Denis Diderot, *Rameau's Nephew and Other Works*, trans. Jacques Barzun and Ralph Bowen (New York: Bobbs-Merrill, 1964), 160.

80. Vartanian, "Diderot's Rhetoric of Paradox, or, the Conscious Automaton Observed," *Eighteenth-Century Studies* 14:4 (Summer 1981), 379–405, at 385.

81. Ibid., 384, 387.

82. "Des huîtres aux grands animaux," 103.

83. Tunstall, "Eyes Wide Shut: *Le Rêve de d'Alembert*," in *New Essays on Diderot*, ed. James Fowler (Cambridge: Cambridge University Press, 2011), 141–57, at 147 and 150.

84. As Vartanian points out, "Diderot's examples of the 'perte de la conscience du soi' were not intended to restrict human automatism to aberrant mental states. . . . Actually, he was drawn to, indeed, fascinated by, such phenomena because, being persuaded in advance by the truth of automatism, he found in them the best proof that he was right. In trance-like or 'cataleptic' behavior, any observer, and not just the materialist philosopher, can recognize the underlying man-machine"; "Diderot's Rhetoric," 391n15.

85. Diderot, *Éléments de physiologie*, 499–500.

86. Ibid., 500–501.

87. See Jacot Grapa, *Dans le vif du sujet*, 31; and Vidal, *Sciences de l'âme*.

88. Roach, *The Player's Passion: Studies in the Science of Acting* (Ann Arbor: University of Michigan Press, 1993), 154. On Diderot's notions of corporeal and creative memory, see also Angelica Goodden, *Diderot and the Body* (Oxford: Legenda, 2001), 89–113, and *The Backward Look: Memory and the Writing Self in France 1580–1920* (Oxford: Legenda, 2000), 84–109.

89. "I hear you, reader: you've had enough, and in your opinion we should get back to our two travelers. Reader, you are treating me like an automaton, and that is not polite"; *Jacques le fataliste* [1784], in DPV, vol. 23, 84. Diderot also used *automate* negatively in the *Discours de la poésie dramatique* (1765), where he applied it to those who lacked imagination; *Discours de la poésie*, in DPV, vol. 10, 360, discussed in Gerhardt Stenger, *Nature et liberté chez Diderot après l'Encyclopédie* (Paris: Universitas, 1994), 31. Studies of automatons that touch on Diderot include Victor Sage, "Diderot and Maturin: Enlightenment, Automata, and the Theatre of Terror," in *European Gothic: A Spirited Exchange, 1760–1960*, ed. Avril Horner (Manchester, U.K.: Manchester University Press, 2002), 55–70; Minsoo Kang, *Sublime Dreams of Living Machines: The Automaton in the European Imagination* (Cambridge, Mass.: Harvard University Press, 2011); and Julia V. Douthwaite and Daniel Richter, "The Frankenstein of the French Revolution: Nogaret's Automaton Tale of 1790," *European Romantic Review* 20:3 (2009), 381–411.

90. Jonathan Crary, *Techniques of the Observer: On Vision and Modernity in the Nineteenth Century* (Cambridge, Mass.: MIT Press, 1990), 60.

91. *Essai sur les règnes de Claude et de Néron, et sur les mœurs et les écrits de Sénèque (Essai sur Sénèque)* [1778], in DPV, vol. 25, 336.

92. *Réfutation*, 557.

93. Ibid., 576.

94. Diderot, *Le Neveu de Rameau ou Satire seconde* [1761–82/1805], in DPV, vol. 12, 76.

95. *Réfutation*, 583.

96. Gaukroger, *Natural and the Human*, 138.

97. "To explain the mechanism of memory, one must see the soft substance of the brain as a mass of sensitive and living wax, but susceptible to all kinds of forms, never losing any of the forms it has taking and endlessly taking new ones that it preserves. Here is the book. But where is the reader? The reader is the book itself"; *Éléments de physiologie*, 470; translation from Joanna Stalnaker, "Diderot's Brain," in *Mind, Body, Motion, Matter*, 230–53, at 246. The same passage is discussed in Charles T. Wolfe, "'The Brain Is a Book Which Reads Itself': Cultured Brains and Reductive Materialism from Diderot to J. J. C. Smart," in *Mindful Aesthetics: Literature and the Science of Mind*, ed. Chris Danta and Helen Groth (New York: Bloomsbury, 2014), 73–89.

98. *Salon de 1767*, in DPV, vol. 16, 233. I discuss these questions more fully in "Le sublime, le grotesque, et l'animal dans les théories esthétiques de Diderot," in *Le sublime et le grotesque*, ed. Jan Miernowski (Geneva: Librairie Droz, 2014), 181–207.

99. *Réfutation*, 624.

100. See Sarah Cohen's discussion of this point in "Chardin's Fur: Painting, Materialism, and the Question of Animal Soul," *Eighteenth-Century Studies* 38 (2004), 39–61.

101. Diderot used the term "magician" to describe Chardin in the *Salon de 1765*, in DPV, vol. 14, 135.

102. Saint Girons, "Génie," 496.

103. *Salon de 1767*, 229.

104. Ibid., 179–80, 172.

105. Dieckmann, "Diderot's Conception of Genius," *Journal of the History of Ideas* 2:2 (1941), 151–82, at 152.

106. McMahon, *Divine Fury*, 96.

107. *Réfutation*, 583–84.

108. See Jacques Chouillet, *La formation des idées esthétiques de Diderot, 1745–1763* (Paris: A. Colin, 1973), 141; and Kaitaro, *Diderot's Holism*, 39–50.

109. See Charles T. Wolfe, "'Cabinet d'Histoire Naturelle,' or the Interplay of Nature and Artifice in Diderot's Naturalism," *Perspective on Science* 17:1 (2009), 58–76.

110. Brewer, *Discourse of Enlightenment*, 104.

111. *Lettre sur les sourds et muets*, 197–98.

112. For Diderot, "watching oneself think" had none of the hallucinatory quality it would have for later authors like Guy de Maupassant; see Bertrand Marquer, *Naissance du fantastique clinique: La crise de l'analyse dans la littérature fin-de-siècle* (Paris: Hermann, 2014), 111–32.

113. *Lettre sur les sourds et muets*, 161–62; translation adapted from *Letter on the Deaf* in *Diderot's Early Philosophical Works*, 187.

114. Translation proposed in Marion Hobson, "Diderot's *Lettre sur les sourds et muets*: Language and Labyrinth" (orig. French, 1976), reprinted in Hobson, *Diderot and Rousseau: Networks of Enlightenment*, ed. and trans. Kate E. Tunstall and Caroline Warman, SVEC 2011:04, 215–59, at 235.

115. Fontenelle, "Eloge du père Sébastien [Jean] Truchet, Carme" [1729], in *Œuvres complètes*, 9 vols. (Paris: Fayard, 1996), vol. 7, 149–59, at 156–57. See also "Les Théâtres d'automates," in Alfred Chapuis and Édouard Gélis, *Le Monde des Automates, étude historique et technique* [1928], 2 vols. (Geneva-Paris: Slatkine, 1984), vol. 1, 335–46.

116. See Jessica Riskin, "Machines in the Garden," *Republic of Letters: A Journal for the Study of Knowledge, Politics, and the Arts*, 1:2 (2010), http://arcade.stanford.edu/rofl/machines-garden

117. Jean-Baptiste de Saint-Jean, "Tableau animé représentant le château de Saint-Ouen," N inventaire: 01407–0002-, http://www.arts-et-metiers.net/musee/tableau-anime-chateau-de-saint-ouen. The museum's website also provides links to photos of the gears that operated this painting. Another mechanical painting by Saint-Jean, "Tableau animé représentant un parc de château" (N inventaire: 01407–0001-), depicts the arrival of a horse-drawn carriage, escorted by cavaliers and soldiers, at the steps of an elegant château; its frame carries the arms of Marie-Antoinette, *dauphine*. See http://phototheque.arts-et-metiers.net/?idPageWeb=95&popUp_infosPhoto=1&infosIdPhoto=26578&interfaceParent=tableLumineuse&PHPSESSID=83d510166190e6ceb66d358704d8dccb.

118. *Lettre sur les sourds et muets*, 159–60; *Letter on the Deaf*, 185.

119. *Lettre sur les sourds et muets*, 169.

120. Fellows, "Diderot, Hawkes, and the *Tableau mouvant*: From the Motion Pictures of Interior Animation to the Luxury of Still, Exterior Projection," *Diderot Studies* 18 (1975), 61–79, at 67.

121. *Salon de 1767*, 70.

122. "Sur le Génie" [1774, unpublished], in *Œuvres complètes de Diderot*, ed. J. Assézat, 20 vols. (Paris: Garnier Frères, 1875–77), vol. 4, 26–27, at 27.

123. Diderot imagined constructing a machine or automaton to rival Raphael in the *Salon de 1767*, 179–80. In the *Paradoxe sur le comédien*, he described the great actor as a resonating instrument capable of taking on any tonality, and added, "I highly esteem the talent of a great actor; such a man is rare, as rare and perhaps more rare than the great poet"; *Paradoxe*, in DPV, vol. 20, 93–94.

124. On the controversy stirred up by Boulanger's theories, see Paul Sadrin, *Nicolas-Antoine Boulanger (1722–1759) ou avant nous le deluge*, SVEC 240 (1986), 222–32; and Alan Charles Kors, *D'Holbach's Coterie: An Enlightenment in Paris* (Princeton, N.J.: Princeton University Press, 1976), 38.

125. See Christophe Paillard's remarks in *Lettre sur le commerce des livres* [1763], ARTFL Electronic Edition, ed. Christophe Paillard (2009), 43n33. Diderot referred elliptically to a "new anti-Christian library" in his September 24, 1767 letter to Sophie Volland, in *Correspondance*, 770. Mark Curran argues that Boulanger had a direct influence on the materialist thought of d'Holbach: *Atheism, Religion and Enlightenment in Pre-revolutionary Europe* (Woodbridge, Suffolk, U.K.: Boydell, 2012), 28.

126. "Sur la Vie et les ouvrages de Boulanger" [1765], in DPV, vol. 9, 449. Further citations to this work appear parenthetically in the text.

127. Angelica Goodden, "Diderot, Rousseau, and the Art of Craft," in Fowler, *New Essays on Diderot*, 59–73, at 63. I am borrowing an expression from Barbara Stafford and Frances Terpak, *Devices of Wonder: From the World in a Box to Images on a Screen* (Los Angeles: Getty Research Institute, 2001).

Chapter 5

1. Citation from Leo Braudy, *The Frenzy of Renown: Fame and Its History* (Oxford: Oxford University Press, 1986), 372. On the enthusiasm of some of Rousseau's readers, see Lilti, *Figures publiques*, 164–77; Robert Darnton, *The Great Cat Massacre and Other Episodes in French Cultural History* (New York: Basic Books, 1984), 242–43; and Nicholas Paige, "Rousseau's Readers Revisited: The Aesthetics of *La Nouvelle Héloïse*," *Eighteenth-Century Studies* 42:1 (2008), 131–54. On reading-induced "conversion experiences" among readers in the seventeenth and nineteenth centuries, see Adrian Johns, "The Physiology of Reading," in *Books and the Sciences in History*, ed. Marina Frasca-Spada and Nick Jardine (Cambridge: Cambridge University Press, 2000), 291–314.

2. Rousseau declared his resolution to live as a solitary in his 1761 correspondence with Malesherbes, discussed by Erik Leborgne in "Le Portrait clinique de Rousseau dans *De la solitude* de J. G. Zimmermann," *Annales Jean-Jacques Rousseau* 48 (2008), 237–50, at 244–48. See also Lilti, "Solitude de l'homme célèbre," in *Figures publiques*, 153–219.

3. See Le Menthéour, *La Manufacture de maladies*, esp. the chapter "L'Invention de la rêverie," 67–104.

4. The first citation is from Madelyn Gutwirth, *Mme de Staël, Novelist: The Emergence of the Artist as Woman* (Champaign: University of Illinois Press, 1987), 299. The second is from Angelica Goodden, *Madame de Staël: The Dangerous Exile* (Oxford: Oxford University Press, 2008), 16.

5. Lydia Marie Child, *The History and Condition of Women in Various Ages and Nations* (1835), cited in Bonnie Smith, "History and Genius: The Narcotic, Erotic, and Baroque Life of Germaine de Staël," *French Historical Studies* 19:4 (1996), 1059–81, at 1061. On the admiration that other French women authors expressed for Staël, see Mona Ozouf, *Women's Words: Essays on French Singularity*, trans. Jane Marie Todd (Chicago: University of Chicago Press, 1997), xvii–xix.

6. Staël, *De la littérature considérée dans ses rapports avec les institutions sociales* [1800] (Paris: Garnier-Flammarion, 1991), 339.

7. This passage, from the journal Staël wrote while traveling in Germany in 1808, is cited by Simone Balayé in "Le génie et la gloire dans l'œuvre de Mme de Staël," *Rivista di letterature moderne e comparate* 20 (September–December 1967), 202–14, at 211.

8. Jane Darcy, *Melancholy and Literary Biography, 1640–1816* (New York: Palgrave Macmillan, 2013), 1–2, 96.

9. Ibid., 1.

10. See Radden's introduction in *Nature of Melancholy*, 3–51. For an example of modern psychoanalytic theories of melancholy brought to bear on early modern literature, see Juliana Schiesari, *The Gendering of Melancholia: Feminism, Psychoanalysis, and the Symbolics of Loss in Renaissance Literature* (Ithaca, N.Y.: Cornell University Press, 1992).

11. Guerrini, *Obesity and Depression*, 5.

12. The first quote is from Massimo Riva, "Malattia dell'immaginazione e immaginazione della malattia: Ipocondria e malinconia nella letteratura italiana del Settecento," *Lettere Italiane* 39:3 (1987), 346–77, cited and trans. Nancy Isenberg, "Without Swapping Her Skirt for Breeches: The Hypochondria of Giustiniana Wynne, Anglo-Venetian Woman of Letters," in *English Malady: Enabling and Disabling Fictions*, ed. Glen Colburn (Newcastle: Cambridge Scholars Publishing, 2008), 154–76, at 161. The second is from Eric Gidal, "Madame de Staël and the Sociology of Melancholy," in *English Malady*, 20–40, at 31. As Glen Colburn notes in his introduction to this volume, melancholy was "a malleable cultural metaphor that could be adapted to a wide range of social diagnoses" (*English Malady*, 2).

13. See Claire Crignon-De Oliveira and Mariana Saad, "La Mélancolie et l'unité materielle de l'homme—XVIIe et XVIIIe siècles: Introduction," *Gesnerus* 63 (2006), 6–11.

14. Schmidt, *Melancholy and the Care of the Soul: Religion, Moral Philosophy and Madness in Early Modern England* (Burlington, Vt.: Ashgate, 2007), 186.

15. Anon., "Mélancolie ("Économie animale)," in ENCYC, vol. 10: 310.

16. Ibid., 471.

17. Louis-Courvoisier, "Rendre sensible une souffrance psychique." On self-descriptions by British melancholiacs, see Allan Ingram, "Death in Life and Life in Death: Melancholy and the Enlightenment," *Gesnerus* 63 (2006), 90–102.

18. Mark S. Micale, *Hysterical Men: The Hidden History of Male Nervous Illness* (Cambridge, Mass.: Harvard University Press, 2008), 20, 24.

19. Lorry, *De melancholia et morbis melancholicis* (Paris: Cavelier, 1765), cited and trans. Jean Starobinski, *History of the Treatment of Melancholy from the Earliest Times to 1900* (Basel, Switzerland: J. R. Geigy, 1962), 48–49. The original French version of Starobinski's book, *Histoire du traitement de la mélancolie des origines à 1900*, has been reprinted in *L'encre de la mélancolie* (Paris: Éditions du Seuil, 2012), 13–158.

20. Starobinski, *History of the Treatment of Melancholy*, 66–67.

21. Starobinski also underscores the difference in the treatments given to melancholiacs from different classes: the wealthier ones traveled, whereas the less wealthy were sent to asylums; ibid., 70.

22. Beaumarchais, *The Marriage of Figaro*, in *The Broadview Anthology of Drama: Plays from the Western Theatre, Volume 1: From Antiquity Through the Eighteenth Century*, ed. Craig S. Walker and Jennifer Wise, trans. John Van Burek and Jennifer Wise (Peterborough, Ont.: Broadview Press, 2003), 743; *Le Mariage de Figaro*, in Beaumarchais, *Œuvres*, ed. Pierre Larthomas (Paris: Gallimard, Editions de la Pléiade, 1988), act III, scene 9, 436. The count is implying here that Suzanne will soon suffer from nervous distress because he intends to thwart her planned marriage to Figaro. Sabine Arnaud points out that Beaumarchais also used the vapors as a plot device in *Le Barbier de Séville* (1775)—as did other playwrights of the period; *On Hysteria*, 138.

23. Lambert described the vapors as one of the "ridiculous" fashions embraced by some aristocratic women; *Réflexions nouvelles sur les femmes*, 172. Later in the century, Mercier sarcastically described the vapors as "the torture of all those effeminate souls who have been thrust by inactivity into dangerous modes of voluptuousness"; *Tableau de Paris*, 12 vols. (Amsterdam, 1782–88), vol. 1, 164–65. On the association of the vapors with elite culture, see Elizabeth A. Williams, "Hysteria and the Court Physician in Enlightenment France," *Eighteenth-Century Studies* 35.2 (2002), 247–55; and Arnaud, *L'Invention de l'hystérie / On Hysteria*.

24. Tissot, *Essai sur les maladies des gens du monde*, 84–85.

25. *Avis au peuple sur sa santé* [1761], 6th ed., 2 vols. (Lausanne: Chez François Grasset, 1775), vol. 1, 198–99.

26. According to his correspondence with Zimmermann, Tissot planned for several years to write a treatise devoted exclusively to the vapors; see particularly Tissot's letter of January 19, 1764, in *Correspondance 1754–1797*, 256. Antoinette Emch-Dériaz remarks in a note to this letter that, according to unpublished documents in the Fonds Tissot, he renounced that idea for fear of censorship—and instead wrote the *Traité des nerfs*.

27. *Traité des nerfs*, vol. 1, xvi.

28. Anon, "Vapeurs (*en Médecine*)," in ENCYC, vol. 16: 836–37, at 836.

29. Rieder, *La figure du patient*, 93–111. Rieder also notes that Charrière was unusually outspoken in critiquing mainstream medical discourse (161–62).

30. Belle de Zuylen, letter to Constant d'Hermenches, September 9, 1762; cited in ibid., 95.

31. Stolberg, *Experiencing Illness*, 182–83.

32. Rieder, *La figure du patient*, 161.

33. *Caliste, ou Continuation des lettres écrites de Lausanne*, in Isabelle de Charrière / Belle de Zuylen, *Oeuvres complètes*, vol. 8, 233. See Tili Boon Cuillé's analysis of this novel in *Narrative Interludes: Musical Tableaux in Eighteenth-Century French Texts* (Toronto: University of Toronto Press, 2006), 131–43.

34. Arnaud emphasizes that some contemporaries refuted this salutary interpretation: "the Revolution was presented in newspapers and pamphlets as a form of hysteria, an epidemic of convulsions or political vapors" (*On Hysteria*, 37). She also notes that similar pathological rhetoric was used by opponents of the French Revolution across the English Channel, like Edmund Burke.

35. Petit, "Discours sur l'influence de la Révolution française sur la santé publique" [1796], in *Essai sur la médecine du coeur* (Lyon: Chez Garnier et Reymann, 1806), 133–34; discussed in Arnaud, *On Hysteria*, 236–37. On melancholy's historical association with aristocratic boredom and idleness, see Wolf Lepenies, *Melancholy and Society*, trans. Jeremy Gaines and Doris Jones (Cambridge, Mass.: Harvard University Press, 1992).

36. Cited in Goldstein, *Console and Classify*, 101.

37. Staël, *De la littérature*, 241–42. See Eric Gidal, "Civic Melancholy: English Gloom and French Enlightenment," *Eighteenth-Century Studies* 37:1 (2003), 23–45, and "Madame de Staël and the Sociology of Melancholy," 29–30.

38. "Mon portrait," in Rousseau, *Œuvres complètes*, vol. 1, 1123; cited in Lilti, *Figures publiques*, 186. "Mon portrait" is a set of autobiographical fragments that Rousseau probably wrote in 1761–62.

39. Le Menthéour, *La Manufacture de maladies*, 126, 138.

40. *Rousseau juge de Jean-Jacques, Dialogues* [1780], in *Œuvres complètes*, vol. 1, 806.

41. Jan Miernowski, "Rousseau ou le Misanthrope manqué. L'écriture au risque de la haine," *Annales de la Société Jean-Jacques Rousseau* 48 (2008), 277–315.

42. Letter from Malesherbes to Rousseau, December 25, 1761; cited and discussed in Le Menthéour, *La Manufacture de maladies*, 150–51. See also Laurent Cantagrel's analysis of this episode in *De la maladie à l'écriture. Genèse de la mélancolie romantique* (Tübingen: Niemeyer, 2004), 113–43.

43. Zimmermann, *Traité de l'expérience*, 480–81.

44. See Leborgne, "Le Portrait clinique de Rousseau," which reproduces several passages from the more complete and accurate translation of Zimmermann's text that was later done by A.-J.-L. Jourdan, *De la solitude, des causes qui en font naître le goût, de ses inconvénients, de ses avantages et de son influence sur les passions* (Paris: J.-B. Baillière, 1840).

45. Fabre, *Essai sur les facultés de l'âme, considérée dans leur rapport avec la sensibilité et l'irritabilité de nos organes* [1785], 2nd ed. (Paris: Delalain, 1787), 202–5.

46. Ibid., 203–4. Fabre was also intent on refuting Mesmer's theories (218–41).

47. Rousseau, *Les Confessions* [1782–89], in *Œuvres complètes*, vol. 1, 218–19; *Confessions*, in *Collected Writings of Rousseau*, vol. 5, 184. The former work in the note is hereafter cited in the text within parentheses as "LC," and the latter is cited as "TC."

48. "Préface à Narcisse," 967; "Preface to Narcisse," 192–93.

49. This psychological interpretation of Rousseau's physical ailments is proposed both by the editors of the Pléiade edition of the *Confessions* (in *Œuvres complètes*, vol.